The World Of Salt Shakers

Second Edition

by
MILDRED & RALPH LECHNER

COLLECTOR BOOKS
A Division of Schroeder Publishing Co., Inc.

Dedication

This book is dedicated
to the memory of

Doris (Bobbie) Lawson
and
Charles Edward Lawson

The current values in this book should be used only as a guide. They are not intended to set prices which may vary from one section of the country to another. Auction prices as well as dealer prices vary greatly and are affected by condition as well as demand. Neither the Author nor the Publisher assumes responsibility for any losses that might be incurred as a result of consulting this guide.

Acknowledgments

As every author knows, the writing and compiling of a technical book such as this is dependent upon many individuals.

Presenting a comprehensive pictorial story of Victorian era antique glass could only be accomplished by having access to some of the major salt shaker collections in the United States.

Through the interest and thoughtfulness of the Antique Art Glass Salt Shaker Collectors Society (AAGSSCS), various members took the time to make their salt shaker collections available to our camera.

Some individuals risked their rare and irreplaceable glass shakers by shipping them to us for photographing. Others went to the trouble and expense of having pictures taken and mailing them to us because we were unable to take the time to travel and do the photographic work.

We can't begin to count the numerous long distance telephone calls made by caring individuals in order to properly record and establish the technical details associated with some of the rarities involved.

Therefore, we wish to express our gratitude and appreciation to the following individuals who have in one way or another contributed their time, support, and consultation to this book. They deserve to be individually acknowledged.

Victor W. Buck, Upland, California. One of the leading authorities of art glass and pattern glass in Southern California. A discriminating collector, appraiser and fine glassware dealer for many years, he produced and sponsored numerous antique shows at the Los Angeles County Fairgrounds. Victor and his wife Mary have been close friends and advisors to us for approximately 25 years. They have contributed much toward our overall collection realizations.

B. Douglas and Margaret Archer, Kernersville, North Carolina. Absolutely wonderful people; and close personal friends and consultants for over 20 years. Doug is curator of the Archer Glass Museum in Kernersville. The glassware on display in the museum is outstanding. It is well worth the stop for any collector traveling through the Greensboro – Winston-Salem area. Both Doug and Margaret are recognized authorities on antique glass candlesticks, having written several books on this subject.

Carl Just, York, Pennsylvania. An outstanding collector of fine glassware for many years, Carl is a retired patent attorney who helped us greatly with the patent section of this book. We had the pleasure of appraising his almost 1,200-piece salt shaker collection in 1986, at which time he allowed us to photograph some of his outstanding shakers.

Marilyn and Charles Lockwood, New York. Personal friends and supporters of our writing efforts, they made their excellent collection available to us for photographing. In addition, they submitted essential last minute photos for this book. They are past co-presidents of the AAGSSCS. In our opinion, the success of the society is a direct result of their early leadership.

Dick and Mary Ann Krauss, Ohio. Good friends and current co-presidents of the AAGSSCS; discriminating collectors and contributors to this book. Very knowledgeable and thoughtful people. Our readers have them to thank for the Blue Aurene salt shaker photos in our book.

Dottie and Bill Avery, Maitland, Florida. Founders of the AAGSSCS. They performed the detailed coordination efforts associated with obtaining photographs from various members that work with the society's "Unknown Shaker Identification Project." In addition, Bill did some excellent personal photographic work for us.

Bob and Carole Bruce, Southern California. Made their collection available to us in 1986 for several hours of photography. Bob also performed personal photographic efforts from his collection for us to add to this book. Good friends and thoughtful people.

Bennie and Bobbie Lawson, San Luis Obispo, California. Knowledgeable consultants and close supporters of both our collecting and writing efforts for many years. Bennie has contributed several rare salt shakers to our collection.

Barbara White, New York. Barbara contributed some unknowns to this book. She is a most knowledgeable collector and researcher. We always enjoy the exchange of technical information at each annual convention of the AAGSSCS. Just a lovely lady.

Ann and Howard Hoffman, Waverly, New York. Close friends, consultants and supporters of our writing efforts. Ann specializes in opaque white opalware.

Linda McCullough, Richmond, Virginia. A good friend and supporter as well as an outstanding teacher of English in the public school system. We thank you for your consultation and editorial expertise.

Vi and Vince Baffa, Fontana, California. We thank for your friendship and consultation over the past 25 years. Your contribution to this book is especially appreciated.

TABLE OF CONTENTS

Special Acknowledgment

Stan and Shirley McElderry of Iowa contributed a lot of special assistance to both the early and final preparation of this book.

It all started in the early 1980's as an author to reader relationship via letters and an occasional telephone conversation. Over the years our acquaintance developed into a very close friendship. With two such down-to-earth people, how could it have been otherwise!

As we would travel around the United States antiquing and doing future book research, we always tried to make an annual stop to engage in salt shaker talk and exchange meaningful ideas and data relative to the field of both art glass and the accumulation of those many unknown shakers we had never seen before, pieces that continued to make their appearance at the various antique shops, shows, auctions and flea markets. A full hour of discussion concerning a single shaker became quite commonplace between us.

The final months of the writing and photographing required to assemble this book was greatly enhanced by the special voluntary efforts from these folks who never stopped for a minute to think of the personal impact that might be involved.

To you, Stan and Shirley, we wish to convey a special thank you for being there.

Foreword

When my wife and I started collecting Victorian art glass in the 1950's, salt shakers and salt dips were plentiful in almost any type of glass made. We would pick up one from time to time but never really got serious about them except as an excellent example to include in our art glass collection.

About this time frame we became acquainted with Ralph & Mildred Lechner, and we made many trips together in quest of different examples to further our respective collections. As time went by, the Lechners zeroed-in on salt shakers as excellent examples that did not require a lot of display room, and generally were lower in cost than most other quality items within a particular category. With Ralph's engineering analytical mind, and Mildred's keen eye and tenacity, they made a deadly combination that acquired antique salt shakers in a way that seemed almost miraculous.

As the years passed, my wife, Mary, and I deviated from time to time in our collecting habits; but not the Lechners' interest in the ubiquitous salt shaker; they never wavered. In thousands of miles of travel and thousands of antique shops, swap meets, yard sales, etc., and coupled with their viewing about every major salt shaker collection in the country, it is understandable why they are considered "The Authorities" in the field of Art and Colored pattern glass shakers. They have worked long and hard and laid a firm foundation.

There are many books on the collector market today; a large percentage of them are inadequate because they only touch the surface of their subject. Anyone who is familiar with the Lechners' first book, *The World of Salt Shakers*, is well aware that this is not true of them. They have included all pertinent information in this book in an honest effort to educate the reader and help him/her to understand whether the person is a novice or a professional. There are over one thousand shakers illustrated in excellent color and enough description to educate without confusing. Rarity and value are based upon their many years of study/research and specialization.

No doubt a few more different shakers will surface as time passes, but for the most part they will only be variations of those shown in this book. I am honored and pleased to have been a friend and associate of the Lechners over the years. I cannot recommend any effort of theirs too highly.

Victor W. Buck
Upland, California

In reviewing this manuscript, I well remember the years of research that Margaret and I spent trying to put together meaningful and accurate information on glass candlesticks. All of the confusion of true identity of a piece of glass, all of the times that we encountered items inadequately labeled, and most of all when we thought that we had identified an item correctly, to find that it had been identified incorrectly, came into my thoughts. This brings me to the point of the research that Ralph and Mildred did for this book. Over 30 years of dedicated effort has made this text a joy for me to read. I feel that the information transcribed herein is a remarkable accomplishment. The reason behind this statement is based on the fact that one can spend a lifetime researching a single glasshouse, where the Lechners have had to dip into the history of 50 or more glasshouses for this work.

For the novice salt shaker collector, this text should correct most of their misgivings of identifying their collections; for the advanced salt shaker collector it should inspire them to hunt for the once-in-a-lifetime find. To identify is to cherish.

Douglas Archer, Curator
Archer Glass Museum

Antique & Art Glass Salt Shaker Collectors Society

A rather long name for a group of people who truly feel the joy of collecting, identifying and researching salt shakers.

For many years there have been individuals, mostly unknown to each other, who were building their own private collections without the aid of a book to go by. Books that were available gave references to other glass items as to patterns, manufacturers and famous people in the glass industries of years gone by.

With the publication of Dr. Arthur G. Peterson's book *Glass Salt Shakers: 1,000 Patterns* in 1970, and Mildred & Ralph Lechner's *The World of Salt Shakers* in 1976, we now had a source for information, and salt shaker collecting took on a new meaning. This was a meaning that brought people together to share their knowledge of collecting available information.

This basically is what the AAGSSCS organization is all about — bringing collectors together and sharing information. Our newsletter and annual conventions highlight this theme. Our shaker "Identification Project" is chaired by a committee of some of the most knowledgeable collectors and writers in the country and aided by all the society members. This is an ongoing project which focuses on the research of patterns, manufacturers and the people involved. This project is truly a labor of love and one in which everyone benefits.

This book will truly open wide the wonderful world of salt shaker collecting and will be a valuable aid to both the beginning and advanced collector. Available is everything that you always wanted to know about prices, patterns, availability and manufacturers. It will be an excellent guide in your quest for that next shaker.

Dick and Mary Ann Krauss
Co-Presidents 1989-1991

A Brief History

How did the AAGSSCS get started? It involved mixing an interest in a rediscovered book; a meeting with its author and finding that no club existed, plus mustering the initiative to start a national club for fellow salt shaker collectors.

Soon after moving to Florida in 1980, we received the book *Salt and Salt Shakers* from a friend who had been keeping it for Dottie since 1960. It was inscribed to Dottie by the author, Dr. Arthur G. Peterson, but few clues as to why. We located Dr. Peterson in Du Bary, Florida and arranged to meet him and his wife.

Dr. Peterson showed us many of his shakers which sparked an even greater interest and introduced us to his second book, *Glass Salt Shakers: 1,000 Patterns*. He told us that we certainly could begin a collection but "the shakers will be a little harder to find, and quite a bit more expensive than they used to be." He was not aware of any club for collectors.

Only a short time passed before we attended auctions, antique shakers were available and then the inevitable happened. We began to build a collection. We found *The World of Salt Shakers* by Mildred and Ralph Lechner as another source of information, and the series of books on Victorian glass by the late William Heacock opened our eyes further to the variety of beautiful colors and interesting and intriguing patterns in old glass. But no one knew of a club!

A small ad in the *Antique Trader Weekly* inviting anyone interested in forming a club for collectors of salt shakers brought responses from approximately 20 people and so it began. A very informal newsletter exchanged addresses and general information, and by way of the grapevine, others learned of the club's existence. Before long, members were getting together and enthusing over this and that shaker and discovering that other collectors were delightful people who became firm friends. Eventually, a get-together of a few members led to more formal meetings and an established organization now known as the Antique and Art Glass Salt Shaker Collectors Society.

The contribution of Dr. Peterson and the Lechners with their publications have served as the foundation for identifying and cataloguing salt shakers. However, hundreds of unlisted shakers, not described in current glass literature, have been found by the club members. As a result, the society began a project in 1988 to collect pictures and information on all these unknowns. Publication of pictures in our quarterly newsletter, *The Pioneer*, has given the society a meaningful and worthwhile purpose. At each annual convention, the members name the shakers for which no pattern name has been found.

This book contains some pictures and information from various members of the society that have never been published before. If anyone is interested in society membership and the participation of sharing knowledge and meeting wonderful people, write to the AAGSSCS, 2832 Rapidan Trail, Maitland, Florida 32751 for more information.

Dottie & Bill Avery, Founders

INTRODUCTION

Our first book, *The World of Salt Shakers* has been out of print for several years. Since its initial publication in 1976 (with an updated edition in 1982) Mildred and I continue to get numerous inquiries/requests as to the production of a second book dealing with antique art and pattern glass salt shakers that were primarily manufactured by American glasshouses during the nineteenth and early twentieth century period.

For over three decades, as both collectors and authors, we have studied and specialized in obtaining detailed information relative to this type of glassware. Our primary goal has always been to establish identification & attribution of the many remaining pattern designs. While we have always wanted to do a second book, our past vocational demands, the need to decide when to set additional research aside and go to press, coupled with some intermittent health anomalies, has delayed our bringing such a comprehensive book to a satisfactory fruition. We believe that our efforts have finally progressed to the point where a meaningful guide has been compiled.

In keeping with the same objectives and guidelines established by our first book, we have once more documented information that will be the most useful to both collectors and dealers alike. Such criteria consist of the following:

1. Distinct pattern detail through close up photography.
2. Pattern name listing.
3. Known production colors manufactured.
4. Approximate date(s) of first manufacture.
5. Type of glassware.
6. Manufacturer attribution if established.
7. Existence of reproductions if known.
8. Physical height measurements of each shaker.
9. Alphabetical listing by glasshouse and pattern name.
10. A "Potpourri" section of unidentified shakers listed in alphabetical order by pattern name.
11. Retention of pattern names established by previous authors that are clearly accepted by today's collectors and dealers.
12. Assignment of pattern names to unknown and previously unlisted shakers.
13. A current retail market value guide.

ATTRIBUTIONS

Conversations with various knowledgeable antique glassware collectors and dealers throughout our collecting years has highlighted various points of common concern.

For example, every collector/dealer sooner or later wants the answer to "Who Made It?" This, of course, brings forth the question of attribution. Unfortunately, this is one of the most difficult questions to answer with absolute certainty, and can result in some serious blunders, particularly as related to pattern glass.

It is an absolute fact that American factories/glasshouses copied each other's popular patterns, traded and sold molds, were absorbed into larger corporations that reissued patterns at a later date (sometimes at a different factory), and pirated away and employed skilled glass designers and workers from other competitive glasshouses; all of which makes attribution extremely difficult and in some instances impossible.

The attribution techniques that we have employed involve no new innovations. Since we are no smarter than the many authors and writers that have preceded us, we have employed a liberal portion of conservatism in arriving at the attribution conclusions that we are projecting. Simply stated, if we didn't know which glasshouse manufactured a particular item, you will find it listed within the "Potpourri" section of this book.

There are more pluses than minuses to the approach; i.e., the pattern has been named and illustrated; the glass typed; approximate age established (circa); physical dimensions and pattern description is described along with its current retail value; and known colors of manufacture are listed.

In some instances, we may offer an opinion as to who made it based upon cautious analysis, museum attribution and/or knowledgeable authorities. However, THE OPINION GIVEN SHOULD NOT BE TAKEN TO REPRESENT ABSOLUTE/POSITIVE.

PATTERN NAMES

A major portion of the pattern names associated with antique glass salt shakers have been primarily established by Minnie Watson Kamm, E. G. Warman and Arthur G. Peterson.

Generally speaking, Peterson continued to promulgate many of the names assigned by Kamm and Warman in his various publications; also, due to his own personal research, he innovated his own pattern names to a very high percentage of the shakers that are listed in his 1970 book, *Glass Salt Shakers: 1,000 Patterns.*

William Heacock in his first six Victorian pattern glass books continued to endorse and use a majority of the pattern names utilized by the above three authors.

When Mr. Heacock published his seventh Victorian pattern glass book, relative to ruby-stained pattern glass, he began to change the names of many recognized patterns that we salt shaker collectors have hunted for years to locate. The changes were brought about by the fact that his research had uncovered original manufacturers names (OMN).

While this is very commendable effort, the fact still remains that these pattern names have become entrenched, recognized and accepted by today's collectors for almost four decades. We too believe that it would be wonderful to revert back and list OMN but such actions are bound to create confusion by disrupting communications between the salt shaker collectors/dealers that use established pattern names to communicate and interact.

By way of further explanation, let's use a hypothetical example:

I have for sale a "Sawtooth & Star" (Kamm/Peterson named) shaker, but I advertise it for sale as "O'Hara Diamond" (Heacock renamed due to OMN discovery). What does the reader think the chances of selling it would be? Obviously, most collectors/dealers would be unable to visualize the pattern that is being offered for sale.

In our opinion, it is not in the best interest of the collectors and dealers for us to begin changing established patterns by listing recently discovered OMN in place of currently recognized and accepted salt shaker patterns. Therefore, we have elected to not add to the confusion by engaging in pattern name changing due to an OMN discovery.

However, if we do uncover OMN pattern data, we will list it as an adjunct to the already established pattern name. In those cases where there appears to be no conflict with previously established patterns, an OMN will be listed within our descriptive text and carried over into the index of this book.

With the above in mind, the reader is invited to take advantage of the detailed data presented along with our cross indexing format.

SALT SHAKER MEASUREMENTS

We have taken the extra time to include the vertical height measurements (to within + or - ⅛") of each shaker that we have illustrated in this book. The data was taken by the use of an ordinary desk ruler; more precise measurements than this are meaningless due to mold variances and the production techniques that were used.

All measurements were taken with the screw-on metal top removed. In the case of two piece metal tops, height measurements were taken to the top of the cemented-on threaded metal collar.

The obvious reason for not measuring shakers with their top in place is due to the fact most of the time it is impossible to tell whether the top to be measured is original or not. Also, the method employed establishes uniformity of data.

GLASS TERMINOLOGY

It might seem that this subject has been covered numerous times because for several decades almost every major antique glass publication contains a specialized vocabulary and idioms to describe their subject glassware. So! Why do it again?

This may seem redundant, but we believe that it is important to convey to our readers precisely what we are referring to in this book when we use such terms as **cased, overlay, plated, lined, flashed,** and **marbleized** to describe a particular piece of glassware. Therefore, here we go with a conspectus:

The words *cased, overlay, lined, plated* or *flashed* refer to a piece of glassware that contains two or more contrasting glass layers. Flashed glass has only two glass layers, one of which is thin colored and the other crystal (clear). Cased or Overlay glass contains fairly thick layers.

Stained Glass refers to all or part of a glass surface that has been stained with a colored fluid process, which may have been accomplished by dipping, spraying or the brushing on of hot glass and then firing it to bake on the color.

Variegated/Marbleized or *Slag-Like* refers to a glass technique that creates outstanding color variations within a piece of glassware by the incomplete mixing of various colors.

Homogenous is glassware that consists of a glass mix containing a uniform color throughout it from one surface to the other.

Frosted, sometimes called *Camphor Glass*, refers to crystal clear glass that has been acid treated/grit blasted to obtain a frosted look, thus making the glass translucent.

Annealing Crack is a fracture caused by internal stresses that have built up within a glass piece during its manufacture.

Crackled refers to glass that has been deliberately fractured after having been formed and then reheated to seal the cracking; thus forming a unique, permanent design.

Mold Blown, hot glass that is blown into a mold and forced to conform to the pattern of the mold by use of air pressure.

Pressed Glass, glass that is put into a mold and forced to conform to the mold pattern by use of a mechanical plunger.

Pontil Rod, a rod used by a glass worker to hold the glass while it is being formed.

ART GLASS DEFINED

While entire books are available that cover this type of glassware, the ability to come up with a concise definition is most difficult.

This glassware encompasses a vast assembly of fabricating techniques and limitless coloring that began in the early 1880's and carried forward into the early 1930's.

The fabrication of art glass was extremely demanding and required a high degree of skill, patience and craftsmanship associated with hand manipulation.

Art glass is a product of almost limitless materials. It has unusual color and detailing. It has an artistic glamour that represents the epitome of beauty. Finally, it is a product that is recognized by the art glass community as art.

Many of the designs and decorating techniques that were used by the Mount Washington/Pairpoint glass factories, while not formally listed in past art glass reference books, really fall within the parameters of an art glass category. Examples that show innovation, craftsmanship and quality are: Flat End Egg, Flat Side Egg, Fig, Cockle Shell, Tomato, Chick Head, Flower And Rain, Bird Arbor, Game Bird, Two Flower Sprig, and Squatty Lobe. All of these examples satisfy the definition of art glass and accordingly command art glass prices.

As we mentioned in the first book, the collecting of art glass shakers such as New England Peachblow, Agata, Burmese, Holly Amber (Golden Agate), Webb Peachblow, Stevens & Williams Peachblow, Pomona, Rose Amber (Amberina), Wheeling Peachblow, Tiffany, and Steuben, is difficult.

When located, the cost will usually be high, and you will be faced with the dilemma of how much to pay, and whether to purchase or not. Art glass shakers are highly collectible and fall into the categories of Rare, Very Rare and Extremely Rare.

Our years of collecting this type of ware has proven that art glass shakers were not produced in production quantities, in fact, such items as Tiffany and Steuben were only produced to satisfy special orders and most collectors will probably have to be satisfied with viewing one through photographs, perhaps a museum or this book. The only art glass shakers (to our knowledge) that were produced in production quantities are Mt. Washington Burmese and Wheeling Peachblow. Despite this fact, the quality that these glasshouses maintained was very high.

The only advice that we can offer is to recommend that a few art glass shakers be acquired in order to add depth and value to a collection.

PEACHBLOW ART GLASS

The name "Peachblow" is just as magic today as it was during the Victorian period when this glassware was first produced.

Peachblow glass was manufactured by three American and two English glasshouses during the mid-1880's. There are photographic examples of all five types within this book.

Today's collectors and dealers refer to each type of Peachblow by the name of the company that first produced it. Thus, this ware is listed in this book as New England Peachblow, Mt. Washington Peachblow, Webb Peachblow and Stevens & Williams Peachblow. An exception is the Peachblow that was produced by Hobbs, Brockunier which is called Wheeling Peachblow, after the name of the city in West Virginia where the factory was located at the time of their Peachblow production.

In addition, the reader will find the original manufacturers name (OMN), if known, for each type of Peachblow shaker listed within our individual descriptive text.

For additional details of this type of glassware, we recommend A. C. Revi's book *Nineteenth Century Glass* and John Shuman's book *American Art Glass* by Collector Books.

PRINCIPAL SALT SHAKER FACTORIES

While glass salt shakers were produced by a majority of the glasshouses that existed between 1875-1910, these glass manufacturers deserve special mention. The following selections were based upon the consistent large quantity, variety of design, and quality of shakers that they produced.

MT. WASHINGTON GLASS CO/PAIRPOINT CORPORATION

Began in 1869 as the Mount Washington Glass Works at New Bedford, Massachusetts and was owned by William L. Libbey, who resigned in 1872 to become an agent for the New England Glass Co.

After an 1873 closure (due to a depression) the company was reorganized and reopened in 1874 with A.H. Seabury as president and Frederick S. Shirley as manager.

In 1876 the company name was changed to the Mt. Washington Glass Company.

In 1894 Mt. Washington merged into the Pairpoint Manufacturing Company which in 1900 changed its name (due to financial difficulties) to Pairpoint Corporation. The company operated as Pairpoint Corporation until its closing in 1938.

Frederick Shirley innovated and patented many types of ornate and fancy glassware which contributed significantly to this firm's success and expansion. Burmese, Peachblow, Mother-of-Pearl Satinware & Rose Amber (Amberina) are among several types that are outstanding in both beauty and quality which are attributed to the Mt. Washington Glass Co.

In 1880, the Pairpoint Manufacturing Company was formed and located on land adjacent to the Mt. Washington Factory. Pairpoint was specifically created for the purpose of manufacturing and providing a complete line of fancy silverplated articles such as stands and condiments holders that were needed by Mt. Washington for their various glass items.

Despite this capability, it is not at all unusual to find Mt. Washington glassware in metal holders that were made by other silverplating houses that were in existence at the time.

This should not cause alarm or confusion for today's collector when one stops to rationalize that Mt. Washington took such actions in order to realize cost savings that could be obtained by the use of competitive bids from outside vendors. In addition, other silver factories purchased various glass condiment pieces for insertion into their own silverplated holders.

After the 1894 merger of Mt. Washington into the Pairpoint Manufacturing Company, Pairpoint continued to produce both glassware and silver-plated items. During the normal course of production runs, Pairpoint periodically manufactured the earlier Mt. Washington glassware designs along with their own new lines such as Crown Milano, Royal Flemish, Napoli, Albertine, etc. As a result of this method of operation, it is difficult (sometimes impossible) to date/separate the ware that was produced by these two firms.

There are many variations of the "Egg, Flat End" salt shaker that were produced by Mt. Washington and Pairpoint for at least a decade or more. The reader will find several of these egg pattern variants shown in this book.

It is because of examples such as the above, that we have decided to list all the known glass patterns that these two firms produced under the central name of Mt. Washington/Pairpoint. It is our opinion that this attribution approach will eliminate many errors as to who made it.

Realistically, it doesn't make that much difference, since these two factories were closely entwined from Pairpoint's beginning in 1880.

The glassware produced by these houses ranks among the finest ever made in America. Many of their glass designs were also sold to such famous glass decorating houses as C. F. Monroe and the Smith Brothers. This sometimes creates further attribution confusion for today's collectors and dealers.

Consolidated Lamp & Glass Company

This glasshouse was established in 1893 at Fostoria, Ohio. The main offices were located at Pittsburgh, Pennsylvania. First glass production took place at Fostoria, Ohio and continued well into 1895; at which time a fire dictated the movement of the factory to Coraopolis, Pennsylvania.

Having moved from the Hobbs Glass Company in Wheeling, Nicholas Kopp assumed the position of factory manager at the age of 23.

This man is credited with designing many of Consolidated's shapes and various color shadings until he left the firm to join the Pittsburgh Lamp, Brass and Glass Company around 1902.

There is little doubt that the glory years of Consolidated Lamp was from 1894 to approximately 1905. After this period, history shows that Consolidated had various shutdown periods, but managed to remain in business (despite various owner/management changes) until 1964.

In terms of variety, the number of patterns produced seems to be almost infinite. Salt shaker collectors will find that much of this ware is still available today.

Thanks to Kopp, this glasshouse specialized in many colored opaque patterns as well as cranberry, ruby, rubina and cased items. The unusual yellow cased salt shakers (innovated by Kopp) are one of the rarity colors sought after by today's collectors. The Cone, Lacy Scroll, Bulging Loops & Bulging Three Petal patterns were made in this cased yellow color.

It seems plausible that the vast variety of designs and colors that this glasshouse produced was further triggered by competition from Dithridge & Company.

Dithridge & Company

This glasshouse was an outgrowth of the Fort Pitt Glass Works of Pittsburgh, Pennsylvania, which was owned by R. B. Curling. Beginning around 1850, Edward D. Dithridge worked for Mr. Curling as a glass blower. By 1860 Dithridge was the principal stock holder in the company.

During 1863, Edward Dithridge became the sole owner and changed the firm's name to Dithridge & Company. The Fort Pitt Glass Works connotation was retained as part of their advertising along with the Dithridge & Company name.

Ultimately this factory became famous for the manufacture of a variety of novelty items (patterns) with salt shakers and condiment sets being produced in abundance in many unusual shapes and colors.

During the 1890's, much of their ware was in direct competition with the Consolidated Lamp & Glass Company of Pittsburgh.

History shows that Dithridge produced high quality glassware, and was the recipient of several patents associated with lamp design and manufacture. They also produced opalware, and cased and colored glassware; sometimes with hand applied decoration.

After 1903, Dithridge & Company ceased to exist, going out of business due to absorption by the Pittsburgh Lamp, Brass and Glass Company.

The Dual Mold Process

In the first edition we referred to some of the illustrated salt shakers as having been produced by a technique involving a dual mold process. This resulted in the receipt of letters from some our readers asking for more detail regarding this type of process.

To the best of our knowledge, there is no single publication that provides a concise description of the steps that are involved.

We make this statement due to the fact that no individual craftsman developed and patented this invention within a single glasshouse. Nor was the total process brought to fruition within a few years.

Our studies show that the first United States patent for making cast and blown glassware within the same mold was issued during June 1868, to James S. and Thomas B. Atterbury via patent No. 139,993.

This invention enabled the combining of two operations within one mold, which lessened the need for hand manipulation and reduced production costs considerably.

A next step forward by the Atterbury brothers was a mold for making pressed and blown glass in the same mold from one piece of glass; a patent was issued during June 1873.

This type of mold was especially adapted for making pitchers, bulging bodies and other vessels having narrowed necks. Prior to this invention, according to the patentees, "it had only been considered practicable to produce such articles by the process of blowing alone."

We found that other writers have placed major emphasis on Philip Arbogast's 1882 Patent No. 260,819 for the manufacture of glassware using two molds.

One was a Press Mold for pressing the mouth or neck to finished form, with a dependent mass of glass, in which the plunger made a conic cavity to facilitate blowing the body after the semi-finished glass article was shifted to a separate mold. However, Arbogast realized that his process would have little commercial value unless he could mechanize it.

It turned out that he was unable to develop a successful machine, so in 1885 he disposed of his patent to Ripley & Company of Pittsburgh. This company, in turn, experimented with pieces of pressed and blown tableware but there was such strong union opposition that the company abandoned the machinery that it had acquired for this purpose.

Daniel C. Ripley continued his special interest in improving molding techniques. In 1887 he obtained Patent No. 364,298, which involved pressing the mouth and neck in a finished form, and then reheating and blowing the lower portion into a bulbous body and at the same time uniting this to a previously pressed foot or base.

Two other patents were obtained by Ripley in 1891–1892 (Patent No. 458,189 and 477,366) which further improved the process. For example, the blank could be transferred from the press mold to a separate blow mold where the unfinished body

portion wholly below the completed neck and handle was expanded to the desired bulbous shape.

A classic example of a dual mold process lies in the description of Onyx Glassware, which was produced by Dalzell, Gilmore and Leighton Company of Findlay, Ohio, primarily during 1889.

This glass was made from a sensitive mixture containing metallic constituents capable of producing silver, ruby and other lusters. The coloration came about when the still glowing mass was subjected to heat and gaseous fumes. Two molds were used, one to produce the raised ornamentation and the other to bring the article to full size and ultimate shape.

The difficulties encountered in controlling the color and annealing cracks resulted in the short production run of less than a year.

As a result of the above scenario, it is pretty obvious that the driving force behind the use of dual molds was to reduce production costs. Quality glassmaking is very labor intensive, and there were numerous glasshouses during the Victorian era that were highly competitive with each other. It is a standing monument to these American factories that they were able to keep their quality high and still produce a profit.

For an in-depth overview of molding techniques, we recommend *American Glass* by the McKearins, *Nineteenth Century Glass* by A.C. Revi and A.G. Peterson's series of books, especially his *Glass Patents & Patterns*.

SALT SHAKER TOPS

The tops available to today's collector are seldom original, due to the deleterious effect that the Victorian era salt had on the original metal tops.

The various metals used included pewter, tin, brass, sterling silver, nickel and several alloys.

Despite the continuous design efforts, none of the tops that were made turned out to be impervious to the corrosive actions of the salt that they were expected to dispense.

As the original tops corroded away, substitutions have been employed by the individuals that resell this ware to today's collecting world. In fact it is becoming all too common to find antique shakers for sale with their tops entirely missing.

Should a collector purchase an old glass shaker if the top is missing? It is our opinion that it is a mistake not to purchase a desired shaker simply because the top is missing. Through a diligent search, we have many times secured a suitable old top for a shaker that was purchased at an earlier date.

Obviously, there are some exceptions which must be observed. In the instance where a shaker's identity would be obliterated due to lack of the original top, as would be the case with such items as:

Mt. Washington Fig, Mt. Washington Chickhead, C. F. Monroe Chick-on-Pedestal, Mt. Washington Tomato, Flat End Egg, Little Owl, Atterbury Twin, Mr. Washington Cockle Shell, etc.; these types of shakers are unique and of a special nature; therefore, they will have little, if any, value if their original tops are missing.

While one should remain aware of the above exceptions, it is the glass itself that determines whether or not a purchase should be made. When you locate a desired shaker that has no top, it never hurts to bring it to the attention of the seller. Quite often this can form a basis for negotiation of the original asking price.

CONDIMENT SETS

In our first book we were only able to document a few condiment sets due to printing and illustration space constraints. As a result, we were unable to address this aspect of salt shaker collection in very much detail.

The Victorian era condiment sets were produced in various configurations. The most common type consisted of a salt & pepper which is enclosed within a specially designed glass or silver plated metal stand/holder. Next, is a type of set consisting of salt, pepper and mustard.

Some of the more elaborate condiment sets contained four items: salt, pepper, mustard and an oil/vinegar bottle having no handle.

There is also the type of set that consists of salt, pepper, and a large handled oil or vinegar bottle having a glass stopper and (usually) matching glass tray or holder. This latter ware has been dubbed a "cruet set" and will not receive much attention in this book. Cruets and cruet sets have been pretty well covered by previous authors such as Dean L. Murray and William Heacock.

The condiment set designs that we illustrate are difficult to find in a satisfactory condition due to consistent usage that resulted in abnormal chipping and breakage. It is important that a potential buyer carefully check both the condiment dispensers and their associated glass holder prior to purchase.

In the case of condiment dispensers that come with silverplated metal holders, a careful check should be made as to how well the glass shakers, etc., fit into the holder from which they are being offered for sale. Our experience has been that some sellers can be very enterprising when it comes to creating their own version of a stand or holder. If in doubt, start asking questions. Sometimes if the seller is subjected to detailed scrutiny, they will admit that they aren't sure if the metal holder is original or not.

A classic example is shown within the Mt. Washington/Pairpoint portion of this book relative to the Cockle Shell shakers with their extremely rare accompanying stand/holder.

COLLECTING SALT SHAKERS

While the majority of the antique salt shakers presented in this book are a part of our personal collection, there are some shaker pattern/types shown that were generously made available to us by other collectors.

Over the past decade, we have had the opportunity to view, photograph and appraise several of the major salt shaker collections that are owned by members of the Antique and Art Glass Salt Shaker Collectors Society of which we are also members. Such interactions have imparted to us a broadened perspective of many of both the listed and unlisted types of patterns and colors that are available to today's collectors. This effort has also enabled us to present a more accurate and comprehensive listing of pattern variations that were produced.

Since salt shakers were generally produced in the majority of pattern and many types of art glass, the use of this book for "identification criteria" is not limited to just salt shaker collectors alone.

Our original decision to collect shakers was primarily based upon the fact that this ware represents a major cross section of the American glassware that was produced during the Victorian era. Another factor that entered into our decision was the realization that the physical collecting space consumed is reasonable along with the monetary expenditure involved.

Fortunately, the quality of design and craftsmanship of old shakers was retained by a majority of the glasshouses. Therefore, by the use of discriminating collecting guidelines, today's collector can accumulate a fair sized collection that will continue to appreciate in value over time. This is not a speculative statement, just look through the various "Pricing Guides" of the past, and you will glean the pricing trends that have taken place relative to the entire antique glassware universe.

The collecting of antique glass salt and pepper shakers really took-off after Arthur Peterson published his first book, *Salt and Salt Shakers*, in 1960.

While we became antique glassware collectors in the late 1950's, we didn't begin to collect any particular category of glass until 1962 when it became apparent that quality glass pieces from the Victorian era were available in the form of salt shakers.

Over the last 30 years the Peterson books have become the salt shaker collectors' bible; it is impossible to address this subject without referencing the many pattern titles that he created. As a result, there are very few of the so-called "Peterson shakers" that are not at least scarce in today's antique shops and flea markets. The reader will find few shakers listed in this book that are not labeled as such.

Like any other type of antique, the scarcity factor is related to current collectability trends. With the establishment of the Antique Art Glass Salt Shaker Collectors Society by Dottie and Bill Avery in the early 1980's, the interest, demand and competition among collectors has intensified even more.

It is our current experience that one can attend almost any major antique show and see less than half a dozen antique salt shakers for sale. The same holds true for today's antique shops.

Since any publication must address both the beginner and the advanced collector, this book has been so oriented. Don't allow the words "scarce" and "very scarce" to alarm you. If you follow the guidelines and suggestions we have offered, a quality antique salt shaker collection can be obtained.

DON'T BE IN A HURRY! BE DISCRIMINATING IN WHAT YOU BUY! STRIVE FOR QUALITY AND NOT QUANTITY! If you do, we promise that you will derive much enjoyment from your collection with the knowledge that it will appreciate in value over time.

If we can be of any help to our readers, feel free to contact us. We only ask that you enclose an SASE in order to assure that a return reply will be received.

VALUE GUIDES

Another subject of concern is the establishment of current retail market values for each piece of ware that is listed within a book.

Practically every author that has ever provided a value guide will at one time or another receive questions or criticisms of the pricing data contained therein.

Unfortunately, the preponderance of negative remarks received are often the result of misunderstanding and misinterpretation by the various readers involved.

For example, a common reader misconception

results from the attempted sale of an item to a dealer at the full retail value projected within a value guide. The dealer response will usually be "Thanks, but no thanks!"

Dealers are simply unable to stay in business if they purchase their resale stock at full retail value. Therefore, don't waste your time by approaching them to buy based upon this type of pricing.

On the other hand, some dealers (particularly the newer ones) will acquire a piece at a reasonable price and immediately price the item at the top listed dollar value without taking into consideration such important factors as condition, collectability, quality, type of glass, age and scarcity factor.

It should be noted that age and scarcity factor DO NOT determine the individual retail value of any piece of ware.

Keep in mind that those individuals that are willing to pay high prices are usually very knowledgeable people, and they are fully cognizant of the aforementioned attributes. In fact, they use them as a yardstick to make an important purchase. The fact is that they usually know exactly what they are looking for.

As a bottom line, a value guide is not absolute. It should be used only as a guide while taking all of the previously mentioned factors into consideration.

SALT SHAKER EVALUATION GUIDELINES

Salt shakers, unlike many other types of glass collectibles, are somewhat unique. Therefore, it is necessary to establish certain fundamental ground rules and guidelines in order to accomplish fair and uniform appraisal and evaluation of this glassware. Such special considerations are enumerated hereinafter:

1. Roughness and chipping under the tops of salt and pepper shakers should not form a basis for downgrading their value. This is proper because a majority of the shakers are mold blown and were taken off the pontil rod at the top. Such a manufacturing technique left roughness and chips which were not polished out by the manufacturing glasshouse because they are hidden from view by the shaker tops.

2. Despite much of their artistic beauty, the old glass shakers will, on occasion, have rough mold lines. This was not an uncommon manufacturing flaw, and is not cause for degradation of a shaker's appraisal value.

3. In the case of hand painted (fired-on)

decorations, it is rare that one will find the decoration to be in perfect (mint) condition. This is true because these items were in continuous use at the dinner table, and therefore subjected to frequent washings. The soaps that were used during the Victorian era were quite harsh so there will almost always be some wear of the various applied decorations. As long as portions of the decoration have not been obliterated, this should not form a basis for downgrading a shaker. Obviously, this is a judgment call to be exercised on an item-by-item basis.

4. Slight chipping or roughness on the bottom of a shaker, if hidden from view when it is placed upright upon the table, should only cause the imposition of minor value degradation (usually ten percent). It should be kept in mind that during their days of usage, salt shakers were often pounded on their bottom due to coagulated salt problems.

After application of all evaluation guidelines, the individual values arrived at should represent what a collector would expect to pay if that item were purchased today at retail in an antique shop.

Final appraisal values should be arrived at based upon the consistent application/analysis of condition, type and quality of glass, collectability, color and scarcity factors.

SALT SHAKER FRAILTIES

It is important that we pass along to our readers those salt shaker patterns that we have found to be consistently difficult to find in an acceptable condition.

Over the years, experience has shown that certain types of glass designs and patterns are predisposed to excessive chipping, annealing cracks, or abnormal decoration wear.

Therefore, it is recommended that before purchasing, the following shakers be examined very closely by the use of a ten power magnification loupe.

Agata ....excessive stain decoration wear
Beaded Triangle (chocolate) ....base motif chipping
Cactus (chocolate) ....motif and base chipping
Dewey (chocolate) ....annealing cracks on feet
Geneva (chocolate) ....motif chipping
Holly Amber ....annealing cracks
Inverted Fan & Feather ....base and motif chipping

Klondike......Chipping on frosted part of motif
Leaf Bracket (chocolate) ....annealing cracks on feet
Mt. Wash. Peachblow...........annealing cracks
Green Opaque (N.E. Glass) ....excessive mottled stain wear
Royal Ivy ....excessive chipping on/around motif
Shuttle (chocolate) ....motif chipping
Wild Rose with Bowknot ....motif chipping mainly in chocolate glass pieces
Eagle Glass Co. Shakers...........excessive wear on their hand painted decorations
Wave Crest Shakers ....transfer-type decorations subject to excessive wear

Watch out for hidden so-called paint-over repairs. These are attempts (sometimes by the seller) to mask chipping damage by painting over it. *Always* use magnification assistance to examine all gilt areas of every pattern prior to purchasing. This precaution is especially applicable to the custard patterns such as Inverted Fan and Feather and Ivorina Verde (Winged Scroll).

We recommend the use of a portable (battery operated) black light for revealing minute cracks and repair efforts. Such a light is a good investment. The first time this device saves you from making a bad purchase, it will have more than paid for itself.

SAFEGUARDING YOUR COLLECTION

It will come as no surprise to salt shaker collector's that glassware from the Victorian era can amount to quite a significant investment.

As a collection grows in both size and stature, it is in a collector's best interest to establish a reasonable amount of protection. Almost every month we see an advertisement in one of the many antique periodicals proclaiming the loss of valuable antique property.

Physical protection involves the use of proper security measures in order to avoid possible losses due to theft. We have found that the implementation of a few simple steps can provide reasonable safeguards at a minimal cost. Perhaps the best way to make our point is for us to list what we have done to protect our own salt shaker collection.

1. Avoid verbal advertising to friends, acquaintances and your neighbors that you own a valuable collection. If they know that you do have a collection, do not mention its monetary worth.

2. If possible, see to it that the place where your collection is displayed/stored is in an area that has no windows.

3. Install an adequate burglar alarm system that contains both a motion detector and window/door monitors.

4. Obtain a small vial of ultra violet marking ink that is invisible in ordinary light, and mark or dot code so that it will show up for identification when exposed to black light.

5. Register your property marking code with your local police.

6. If you buy and sell glassware through the mail or at shows or flea markets, be sure that your business is conducted by means of a rented post office box.

7. Make certain that your business cards list only a post office box address.

8. Conduct all written correspondence from your post office box address; as we do with our book readers.

9. Contact your local police and have them make a security inspection of the place where your collection resides.

PROFESSIONAL APPRAISAL OF YOUR COLLECTION

As the serious collector accumulates a sizeable salt shaker collection, the monetary investment involved can become rather significant.

Sooner or later a point will be reached where it makes good sense to protect a collection by the acquisition of insurance coverage; particularly for the more expensive and rare art glass items.

To our knowledge, no insurance company will accept a collector's personal appraisal of his/her collection no matter if the owner involved is a recognized expert. Therefore, if you want your collection insured, you must obtain a written independent appraisal to present to your insurance agent.

Professional appraisers do not work cheap, but a good one is worth the money; not only for insurance purposes, but to aid in the selling of an extensive collection or for future estate settlement.

Keep in mind that most of an appraiser's charges will be associated with turning their collected appraisal data into a properly researched and thoroughly written and signed report. Such a report should be uniformly formatted and provide a pattern name, article description, condition, approximate age, measurement data, the appraised value in dollars and a scarcity and collectability factor (if known) for each item.

SELECTING AN APPRAISER

Before hiring an appraiser, it is important to apply the following criteria, which is nothing more than an application of good common sense.

1. If hired, will the appraiser be acceptable to your insurance company?

2. Does the appraiser under consideration have experience with antique glassware? You obviously wouldn't want to consider one that specializes in furniture or some other unrelated field.

3. Make it clear to an appraiser being considered just what you are expecting; the size of your collection; the requirement for a written and signed report on each item that has been appraised.

4. Ask about the appraiser's method of determining charges. If it turns out to be anything different than by the hour, say thank you and look for another appraiser.

5. Before hiring, arrange for a personal interview and ask for references from previous clients that you may contact.

OTHER APPRAISAL CONSIDERATIONS

1. Quality in personal property is primarily determined by materials used, artistic design, and craftsmanship.

2. The ultimate value of a piece will always show a relationship to quality.

3. Generally speaking, quality + condition + current collectability + age = value.

4. Alteration, excessive refinishing of any piece, is usually damaging, and can devalue an item.

5. In the case of salt shakers, a true evaluation of each item can only be gleaned by the use of a ten power loupe or headband-type magnifier.

6. The only value a broken or badly chipped item has is its value as a study piece.

7. The final appraisal report should be accompanied by a signed transmittal letter containing appropriate facts about the appraised collection and any pertinent concluding remarks.

Outstanding Salt Shaker Rarities

In the establishment of an outstanding rarities group for special illustration, it was necessary to make the selection based upon more than the fact that the shakers are rare and considered to be art glass.

There are many rare & beautiful shakers in this book that have high collectability factors and are most desirable, but in our opinion they didn't have that "extra special something" to warrant highlighting within this portion of the book. Our decision was not made lightly nor was it based upon snap judgments or personal friendships.

We certainly couldn't select our candidates based upon the fact they are considered to be art glass pieces. If we were to do that, half the Mt. Washington/Pairpoint shakers that we have listed would certainly qualify.

Some of the selected shakers have never been recognized for what they are simply because they were not available to previous authors that have produced art glass publications. Couple this with the fact that we are not aware of any published art glass books that have ever used salt shakers as their predominating pictorial examples. Those big art glass vases, bowls, lamps, etc. always grab the spotlight. Since this book is about salt shakers, they will now get the attention that they deserve.

We are particularly grateful to all of those individuals that expended that extra effort to make this section of the book possible for our readers to enjoy. Their names are listed within the "Acknowledgments" section of this book.

Krauss Collection

Hexaglory Condiment Set: Hand Decorated Rubina & Custard Glass.
See Potpourri section for text. Circa 1885-1890.

Outstanding Salt Shaker Rarities

Barrel, Ribbed Mt. Washington Peachblow: Extremely Rare Art Glass. Mt. Washington/Pairpoint Glass Company. 2¾" tall. Circa 1886. (See page 131 for text.)

Pillar, Ribbed Mt. Washington Peachblow: Extremely Rare Art Glass. 3⅜" tall. See page 148, Mt. Washington/Pairpoint, for text. Circa 1886.

Blue Aurene: F. Carder, Steuben. Matched Pair, 2¹³⁄₁₆" tall, 1¼" diameter. Circa 1912-1922.

Curved Ribbing: Plated Amberina. New England Glass Co. 3⁷⁄₁₇" tall; 1¹³⁄₁₆" diameter. Circa 1886.

Findlay Floradine: Dalzell, Gilmore & Leighton Company. Not Onyx Ware! Note opalescent effect on decoration. 2⅝" tall with 2 piece metal top; 1¼" base diameter; 1¹⁵⁄₁₆" wide.

Rose Findlay Onyx: Shaker made by Dalzell, Gilmore, Leighton Company. Same mold as silver onyx shaker. 2⁹⁄₁₆" tall x 1¹⁵⁄₁₆" wide. Base diameter 1¼". Produced in 1889.

Tiffany: Gold Iridescent Shaker. Tiffany Furnaces, Corona, L.I., New York. Hand signed "L.C. Tiffany–Favrile;" 2⅝" tall. Made only to special orders. Has special two piece push-on top. (See Tiffany Furnaces for text). Circa 1900.

Holly Amber: (Golden Agate). Indiana Tumbler and Goblet Co., Greentown, Indiana. 3" tall. Circa 1903.

Outstanding Salt Shaker Rarities

Mary Gregory: Hand decorated cranberry glass. Originally a part of the A. G. Peterson Collection. Shaker 3¼" tall. Circa 1880.

Mary Gregory Type: (Hand decorated quality crystal) outstanding painted snow scene shaker. 3" tall. Circa 1885–1890.

Webb Peachblow: Thomas Webb & Sons, Stourbridge, England. Matched Pair. 2⁵⁄₁₆" tall. Very Rare. Circa 1882–1886.

Queen Ann: Thomas Webb & Sons, Stourbridge, England Cased Peachblow Glass. 3³/₁₆" tall. Circa 1886–1889.

Long Neck Barrel: New England Glass Company; Joseph Locke New England Peachblow. Hand decorated. 3⅜" tall, 1⅝" base diameter. Circa 1886.

Outstanding Salt Shaker Rarities

Peachbloom: Joseph Webb at Phoenix Glass. This is a heat sensitive shaded cased glass. 3¼" tall, 1⁷⁄₁₆" base diameter.

New England Peachblow Barrel: Joseph Locke, "Wildrose" 3⅛" tall, 1⁵⁄₁₆" base diameter. Patented March 1, 1886.

Geranium: Manufacturer unknown. Elaborate decorated opalescent ware. 3" tall, 1½" base diameter. Circa 1884–1890.

Stevens & Williams Peachblow: Brick-red coloring in the intense portion. 2⅝" tall, 1" base diameter.

Rose O'Neill Kewpies: Made in Germany by Kestner. Patented 1913 Rose O'Neill paper label marked. Pink flesh colored 2½" tall. Circa 1913.

Just Collection

Baseball Player: (tribute to Babe Ruth). Figural Salt Bottle. 5" tall, Circa 1924–1932.

Just Collection

Carnival Corn: (Early Carnival Glass) Peacock Colored Carnival Glass. 5" tall, manufacturer unknown.

Attribution by Glass Factory
(Arranged Alphabetically)
Adams & Co.
Pittsburgh, Pennsylvania.
(1851-1891)

First established by John Adams in 1851 at Pittsburgh. By 1861 this glasshouse was considered one the larger factories in the Pittsburgh area. After Adams' death, in 1886, the firm continued under the same company name until it joined the U.S. Glass Company in 1891; therefore, it lost its identity and became known as Factory A of this giant conglomerate. This factory produced numerous crystal patterns prior to the U.S. Glass merger many of which were reissued in various colors at a later date by the U.S. Glass Company.

Thousand Eye: Clear vaseline glass; mold blown and pressed; The pattern consists of horizontal rows of flattened hobnails; between each group is a sharp diamond. This sharpness differentiates the "Thousand Eye" pattern from the other patterns that resemble it. 2¾" tall. Very Scarce. Circa 1875–1880.

Thumbprint, Ruby: Ruby-stained crystal; mold blown. Also called Kings Crown, and made in crystal and amber-stained colors. 2⅞" tall. Very Scarce. Circa 1880 with continuous production at Factory A.

Wildflower: Clear vaseline; mold blown. Also made in crystal, amber, blue, apple green and possibly amethyst; we have never seen a shaker in this latter color. 3⅛" tall. Very Scarce. Circa 1874 (in crystal) with later color production by the U.S. Glass Co.

Cottage: Clear blue glass; mold blown & pressed. The shaker has a wide fine cut panel that is scalloped both top and bottom. The fine cutting is broken up by short vertical sections. 2⅛" tall. Rare. Circa 1874 with later production in 1898 at U.S. Glass Factory A.

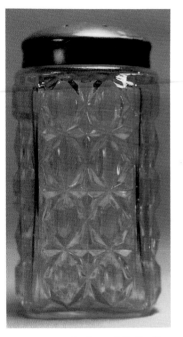

Lockwood Collection

Valencia Waffle: Clear blue glass; mold blown and pressed. Sometimes called "Block and Star." We are illustrating two sides because the pattern is different on each side. Also produced in crystal, amber and apple green. 3" tall. Scarce in color! Circa 1883-1887.

Aetna Glass & Manufacturing Co.

Aetna Glass & Manufacturing Co.
Bellaire, Ohio
(1880-1891)

The Aetna Glass and Manufacturing Company was established on February 7, 1880. R.T. DeVries was the company's president and chief executive officer.

Over this company's life span it manufactured bar glasses, goblets, pressed glass tableware, gas shades, lamps and blown ware.

The factory was closed sometime in 1891.

Hobnail in Square: Crystal and white opalescent pressed glass. The shaker body is completely covered with embossed squares; centered within each square are protruding conical-shaped hobs. Also made in crystal and other colors. 2⅞" tall. Arthur Peterson classified this shaker as Rare. Pattern name by Kamm. Circa 1887.

Authors' Collection

Atterbury & Co.
Pittsburgh, Pennsylvania
(1859-1893)

Established in 1859 with Thomas B. Atterbury as president. He served in this position throughout the company's existence, which ended in 1893 when the factory became known as The Atterbury Glass Company.

Authors' Collection

Atterbury Twin: White opaque Cryolite glass; mold blown and pressed. Also made in crystal. Patented on October 28, 1873. Designed as a dual condiment dispenser; one side for salt and other for pepper. Requires a two-piece special top and is of little value without it. 3⅛" tall to the top of its inside glass divider. Very Scarce. Circa 1873.

RIGHT: Atterbury Twin: showing divider.

Authors' Collection

Authors' Collection

Rib and Swirl: White opaque opal glass; mold blown. Also made in green and blue opaque. 4" tall. Scarce. Circa 1878-1887.

Big Owl: White opaque opal glass; mold blown and pressed. Also made in crystal. 5½" tall. Rare. Circa 1884-1891.

Bakewell, Pears & Company
Pittsburgh, Pennsylvania
(1808-1882)

Began in 1808 as Bakewell & Ensell. Became Bakewell, Pears and Company in 1836. This firm was the recipient of a number of design patents. From a salt shaker collector's point of view, this factory innovated and received the first design patent specifically for a salt shaker which was in the form of an owl. It was awarded to Harry P. Pears on February 13, 1877. The factory closed in 1882.

The "Little Owl" salt shaker can be found in either crystal or frosted type glass (the frosted considerably harder to acquire). After three decades, we were able to verify that this ware was produced as both salt and pepper shakers. The only difference between the two shakers is in the size of the condiment dispensing holes in the metal top. One is better than twice the diameter of the other.

Because this shaker has always been highlighted as a design patent "specifically" for a salt shaker, we wonder how many collectors have asked themselves about the existence of the companion pepper shaker. Of course, the other problem is the fact that this ware falls into the Rare category and is seldom available for purchase in pairs. After all, it only took us 30 years.

Authors' Collection

Owl, Little: Crystal or frosted translucent; pressed glass. Made as both a salt & pepper shaker. 2¾" tall. Rare. Circa 1877.
BELOW: Little Owl salt and pepper showing size comparison of dispensing holes.

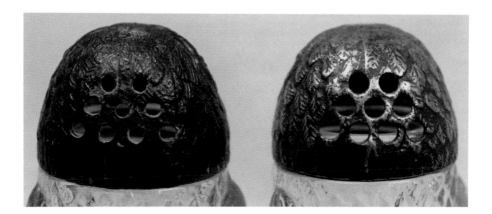

A.J. Beatty and Sons
Steubenville, Ohio
(1851-1891)

This glasshouse produced both cut crystal and pressed and blown ware over their operational history. Not long after the establishment of their Tiffin, Ohio factory they merged their firms with the

U.S. Glass Company and their identities became simply Factory R & Factory S. During the late 1880's Beatty produced a considerable amount of opalescent ware. It is this type of glass that we have illustrated.

Beatty Honeycomb: Clear blue opalescent glass; mold blown. The pattern consists of a solid series of opalescent squares in the form of a honeycomb. The entire motif is in high raised relief. The pattern was named by Ruth Webb Lee in her *Early American Pattern Glass* book. 2⅝" tall. Very Scarce. Circa 1888-1890.

Beatty Rib (Ribbed Opal): Clear blue opalescent glass; mold blown. The pattern consists of 16 protruding opalescent vertical ribs. The ribs are in high raised relief. This is also a Lee pattern name which Peterson changed to "Ribbed Opal," however, most collectors seem to call this item "Beatty Rib." 2⅞" tall. Very Scarce. Circa 1889-1890.

Beaumont Glass Company

Beaumont Glass Company
Martins Ferry, Ohio
(1895-1902)
Grafton, West Virginia
(1902-1906)

The Beaumont Glass Company was formed in 1895 by Percy Beaumont. This glasshouse began in the same manner as Fenton; i.e., decorating and selling glassware that had been manufactured by other glass factories. It must have been profitable because in 1899 the Martins Ferry factory was modified so that it could manufacture glassware as well as decorate it.

This glasshouse produced both pressed and blown ware: a lot of their blown ware was colored opalescent. A 1900 trade ad reveals patterns in "Coinspot" (also produced at Hobbs), "Flower Mold," "Fern" and "Swirl."

In 1902 a new factory was opened at Grafton, West Virginia. After a successful operation, Beaumont sold out in 1906 and the factory name was changed to the Tygert Valley Glass Co.

Coinspot: Cranberry opalescent; mold blown. This shaker has a round cylindrical shape that contains uniform size coinspots. We list the pattern here because it does appear in a trade ad dated 1900. The bottom of this ware is a solid white opalescent with a small amount of the cranberry showing in the center. 3½" tall. Very Scarce. Circa 1900.

Flora: Clear emerald green; mold blown and pressed. This is a very busy embossed floral pattern with gold decoration on the floral sprig and the footed base. 3⅛" tall. Peterson listed this as a Rare pattern in his 1970 salt shaker book. Circa 1895.

Flower Mold, Beaumont's: Clear cranberry; mold blown. The shaker base contains an embossed flower that is equally spaced around its perimeter; the center of this piece contains a band of short vertical embossed ribs. Also produced in blue and green. 3" tall. Rare. Circa 1895.

Yarn, Bulbous: Translucent pink and white spatter; mold blown. This pattern consists of a continuous series of swirls. A very similar pattern was produced by Buckeye Glass Co. Also produced in cranberry and blue opalescent. 2⅝" tall. Very Scarce. Circa 1895.

The Bellaire Goblet Company
Bellaire, Ohio
(1876-1888)
Findlay, Ohio
(1888-1891)

The Bellaire Goblet Company began operations in 1876 at Bellaire, Ohio. The facility was moved to Findlay in 1888. The principal output of the factory was pressed glass goblets, bar glassware and novelties.

The Findlay plant was shut down in early May, 1889, due to a disastrous fire, and did not reopen until early 1890. The company joined the huge U. S. Glass Company in 1891 and operated as Factory M.

Earlybird: Clear blue pressed glassware. One would have to classify this shaker as a novelty piece, and a fragile one at that due to it being in the form of a small footed goblet with a chicken's head protruding from the side of the shaker[1]. Pattern name by Peterson. Usually found in crystal. 2⅞" tall. Very Scarce in crystal; Rare in blue. Circa 1879-1885.

The Bellaire Goblet Company

Log and Star: Clear crystal pressed glassware. The pattern consists of alternating plain and starred cubes in raised relief; very similar to the Milton pattern. Also produced in clear amber and blue in a cruet set containing salt, pepper and handled cruet. 2⅞" tall. Scarce. Circa 1890 with continued production at U.S. Glass after 1891.

Boston & Sandwich Glass Company

Boston & Sandwich Glass Company
Sandwich, Massachusetts
(1825-1888)

Despite the fact that this glasshouse did not completely close until 1888, the Boston and Sandwich Glass Company did not produce glassware after 1887. Over the last six or seven decades there have been many articles and books written about this glasshouse. There have been three very comprehensive hard bound books[1] written and published by Raymond E. Barlow and his co-author Joan E. Kaiser. A fourth volume is currently being compiled.

In our 35 plus years of antique glassware experience, we have never seen a better researched compendium of material dealing with a single glass factory. While some of the material is somewhat controversial, the backup material that is provided is outstanding and should firmly establish many new facts relative to this outstanding American glass house.

As most experienced collectors know, very few salt shakers can be attributed to Boston and Sandwich. In fact, it really boils down to two patterns: the "Christmas Barrel" and "Christmas Panel" salt and pepper shakers.

The so-called "Christmas Pearl" shakers that can be found with an 1877 Dana K. Alden dated top, containing his patented agitator, are a product of the Mt. Washington Glass Company for Alden in fulfillment of special contractual orders.

The "Octagon Waffle" shakers with Alden dated agitator tops were made by several glasshouses to special Alden orders; but not by Boston and Sandwich.

Through the cooperative help of the Archer Glass Museum in Kernersville, North Carolina, we were able to meet with Barlow and Kaiser. The data that follows was obtained as a result of a lengthy discussion.

1. Both the "Christmas Barrel" and "Christmas Panel" shakers were made by more than one glass factory because the Boston & Sandwich factory was unable to handle the order demand placed by Alden.

2. The "Christmas Barrel" molds differed from those produced elsewhere in two ways. (1) There is an intaglio rayed star on the bottom of the Sandwich shakers. (2) Because of different molds, shakers made by other factories will be found to lack a continuous inside curvature; instead, there will be flat spots when the inside of the shaker is felt with the index finger.

3. Alden ran glass journal trade ads up into the early 1890's that stated how many thousands of the Alden shakers were produced during the previous year. These trade ads, along with much

other new information, will be published in the forthcoming Barlow/Kaiser book.[2]

Now let's get even more controversial. There are opaque opalware "Christmas Barrel" shakers that were hand decorated by Mary Gregory.[3] She did not paint small children; the pieces that are attributable to her are hand-painted "house in the snow" winter scenes.[4]

The "Christmas Barrel" mechanical rotary agitator was design patented by Hiram J. White on December 25, 1877 and assigned to Dana K. Alden of Boston, Massachusetts via Patent No. 198,554. White called his invention an "Improvement In Table Salt Bottles." The majority of his patent descriptive text deals with stirring and breaking up caked salt within a vessel.

It is important to keep things in proper perspective. Remember that there were just as many "Christmas Barrel" and "Christmas Panel" pepper shakers made; they only differ in that their tops are undated and they do not have the 1877 patented Alden agitator.

The various Christmas shaker molds were controlled by Alden. However, it is not clear whether this control was by way of lease or ownership.

All the Alden shakers (particularly the "Christmas Barrel") have a high collectibility factor. Only certain colors are really difficult to obtain, but not if you bring money. Also, those with hand-decorated scenes are very scarce to rare.

At a recent glassware show, it was of great interest & significance to observe the sale of a pair of clear cranberry colored "Christmas Barrel" shakers (both containing agitators) for $750.00. A companion pepper shaker was not part of the deal. Strange? Oh, Well!! The poor lowly pepper shaker is hardly in the running.

Should the complete "Christmas Barrel" Alden salt and pepper condiment in its original metal stand that we are illustrating contain two salt shakers and no pepper? We don't think so! Let's get our values and perspectives straight.

The glass quality in the "Christmas Barrel" shakers leaves a lot to be desired; the prices being projected for the clear glass shakers are unwarranted because they often contain excessive bubbles, mold marks and off-center molded compartments.

Christmas Barrel Condiment: Clear cobalt blue; mold blown; The pattern amounts to a short, bulging barrel-shaped shaker having a protruding ring just below the metal top. We are illustrating a complete condiment set in the original "Alden silverplated holder." While not much in terms of overall quality, it is indeed a rarity as a complete set. The salt shaker is on the right with its patent dated rotary agitator top. The companion pepper contains no agitator and the top is undated. The shaker bottoms contain an intaglio rayed star. The stand lifting handle has a ring at the top. 1⅝" tall. Rare. Circa 1877.

Christmas Barrel Condiment Variation: Clear cobalt blue; mold blown. The only thing different about this set from the previous one is that the brassy metal holder has a completely different physical make up. The stand/holder measures 4⅜" tall and 4¼" long; the bottom is marked Alden Griffith & Co., Boston, Mass. We have no way of knowing which stand configuration was first produced; but as we have previously stated, the product is pretty much utilitarian and the collectibility factor is very high. So there you have it! At least two (maybe more) metal holders were produced by Alden for the Christmas Barrel salt and pepper shakers. 1⅝" tall. Rare.

Boston & Sandwich Glass Company

Panel, Christmas: Clear electric blue; mold blown. The pattern consists of ten plain vertical panels with a double glass ring just below the shaker metal top. This is the tallest one that we have seen, but the height will vary from 2⅞" to almost 4". The size variation is apparently due to heat shrinkage as a result of the manufacturing process. Most of these shakers run 3" tall. As in the case of the Christmas Barrel shakers, the companion pepper shakers are identical except for the absence of the Alden patent dated top with rotary agitator. Because of the size of these shakers the agitator is naturally longer. We are also illustrating three Christmas Panel peppers in vaseline, amethyst, and electric blue to provide the reader with a color overview. Most shaker bottoms will contain an intaglio rayed star. Generally speaking we have found the overall glass quality is much better than that of the Christmas Barrel shakers. Made in all colors. Cranberry and amethyst are the scarcer colors. 3⅞" tall. Very Scarce! Circa 1877.

Boston & Sandwich Glass Company, Attributed to
The following shakers were not
made by Boston & Sandwich

The "Christmas Pearl" and "Octagon Waffle" shakers are illustrated within the Boston & Sandwich section to highlight the fact that this ware should not be attributed to Boston and Sandwich Glass Company.

Pearl, Christmas: White opalware with pastel painted backgrounds; mold blown. This a plain bulbous shaker that narrows at its ringed base. There is also a protruding glass ring just below the metal top. Usually found with hand-painted floral decoration but sometimes with the stork or transfer decoration. The salt shakers will have the Alden patent dated top with rotary agitator; the companion peppers will not be dated. We are illustrating four shakers to show typical decorative variations. These shakers were produced for Alden by the Mt. Washington Glass Company to fulfill special contractual orders. 3⅜" tall. Very Scarce! Circa 1884-1893.

Authors' Collection

Lockwood Collection

Waffle, Octagon: Clear crystal pressed glass; has three sizes: 3⅞", 3" and 2" tall. These shakers are completely covered with deeply embossed squares very reminiscent of a waffle design configuration. Known to have been made by several different glasshouses under Alden production contracts. In the salt shakers, the tops contain the 1877 date with an appropriate sized agitator to fit its height. As a grand finale to our Boston and Sandwich section, we are using a picture that shows from the left: Christmas Pearl, Christmas Panel, Block and Panel, Octagon Waffle (3 sizes) and the Christmas Barrel shakers. Circa 1877-1894.

Buckeye Glass Company
Martins Ferry, Ohio
(1878-1896)

The Buckeye Glass Company was established at Martins Ferry, Ohio during 1878 by Henry Helling and associates. The factory production consisted of everything from shades and pressed glass to free and mold blown opalescent glassware, covering Buckeye's early production years until 1890.

Much of the factory's opalescent and art glass production was brought about by John F. Miller and further influenced by the subsequent short-time employment of Harry Northwood from the LaBelle Glass Works, during 1887.

Miller left Buckeye during 1889. The various glass trade journals ceased reporting the production of further Buckeye opalescent glassware after 1890. Some glass historians believe that this was the result of Miller's departure to the American Glass Company at Anderson, Indiana. At any rate, from an art glass viewpoint, the company was never the same. Buckeye went out of business in February, 1896 as the result of a major fire.

Left: Chrysanthemum Base: Cranberry opalescent; mold blown. The principal pattern consists of an embossed ribbed base; the remainder of the pattern is swirled with white swirling opalescent stripes. Also produced in white, canary and blue opalescent glass; some are satinized and speckled. Pattern name by Peterson. 2⅜" tall. Very Scarce. Circa 1888-1891.

Right: Opal Ribbon, Short: Cranberry opalescent; mold blown. The pattern consists of an embossed reverse swirl; the entire external shaker surface has been acid treated/satinized. Also produced in white, canary and blue opalescent glass. Pattern name by Peterson. Heacock refers to this pattern as "Reverse Swirl." 2¼" tall. Very Scarce. Circa 1887-1990.

Authors' Collection

Authors' Collection

Cambridge Glass Company
Cambridge, Ohio
(1902-1957)

The Cambridge Glass Company began production during 1902. It was built by the National Glass Company to be their new, modern production facility. Molds from various other corporate member factories were routed to this new plant in the interest of (what National viewed as) production efficiency.

After the corporate breakup began around 1904, the factory was leased by its former manager, Mr. Bennett, and began producing new pattern designs. By 1907, Mr. Bennett purchased the factory from the former National Glass Co. stockholders. This action made the facility an independent company.

Cambridge produced both high quality pressed and hand crafted blown ware, the latter predominating after 1917.

During it's operative years, the Company had two trademarks; the letter C inside a triangle for hand crafted blown ware and the words "NEAR-CUT" for its pressed glassware. This highly successful glass house finally had to close during 1957. The Cambridge molds were sold to the Imperial Glass Company around 1960.

Cambridge #1035: Clear crystal pressed glass; This is an octagon panelled shaker with deep intaglio cut flowers & leaves. The piece contains the "NEAR-CUT" trademark. 3⅛" tall. Scarce. Circa 1935-1945.

Star of Bethlehem[1] (Nearcut Star): Ruby stained pressed crystal glassware. This is a simple pattern consisting of a large intaglio star that appears on each side of the shaker; the area surrounding the star has been ruby stained. Pattern name by Kamm. Cambridge catalogued this as their No. 2656 pattern. A complete set of tableware was produced in this pattern. In the ruby stained style, this pattern enjoys a high collectibility factory and is very scarce. 2⅞" tall. Circa 1909.

The Central Glass Company
Wheeling, West Virginia
(1863-1891)

This glasshouse was originally formed by eight glass blowers (gaffers) in 1863 by combining their finances. The first man to head this factory was Mr. John Oesterling who was one of the original eight gaffers. By 1879, under his leadership, the factory was established as a major glass manufacturer.

Central Glass exhibited at the San Francisco Exposition during 1881, displaying many pressed glassware designs. During 1891, Central joined the U.S. Glass Co., and became known as Factory O. However, by 1896 a new, separate company using the name "Central Glass Co." was formed, and in 1898 the works was moved to Summitville, Indiana and went into full production. Central finally closed in 1939 due to their inability to compete with the imported wares.

One of the more important patterns produced by this firm was the "Silver Age" design, more commonly known to todays collector as the "Coin" pattern(s)—Coin & Columbian Coin. They also produced an 1876 Centennial "Bell Salt" that A.G. Peterson named "Liberty Bell."

Coin, Columbian: Crystal with gilded coins; pressed glass. One of the coins contains an embossed bust resembling a silhouette of Christopher Columbus. Also made in crystal with frosted coins. 2⅛" tall. Very scarce. Circa 1891 by Central with later production after merging into U.S. Glass as Factory O.

Ribbed Inside: Clear blue; mold blown and pressed. The pattern consists of inside the shaker ribbing with a footed base. Also produced in crystal, vaseline and amber. 3" tall. Very scarce. Circa 1887-1891.

Liberty Bell: Crystal; mold blown and pressed. Has a special handled metal top that forms part of the bell motif. Without the original metal top, this item has no monetary value. 2³⁄₁₆" tall. Rare. Circa 1875-1877

Central Glass Company

Spirea Band: Dark amber; mold blown and pressed. The pattern consists of two small horizontal diamonds; one just below the shaker top and the other across the body base. Known colors are sapphire blue, vaseline, apple green & crystal. 3" tall. Scarce. Circa 1886-1891.

Thumbprint, Swirl-Based: Clear amber; mold blown and pressed. Formed by a dual mold process with thumbprints on the inside and smooth on the outer surface. The footed base contains a series of small swirls. Known colors in blue, vaseline and crystal. 3" tall. Scarce. Circa 1886-1891

Challinor, Taylor and Company

Challinor, Taylor and Company
Tarentum, Pennsylvania
(1866-1891)

Began operation in 1866, located on the south side of Pittsburgh. In 1884 this glass house moved to Tarentum, Pennsylvania. The factory was incorporated into the United States Glass Company in 1891. This glasshouse specialized in colored and hand painted glassware along with many pressed/blown novelties.

In 1886, David Challinor was awarded a patent for variegated glassware (also known as Marble or Slag glass). The technique was accomplished by melting different glass colors in separate pots and then combining the various colors together. The result was the capability of producing an almost infinite variety of marbelized coloring.

Unfortunately, shortly after the merger with U.S. Glass, the factory burned down and was considered to be a total loss. It was never rebuilt.

Banded Shells: Opaque green glass; mold blown. This is a short vertical lobed shaker containing embossed shells top and bottom. Also made in opaque pink, white and blue. 1⅞"tall. Very Scarce. Circa 1890 with later production as Factory C of the U.S. Glass Co.

Beaded Oval Mirror: Blue opaque glass; mold blown. Also made in various variegated (slag) colors as well as white, green and pink. 3¼" tall. Scarce. Circa 1890 with probable later production after U.S. Glass merger when Challinor became known as Factory C.

Flower Bouquet: Blue opaque glass; mold blown. Known production in white, green and red. 3" tall. Scarce. Circa 1891.

Beaded Oval Mirror   **Seashell**

Forget-me-not: Variegated pink glass; mold blown. Known production in crystal, opaque white, green & blue. Some of them are cased. Also made in a complete cruet set with salt, pepper, cruet bottle and matching tray. 2" tall. Scarce. Circa 1887-1891.

Challinor, Taylor and Company

Forget-me-not, Tall: Variegated pink glass; mold blown. Also produced in opaque green, white and blue. 2⅞" tall. Scarce. Circa 1889-1891.

Horseshoe & Aster: Clear vaseline; mold blown. Other known colors are opaque white, pink, blue & green. 3½" tall. Rare (in vaseline).

Marble Glass Box: Variegated chocolate and off-white; mold blown. No doubt made in the other standard colors, but we haven't verified this. 2⅞" tall. Rare. Circa 1890-1891.

Pleated Skirt: Pink opaque; mold blown. Known production in crystal, opaque white, green and blue. 1¾" tall. Circa 1891.

Just Collection

Seashell: Variegated chocolate and off white; mold blown. Also made in opaque white, blue, pink and green. Very scarce in variegated colors. 3⅜"tall. Circa 1890 with later production after 1891 as Factory C.

Authors' Collection

Slag: Opaque variegated shades of brown; mold blown. Also made in non-variegated colors of blue and green. 3¼" tall. Very Scarce. Circa 1890.

Just Collection

Slag: Variegated blue; mold blown. Also made in non-variegated colors of blue, green, pink and white. 3¼" tall. Very Scarce. Circa 1890.

Authors' Collection

Square S: Blue opaque glass; mold blown. Known production in opaque pink, green and white. 3¼" tall. Scarce. Circa 1890 with later production as Factory C.

Columbia Glass Company
Findlay, Ohio
(1886-1893)

This glasshouse began operations during December, 1886. One of the first patterns produced was their No. 54 Line, "Dew Drop," known today as Hobnail, Double-eye. Columbia merged with the U.S. Glass Company in 1891 where it became known simply as Factory J.

While the plant prospered for a short while, in early December, 1892 all Factory J employees were notified of an indefinite shutdown. It turned out that the plant's last day of production was December 10, 1892. The major problem was caused by the loss of natural gas pressure at Findlay; the City simply turned off the gas supply, forcing permanent closure on January 12, 1893.

Just Collection

Lockwood Collection

Broken Column with Red Dots: Ruby stained crystal. Also made in crystal. Apparently this pattern was also manufactured at Factory E of U.S. Glass. (Also see U.S. Glass) 2⅞" tall. Rare. Circa 1893.

Radiant: Crystal glass; mold blown & pressed. This shaker has a special mechanical top that was patented in 1887 by Metellus Thompson (see patent section). To the best of our knowledge, this ware has never been produced in color. 3" tall. Rare. Circa 1887.

Consolidated Lamp & Glass Company

Consolidated Lamp & Glass Company
Coraopolis, Pennsylvania
(1893-1964)

This factory/glasshouse was established in 1893 at Fostoria, Ohio. It was at this location that Consolidated's first glass production took place and continued well into 1895. Subsequent to this period, production was moved to a new factory located at Coraopolis, Pennsylvania. The factory closed in 1964. See the "Introduction" section of this book for more details regarding this glasshouse.

Authors' Collection

Argus Swirl: Pink cased shading to white; mold blown. Also made in clear cranberry (difficult to obtain) opaque blue and white. 2⅛" tall. Scarce. Circa 1894-1900.

Bulging Loops (rib, eight): Pink opaque; triple cased; mold blown. This pattern has eight bulging ribs. Known colors of clear cranberry, rare cased yellow and opaque white, blue, and green (some satinized). 3⅛" tall. Circa 1895-1904.

Beads & Bulges: Clear cranberry (Kopp's so-called Pigeon Blood); mold blown. Also produced in opaque white, blue and pink. 3⅜" tall. Rare in cranberry. Circa 1894-1900.

Bulging Leaf: Blue opaque; mold blown. The motif consists of two rows of bulging leaves. Also made in opaque, green, pink, white and variegated white. 2" tall. Scarce. Circa 1894-1896.

Beaded Panel, Vertical: Green opaque; mold blown. Also made in opaque white, blue and pink. 2⅝" tall. Scarce. Circa 1895-1903.

Consolidated Lamp & Glass Company

Bulging Petal: Blue opaque; mold blown. The motif has four rows of small bulging petals. Also made in opaque white, blue and pink (some of them cased). 2⅛" tall. Very scarce. Circa 1894-1898

Cone: Blue opaque, mold blown. The pattern consists of cone shaped leaves covering the entire shaker. Known colors in opaque white, pink, green and a rare cased yellow. Any of the aforementioned colors may also be found in satin or cased glass. 2⅞" tall. Circa 1894-1904.

Bulging 3 Petal Condiment Set: Rare yellow cased; mold blown; shakers & mustard. The pattern consists of twelve bulging petals covering the main portion of the condiment dispensers which have a slightly extended base for proper fit into the glass based holder that nestles into a special metal stand. The other version of this set has an all glass base with a metal loop-shaped handle. 2" tall. Very Rare. Circa 1894-1900.

Cord & Tassle, Double: Variegated opaque pink-to-white shading; mold blown. The motif comprises two rows of inter-twining cords and tassels on the upper two-thirds of the shaker. Known colors in opaque white, blue, green and pink (some of them cased). 2" tall. Very scarce. Circa 1894-1900.

Cotton Bale: Blue opaque, mold blown. The pattern name satisfactorily describes this pattern. Also made in opaque white, pink and green (some of them cased). 2⅝" tall. Circa 1894-1895.

Cosmos, Tall: White opaque; mold blown. Each panel contains a grouping of three flowers; the neck of the shaker is painted pink. Known colors in opaque pink, blue, green and yellow (some of them cased). 3⅜" tall. Very scarce. Circa 1895-1902.

Consolidated Lamp & Glass Company

Criss Cross, Consolidated's: Cranberry opalescent; mold blown. This unique pattern consists of a series of small cranberry-colored diamonds that have been formed by interspersed, white opalescent, X-shaped figures. Known colors in white and blue opalescent. 3⅛" tall. Very scarce. Circa 1894-1895.

Daisy, Long Petal: Opaque green; mold blown. The pattern consists of two large daisy flowers each growing above appropriate foliage. Also made in opaque white, blue and pink (some of them cased). 3½" tall. Rare. Circa 1904.

Dahlia, Beaded: Pink cased; mold blown. The motif has six Dahlia flowers amid larger leaves. Also made in opaque white, blue and green. 2⅝" tall. Very scarce. Circa 1894-1900.

Bruce Collection

McElderry Collection

Distended Sides: Clear cranberry; mold blown. A plain dome shaped shaker with an extended base for use in a condiment set. We are also showing this pattern in a hand painted opalware condiment. Note the button handle that makes it accessible from either side. 2⅜" tall. Rare in cranberry. Very scarce in an opalware condiment set. Circa 1894-1900.

Authors' Collection

Authors' Collection

Authors' Collection

Florette: Pastel green opalescent; mold blown. The shape is similar to Consolidated's Half Cone and Argus Swirl. In this case, the motif consists of a series of bulging diamond shapes separated by what appears to be small daisies. Known colors in opaque pink, blue, green and white (some of them cased). 2¼" tall. Rare in opalescent glass. Circa 1894-1989.

Fish: Pink cased; mold blown. The motif consists of four embossed fish standing upright; one on each corner of the shaker. Known colors of red, blue, green & white opaque (some of them cased). 3⅛" tall. Very scarce. Circa 1894-1900.

Flower Assortment: Variegated pink opaque; mold blown. A four panelled shaker with each side containing a different type of embossed floral display. Also made in opaque white and blue (some of them are cased). 3¼" tall. Rare. Circa 1894-1897.

Consolidated Lamp & Glass Company

Flower and Rib: Pink cased; mold blown. This ware has a center crease. The lower half contains a series of bulging petals; the upper half has vertical ribs topped-off by leaves protruding downward from the shaker neck. Also made in opaque white, blue and green (some of them cased). 3½" tall. Circa 1894-1900.

Guttate, Squatty: White opaque; mold blown. Has the same basic pattern as the Guttate shaker. Also made in opaque pink, green, blue & a rare clear cranberry; some of the opaque colors are cased or satinized. 1¾" tall. Very scarce. 1898-1900.

Guttate: Variegated pink to white; mold blown. This eight panelled shaker contains five bulging petals on each panel which are outlined by two rows of vertical beads. Produced in opaque pink, blue and the very rare cased yellow. Shakers found with two-piece metal tops are reproductions. 3" tall. Very scarce. Circa 1894-1900.

Half Cone: Pink satinized & cased; mold blown. This is a divided pattern, with the upper portion smooth and the lower two-thirds having embossed, overlapping cones. Also made in opaque white, blue and yellow; both cased and uncased. Considered to be rare in cased pink or yellow. 2⅛" tall. Rare. Circa 1895-1900.

Half Ribbed: Opaque white; mold blown. The lower portion of this shaker is encircled with continuous embossed small ribs; the upper-half is smooth and contains no pattern. An apparent variation of the Half Cone mold. We have no other color experience to report. 2⅜" tall. Very scarce. Circa 1897-1903

Leaf, Overlapping: Variegated pink opaque; mold blown. The pattern contains six rows of sharply defined leaves that are somewhat reminiscent of a type of thistle. Also made in opaque pink, blue, green, custard and white; some of them are cased. 1⅞" tall. Very scarce. Circa 1896-1900.

Melon, Nine Rib: Clear cranberry; mold blown. No doubt a Nicholas Kopp creation containing nine melon-like ribs. The bottom of the shaker has been fire polished smooth. We have the matching biscuit jar. No other colors have been observed. 1⅞" tall. Rare. Circa 1895-1900.

Pansy, Six: Translucent orange-like cranberry (sometimes called Pigeon blood); mold blown; 2½" tall. The motif consists of six embossed Pansy blossoms encircling the shaker body. Also produced in opaque white, blue, pink and green (some of them satinized and cased). Rare. Circa 1895-1900

Pansy, Three: Opaque blue, mold blown. A variation of the "Six Pansy" pattern. Known colors are opaque white, pink, green and a translucent cranberry Pigeon Blood. 2½" tall. Scarce. Circa 1896-1900.

Consolidated Lamp & Glass Company

Periwinkle: Variegated opaque yellow; mold blown. This rare colored pattern consists of a series of embossed five petal flowers distributed uniformly throughout the entire shaker. Known colors in variegated opaque pink and white; also homogenous pink and a very pretty translucent cranberry. 2½" tall. Rare in variegated yellow. Circa 1896-1903.

Panelled Shell: Pink triple cased; mold blown. This pattern has four large, embossed shells completely covering the shaker. Also made in opaque white, blue and green; some will be cased or satinized. 3" tall. Very Scarce. Circa 1894-1900.

Pineapple: Variegated opaque pink and white; mold blown. The pattern consists of twenty large, embossed pineapple leaves. When viewed from the bottom, five of the large bulging leaves form the shaker's feet. Known colors in pink, green, blue and white (some are cased or satinized). 3" tall. Very scarce. Circa 1894-1898.

Periwinkle Variant: Unusual translucent cranberry (Pigeon Blood) with predominating orange; mold blown. This embossed pattern is a variation of the Periwinkle shaker which has the same basic five petaled flower. However, the variation on this ware is that flowers overlap (one into the other) with smaller and smaller portions of each flower being visible as the pattern progresses toward the top of the shaker. 2½" tall. Very rare. Circa 1896-1903.

Quilt: Opaque blue; mold blown. The pattern has a series of embossed bulging diamonds with a daisylike flower at each diamond point; the bottom has a protruding base for fitting this ware into spaces within a condiment set glass holder. Known colors are opaque white, pink and green; some are variegated, satinized and cased. 2½" tall. Very scarce. Circa 1894-1898.

Rib, Alternating: Translucent pink cased; mold blown. This is a bulging base item having eight large ribs. Also produced in opaque white, green and blue (some of them are satinized or cased). 3⅛" tall. Very scarce. Circa 1897-1903.

Rib, Triple: Translucent blue; mold blown. This pattern has three vertical ribbed segments; bulging ribs at the bottom; nine tapered & curved in the central protion of the shaker, and nine short bulging ribs just below the top. Also made in opaque white, pink and green. 3" tall. Very scarce. Circa 1895-1902.

Rib and Scroll: Opaque lime green; mold blown. Contains large embossed scrolling on the lower portion with individual bulging ribs encircling the top; each rib is ringed by a series of round beads. Also made in opaque white, pink, blue and a lovely translucent cranberry. 3" tall. Very Scarce. Circa 1904-1905.

Consolidated Lamp & Glass Company

Ribbon Band: Illustrated are pink cased and opaque green; mold blown. This pattern was named by E. G. Warman and consists of a narrow ribbon band tied into a bow at the narrow portion of the shaker. Known colors in opaque blue and white; made in both satin and cased configuration. 3½" tall. Scarce. Circa 1896-1903.

Scroll, Bottom: Opaque blue; mold blown. A two bulge shaker with the lower portion encircled with continuous scrolling. Also made in opaque white, pink and green (some of them are cased). 2⅝" tall. Very scarce. Circa 1896-1902.

Scroll, Footed: Opaque green; mold blown. Pattern name by S.T. Millard. Consists of intricate panelled scrolls on all four sides; each side is configured to form a small bottom foot in order to provide upright support. Known colors in opaque blue and pink (some are cased). 3⅛" tall. Scarce. Circa 1894-1900.

Scroll, Lacy: Yellow cased; mold blown. Has a two piece metal top. The pattern consists of sections of lace attached to some of the scrolls that are present throughtout the shaker. Also made in opaque white, blue, pink and green (some of them cased). 3⅜" tall. Very rare in yellow cased. Circa 1895.

Scroll and Net: Pink cased; mold blown. Pattern name by Warman. Consists of an embossed band of complex scrolling at the top and base. Two wide netted vertical embossed panels represent the rest of the pattern. Produced in opaque white, green, blue and pink (some of them cased). 3" tall. Very scarce. Circa 1897-1903.

Swirl, Consolidated's Princess: Pink cased; mold blown. This pattern has eight wide swirling ribs that cover the entire vertical height of the shaker. A four part mold was utilized to manufacture this ware. Known colors are opaque blue, white and a pastel green that fluoresces when exposed to black light. Some shakers will be found in satin. 3" tall. Very scarce. Circa 1896-1900.

Swirl, Two-Way: Clear cranberry; mold blown. The pattern has continuous bulging swirls that flow from left to right. The bulging swirls are wider and more predominate at the base; becoming narrower as they reach to top of the shaker. Also produced in opaque white, blue, pink and green (some are cased). 3¼" tall. Rare in cranberry. Circa 1895-1901.

Torquay: Translucent satinized cranberry (Pigeon Blood); mold blown. This is a pillar-shaped pattern, with a bulging ringed base, containing embossed symmetrical vertical ribbing from top to bottom. Known colors in clear cranberry, cobalt blue and white satin. 3⅛" tall. Rare. Circa 1897-1899.

Triple Bud: Variegated pink; mold blown. The pattern consists of three circular rows of flower-like buds covering about two-thirds of the shaker. This ware is of varied color intensity; the darker pink being predominately within the bottom two budded rows. A very beautiful coloration has been created as a result of this type of shading. Also made in opaque white, blue and green (some of them cased). 3" tall. Rare. Circa 1895-1901.

Consolidated Lamp & Glass Company

Vine Border: Pink cased; mold blown. This is a four sided panelled shaker with each panel outlined by drooping vines. Two panels contain embossed floral decoration; the other two have a pebbly-like finish. Known colors are opaque white, blue and green (some of them cased). 3" tall. Very scarce. Circa 1894-1899.

Authors' Collection

Co-Operative Flint Glass Company

The Beaver Falls Co-Operative Glass Company
(1879-1889)
The Co-Operative Flint Glass Company
Beaver Falls, Pennsylvania
(1889-1937)

The Co-operative Flint Glass Company was an outgrowth from the Beaver Falls Co-operative Glass Company as the result of reorganization and management changes in 1889. The chief executive officer was M. J. H. Ruhlandt.

The firm produced both mold blown and pressed glass tableware some of which were ruby or amber stained by their own decorating department.

Co-operative Flint remained an independent glass house; they never joined the U.S. Glass or National Glass corporations. After a major fire in 1906, the factory was rebuilt and remained in business until its closure in 1937. A.C. Revi reported that some of their molds were acquired by the Phoenix Glass Company.

Lockwood Collection

Authors' Collection

Alden (Sheaf and Block): Ruby stained crystal; mold blown and pressed. The principal motif consists of a large embossed diamond containing four smaller ruby stained diamonds. The design is repeated and equally distributed around the center of the shaker. 3" tall. Very scarce. Also produced in crystal. Circa 1893

Co-op's Royal Variant: Clear ruby stained crystal; mold blown and pressed glass. The pattern is a slight variation of "Co-op's Royal" pattern which is a smooth, round concave shape (completely ruby stained) and a base band of embossed bull's eyes. 2⅞" tall. Very scarce. Circa 1894.

Moon and Star, Jeweled: Amber stained crystal; mold blown. This is a sphere shaped pattern containing embossed circles; each circle contains a hand painted blue intaglio star. This design is completely distributed throughout the shaker. 3" tall. Scarce. Circa 1896.

Sunk Daisy: Clear ruby stained crystal; mold blown & pressed. This a short necked bulbous shaker containing three sunken daisy flowers with alternating embossed oval panels containing small diamonds. The ruby staining encircles each daisy flower. 2⅞" tall. Very scarce in ruby stained. Circa 1890-1901.

Twentieth Century: Clear crystal with gild coloring; mold blown & pressed. The pattern consists of a series of embossed diamonds; each diamond is outlined by small horizontal ribs. Also produced in ruby stained. 3" tall. Scarce. Circa 1901.

Coudersport Tile & Ornamental Glass Company

Coudersport Tile & Ornamental Glass Company
Coudersport, Pennyslvania
(1900-1904)

The Coudersport Tile and Ornamental Glass Company began operations as the Webb Patent Tile Company. The firm was founded in 1900 by the brothers H. Fitzroy and Joseph Webb, relatives of the well known English glassmaker Thomas Webb.

It has been established that this factory produced pressed, mold blown and art glassware. We are illustrating the only known salt shakers that Coudersport Glass produced since there are no trade catalogues that have ever been discovered.

This factory apparently had its problems because there were various management changes throughout it's very short history. When the plant burned down in late 1904, it went out of business as the "Bastow Glass Works". There is an excellent article written by Marilyn Lockwood in the February/March 1989 issue of *Glass Collector's Digest* magazine that provides considerably more detail on Coudersport Glass.

Cane Woven: Opaque custard glass; mold blown; The pattern consists of what appears to be bands of woven cane below a single rope-like band. All of the pattern is in raised relief. Also produced in opaque white, blue and green. Peterson reported that this pattern has been reproduced out of Japan but we have never seen any in shakers. 2½" tall. Scarce in custard. Circa 1901-1904.

Authors' Collection

Authors' Collection

LEFT: Fleur-de-lis in Wreath: Opaque custard glass; mold blown. The pattern consists of three embossed fleur-de-lis; each surrounded by a grouping of scrolls. Also produced in opaque white, blue and green. Pattern name by Peterson. 2½" tall. Scarce in custard. Circa 1900-1904.

RIGHT: Fantasia (Fleur-de-lis with Scrolling): Opaque custard glass; mold blown. The pattern consists of three fleur-de-lis around the top and bottom with intricate scrolling. Also produced in opaque white, blue and green. 2⅜" tall. Scarce in Custard. Circa 1900-1904.

Crystal Glass Company
Bridgeport, Ohio
(1889-1908)

The Crystal Glass Company was opened during 1889, with Edward Muhleman as President, having been purchased from LaBelle Glass Company, which went out of business in 1888. Joseph Locke joined with Crystal in 1891 and is responsible for the design of the Flower and Pleat (Clematis) pattern. Mr. Locke had obtained many art glass patterns while at the New England Glass Co. and subsequently Libbey Glass Co. of Toledo, Ohio. One of those patterns that

he patented was "Pomona." Close examination of the "Flower and Pleat" ware will show that the frosted portion of this pattern closely resembles second grind/ground Pomona. Crystal went into receivership and was closed during 1908.

Avery Collection

Authors' Collection

Bruce Collection

LEFT: Flower and Pleat: Clear and frosted crystal; mold blown. The pattern consists of flowers and leaves at the center of the shaker with the frosted portion resembling a second grind Pomona decoration. This ware was also produced with the flowers and leaves being ruby-stained. 3⅛" tall. Very Scarce. Circa 1892-1893.

RIGHT: Red Block & Lattice: Ruby-stained crystal; pressed glass. If there is no staining present Peterson calls this pattern Button & Star. We have never seen this pattern in opaque glass. 3⅛" tall. Very Scarce. Circa 1892-1894.

Dalzell, Gilmore and Leighton Company
Findlay, Ohio
(1888-1901)

This factory was established as an outgrowth from the Dalzell Brothers & Gilmore glasshouse of Wellsburg, West Virginia, which was closed out during August 1888, after which many of the fixtures were moved to the new Findlay, Ohio plant.

Operations began in early September, 1888, at Findlay. During this firm's production years, Dalzell, Gilmore & Leighton produced everything from tumblers, goblets and kerosene lamps, to fine tableware and outstanding blown ware.

The factory became involved with the National Glass Company after having been purchased by them in October 1899, for the sum of $200,000. Some glass historians have speculated that this sale might not have taken place if it had not been for the introdution of the Onyx ware line, which proved to be a financial disaster due to costly production problems.

The Findlay plant remained in operation by the National Glass combine until fuel problems resulted in the plant's closure at the end of November, 1901.

Today's collectors seek to obtain pieces of the Findlay Onyx and Floradine wares; also, the "Amberette"/"Klondike" items are considered most desirable. All of these patterns have a very high collectibility factor and are difficult (as well as expensive) to acquire.

If the reader is interested in obtaining more detail, we recommend the book "*Findlay Glass*" by James Measell and Don E. Smith, published in 1986.

Authors' Collection

Findlay Onyx: Outstanding Rarity. Opaque silver luster over a creamy opaque white, heat sensitive, opal glass mixture. We are illustrating a pair having matched decoration. To many, the glass appears to be cased; actually the glass is homogeneous. According to Revi the illusion of plating or casing is the result of imperfect turning or developing the opalescence in the metal. The pattern molded article was first annealed & then the silver luster was applied to the raised floral design. It was then fired in a muffle to set the staining. Much of this ware came up with annealing cracks resulting in the factory yield being very low and therefore very costly to produce. To make matters worse, a large amount got out to the jobbers, and subsequently into the consumers homes, only to have production annealing cracks appear at a later point in time. Due to the high collectibility factor associated with this glassware, very little is available to today's collectors. In a thirty year time frame we saw two (singles) available for sale, but close examination revealed annealing cracks and we had to pass them by due to the price that was being asked by the seller. We finally got the opportunity to purchase this matched pair in 1986. We have given the reader this short scenario to alert you to the problems that are inherent with onyx glass. Use magnification before paying the asking price, which will be high! This type of glass was patented by George W. Leighton on April 23, 1889. It was produced for only a short period of time (less than a year). 2⅝" tall. Rare.

Dalzell, Gilmore and Leighton Company

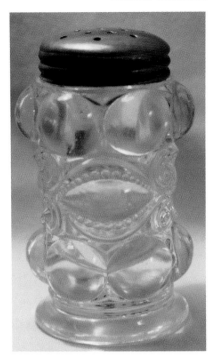

Eye-Winker: Clear crystal pressed glass. The pattern consists of twelve large protruding balls; six at the top and six at the bottom of the shaker. The center of the shaker has three of the Eye-winker designs in high raised relief. Mrs. Kamm states that a collector claimed that the "eye" winks when the piece is moved up and down! Hence, a possible reason for the pattern name. Made in clear crystal only. Peterson reports that the pattern has been reproduced. 3" tall. Scarce. Circa 1889-1895.

Hexagon, Pyramid: Opaque white opalware; mold blown. As the pattern name implies, this is a six panelled hexagon shaker containing a large scallop at the bottom of each vertical panel. Pattern name by Millard. 3" tall. Scarce. Circa 1889-1898.

Rose Findlay Onyx: Outstanding Rarity. (See "Findlay Onyx") All of our previous comments apply to this shaker; the primary difference is in the use of a rose colored luster which places this in the very rare category.

Floradine, Findlay's: Outstanding Rarity. Opaque rose satin homogenous glass with embossed flowers and leaves that radiate an opalescent look; mold and free blown finished. Most art glass books do not differentiate between this type glass and onyx ware, which is a mistake. The mold is different and the glass is completely different; apparently very brittle which rendered a very low production yield at the time it was manufactured. Floradine is of course an outstanding rarity and almost never seen in salt shakers. Produced for less than a year during 1889 and discontinued due to high production and experimental lab costs[2]. 2⅝" tall. Very rare.

Klondike, Curved (Amberette): Frosted translucent crystal with amber stained crossbands; mold blown and pressed. This ware was advertised under the name Amberette but the Curved Klondike name dates back to Kamm and was subsequently adopted by Peterson. It is widely used and recognized by both collectors and dealers today, therefore, we are not going to try to change it to the original manufactures name (OMN) and create confusion. Occasionally the reader will see one of these shakers up for sale, but beware! **Do not** purchase without magnification examination in the motif area. This ware is subject to fine chipping. We have seen very few that are worth the price that is being asked. 3" tall. Finding one in mint condition is rare. Circa 1898.

Robbins (OMN): Opaque white opalware; mold blown. The pattern amounts to six bulging lobes/ribs that flow from top to bottom of the shaker. 2⅝" tall. Scarce. Circa 1889-1900

Rhea-D: (Protruding Panels, Vertical): Opaque white opalware; mold blown & pressed: While "Rhea-D" is the OMN, we believe that "Vertical Protruding Panels" is an ample description of the principal pattern configuration. 2¾" tall. Very scarce. Circa 1889-1900.

Spatter, Findlay: Frosted translucent crystal with external applied random spattering of white, gilt and pale blue paint that has been fixed by firing within a muffle. The pattern is identical to the Silver Luster Findlay Onyx shakers previously described. The height measurements are the same. Very scarce. Circa 1888-1890.

Dalzell, Gilmore and Leighton Company

Thrush: Opaque white opalware; mold blown. This is a short spheroid shaped shaker. As the pattern name implies, it depicts a bird among some branches in high raised relief. Pattern name by Millard. The basic opalware is a very dull, chalk-like white. One of the real rarities produced by this glass house in opalware. 2¾" tall. Very rare. Circa 1890.

Square Twist: Opaque white; mold blown. This is a square based shaker with wide twisted panels from the center to the top. 3¼" tall. Very scarce. Circa 1890-1899.

Dithridge & Company

Dirthridge & Company
Pittsburgh, Pennsylvania
(1863-1903)

This glasshouse was an outgrowth of the Fort Pitt Glass Works that was owned by R.B. Curling. In 1863 the factory name was changed to Dithridge & Company under the ownership of Edward D. Dithridge. In 1903 this glasshouse merged into the Pittsburgh Lamp, Brass and Glass Company. See our write up in the "Introduction" section of this book for more details regarding this glass factory.

Alba Condiment: White decorated opalware; mold blown. The motif has an embossed web-like lower half with the upper part smooth which contains an orange and green floral decoration. Also produced in opaque blue, pink, green and custard; some are cased. 2⅜" tall. Scarce. Circa 1894.

Beaded Bottom: Blue opaque; mold blown. The pattern consists of embossed beads covering the circumference of the base portion of the shaker. Also made in opaque white, pink and green; some will be found cased. Pattern name by Millard. 3" tall. Scarce. Circa 1898-1900.

Beaded Panels, Six: Blue opaque; mold blown. The motif comprised six vertical, bulging panels; each panel is outlined by a single line of beads. Just below the ringed top are twelve short vertical ribs. Known colors in opaque white, green and pink; some are cased. 3⅝" tall. Very scarce. Circa 1897-1901.

Beltway Condiment: White opaque opalware; mold blown. Decorated with hand painted pink, yellow and green florals with this same decoration continued on the glass base holder. We have never seen this condiment set in other opaque colors. Shakers are 2¾" tall. Very Scarce. Circa 1897-1902.

Beaded Top, Scrolled Base: Blue opaque; mold blown. A simple pattern consisting of a row of embossed beads near the top with a single row of embossed scrolls surrounding a bulging base. Also produced in opaque white, green, and pink. 2½" tall. Very scarce. Circa 1898-1901.

Dithridge & Company

Bulge Bottom: White opaque opalware; mold blown. The pattern consists of embossed hand painted poppies and leaves. Known colors in opaque blue, green and pink. 2¼" tall. Scarce. Circa 1894-1897.

Bulging Nine Leaf Condiment: Translucent opalescent turquoise, mold blown. The pattern has nine intaglio leaves encircling the bulging part of the shaker body. The shakers have a single beaded ring near their top; the companion mustard contains two beaded rings. The aforesaid leaf pattern is continued around the circumference of the matching glass base/holder. This pattern was first reported on page 96 of our first book. Also made in opaque white, blue and pink. The shakers are 2½" tall with a neck diameter of ⅞". Rare in opalescent turquoise. Circa 1897-1900.

Bulge Bottom Variant: Opaque white opalware; mold blown. Same pattern as Bulge Bottom except that the base is rounded/oval shaped at the bottom. 2¼" tall.

Bulging Nine Leaf Variant: White opaque; mold blown. This shaker has the same basic motif as the Bulging Nine Leaf Condiment set except that it is taller and has a narrower neck. Also, this shaker has two beaded neck rings. The shaker contains an extended base for insertion into a condiment set glass holder. While we have no additional colors to report, it seems plausible that this ware was made in at least blue and pink. 3" tall with a neck diameter of ¾". Very scarce. Circa 1897-1900.

Cathedral Panel: Pink opaque; mold blown. The pattern has six large embossed leaves encircling the shaker base with a single protruding ring at the top. Pattern name by Warman. Known colors in opaque white, blue, green and custard; some of them are cased. 3" tall. Scarce. Circa 1894-1900.

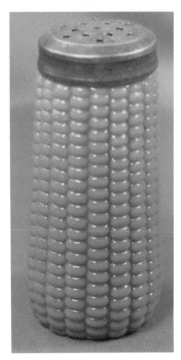

Corn, Sphere: White opaque; mold blown. Contains embossed vertical rows of corn kernels covering the entire spheroid-shaped shaker. Also made in opaque green, blue, pink and custard. 2⅛" tall. Rare. Circa 1896-1902.

Corn: Custard opaque; mold blown. The motif consists of a tapered ear of corn that fluoresces very well under black light. Also made in opaque white, blue, green and a cased pink. 3⅛" tall. Very scarce. Circa 1894-1901.

Corn, Tall: Blue opaque; mold blown. The pattern is configured in the form of an ear of corn that tapers toward the top. Known colors in opaque custard, green, white and pink; some of them are cased. 3⅝" tall. Very scarce. Circa 1895-1901.

Dithridge & Company

Creased Bale Condiment: Pink opaque; mold blown. The motif is reminiscent of stacked bales as the pattern name indicates. Also produced in opaque white, blue, green and custard. Some will be found cased. 3" tall including the mustard. Rare in pink cased. Circa 1894-1900.

Doodad: Green opaque, mold blown. The motif has an intricate embossed scrolled pattern covering the entire shaker. Known colors in opaque white, blue, and pink. Pattern name by Peterson. 3⅝" tall. Scarce. Circa 1896-1902.

Double Deck: White opaque; mold blown. The motif is unusual; starting at the top and continuing downward are 18 vertical rows of corn kernels in raised relief. The base consists of three plain panels; each is outlined by a series of embossed scrolls. Also manufactured in opaque blue, green, pink and custard. Pattern name by Peterson. 2¾" tall. Very scarce. Circa 1897-1902.

Ear: Green opaque; mold blown. The motif reminds one of a human ear; at least Peterson (who named it) thought so. Also made in opaque white, blue and pink. 3" tall. Scarce. Circa 1894-1900.

Double Fan Band: Pink opaque; mold blown. The pattern has two bands of embossed fans; one at the top and the other on the base. The remainder of the shaker is smooth and undecorated. Known colors in opaque white, blue, green and custard; some will be found cased. Pattern name by Peterson. 3⅜" tall. Very scarce. Circa 1894-1900.

Fleur-de-lis, Bulging: Opaque custard with fired-on pink coloring; mold blown. Dithridge listed this ware as their No. 48 pattern which consists of a short, bulging spheroid containing four fleur-de-lis in raised relief. The shaker bottom contains a 1/16" recessed intaglio circle. Also produced in opaque white, blue and green. 1½" tall. Very scarce. Circa 1894-1900.

Floral Sprig Condiment: Cream colored opalware; mold blown. A pillar shaped pattern with a slightly bulging base that has a ⅜" protruding peg which provides stable support when inserted into the matching glass base. Each condiment dispenser has hand painted brown and green budded floral sprigs. No color experience to report. 2⅞" tall including the mustard. Rare condiment set. Circa 1899-1903.

Dithridge & Company

Leaf, Clover: Opaque blue glassware; mold blown. Also made in opaque green, pink and custard. The pattern consists of a band of embossed overlapping clovers in the form of a band that encircles the base of the shaker. Pattern name by Warman. 3⅛" tall. Scarce. Circa 1894-1900.

Heart: Variegated pink-to-white opaque; mold blown. The motif consists of four large embossed hearts; each surrounded by intricate continuous scrolling. The neck contains 32 small vertical ribs. Also produced in opaque white, blue, green and custard; some will be found cased. 2⅞" tall. Very scarce. Circa 1894-1897.

Leaf-Covered Base: opaque custard; mold blown. The motif has a series of embossed overlapping leaves that go approximately half-way up the shaker body; the upper portion is plain. This item is not fluorescent under black light illumination. 2½" tall. Very scarce. Circa 1899-1902.

Leaf, Cornered Base: Blue opaque; mold blown. The pattern has four large embossed leaves; one on each corner of the base. Also made in opaque white, pink, green and custard. 2¼" tall. Scarce. Circa 1894-1900.

Dithridge & Company

Authors' Collection

Authors' Collection

Authors' Collection

Leaf Double: Variegated opaque purple mold blown. Believed to be an experimental piece. Also produced in opaque white, blue and green. 3⅝" tall. Rare in variegated purple. Circa 1895-1901.

Leaf, Standing: Custard opaque; mold blown. The pattern has eight large embossed vertical leaves that slightly overlap each other. Known colors in opaque white, blue, pink and green; some are cased. 2½" tall. Very scarce. Circa 1894-1896.

Leaf, Four: Blue opaque; mold blown. The principal motif comprises four large leaves in raised relief drooping downward from the top of the shaker. Known colors in opaque white, pink, green and custard. 2⅜" tall. Very scarce. Circa 1895-1901.

Authors' Collection

Authors' Collection

Little Shrimp: Custard opaque; mold blown. This pattern has twelve small vertical bulging ribs. Also made in opaque white, blue and green. This shaker has medium fluorescence under black light illumination. 1½" tall. Scarce. Circa 1895-1901.

Authors' Collection

Panelled Four Dot: Opaque variegated pink-to-white; mold blown. This pattern encompasses four large embossed panels equally dispersed around the shaker. The center of each panel contains four small beads/dots in raised relief. Known colors in opaque white, blue, green and custard; some will be found cased. 2³⁄₁₆" tall. Very Scarce. Circa 1894-1896.

Nine Loops, Bulging: Blue opaque; mold blown. The motif has nine bulging vertical loops with small scrolls encircling the neck of the shaker. Known colors in opaque white, pink, green and custard. 3" tall. Very scarce. Circa 1895-1902.

Dithridge & Company

Pansy, Tall: Blue opaque; mold blown. This shaker has two large embossed pansies surrounding the majority of the body; really an unusal design to be called a pansy flower. Also manufactured in opaque white, pink, and green. Pattern name by Peterson. 3⅝" tall. Scarce. Circa 1894-1900.

Leaf, Twisted: Pink opaque; triple cased; mold blown. The motif contains four large vertically twisted leaves in raised relief that run from the base to within approximately ¼" of the shaker top. Also produced in opaque pink, blue, white and green; some are cased. 2⅞" tall. Very scarce. Circa 1894-1900.

Rib, Pointed: Blue opaque; mold blown. The pattern has a group of wide, sharp pointed, vertical ribs that encompass the entire shaker from top to bottom. Also made in opaque white, pink and green. 2⅞" tall. Very scarce. Circa 1896-1902.

Rib, Flared: Blue opaque; mold blown. The motif has a continuous series of embossed ribs that begin at the center of the shaker and bulge ourward as a kind of skirt. Known colors in Opaque white, green, pink and custard. 3" tall. Circa 1894-1900.

Scroll In Scroll: Blue opaque; mold blown. A short, squatty shaker with a creased waist containing ornate scrolling both top and bottom. Also made in opaque white, green, pink and custard. 2¼" tall. Scarce. Circa 1896-1901.

Scroll, Square: Blue opaque; mold blown. This is a four panel shaker with two circular scrolls at the bottom containing four scallop-like feet that protrude above an intaglio cross. Also made in opaque white, pink, green, and custard; some will be found cased. 3⅛" tall. Scarce. Circa 1896-1902.

Spider Web: Pink opaque cased; mold blown. Similiar to the Dithridge Alba pattern, but not the same. The pattern completely covers the shaker with a web-like motif that is reminiscent of a spider's web. Known colors in opaque white, blue, green and custard; some will be found cased. Pattern name by Peterson. 2⅜" tall. Very scarce. Circa 1894-1897.

Sunset: Pink opaque; mold blown. Dithridge listed this as their No. 50 pattern. Warman called it Dithridge. The motif consists of ten large vertical overlapping, scalloped panels. Every other panel contains very small embossed ribbing. Pattern name by Peterson. Known colors are opaque white, blue, green and custard; some will be found cased. 2⅞" tall. Scarce. Circa 1894-1897.

Swirl and Leaf: Pink opaque; triple cased; mold blown. The pattern consists of embossed large swirls separated by individual beads with large leaves at both top and bottom. Also made in opaque white, blue, green and custard; some of them are cased. 3" tall. Rare. Circa 1894-1900.

Dithridge & Company

Teardrop Bulging: Pink opaque cased; mold blown. An ornate pattern consisting of sixteen pointed, bulging lobes; eight at the top pointing downward. Illustrated is a complete condiment set. Known colors in opaque white, blue, pale green and custard; some will be found cased. It is important that the reader realize that the same pattern carries over onto the glass base/holder. 2½" tall. Rare as a complete condiment set. Circa 1894-1901.

Teardrop Bulging Reproduction Condiment: Chalky-white opaque; mold blown. Differences: the repro shakers are ground off to remove pontil roughness; the old shakers were snapped off from the pontil at the top; The milk-white glass has a chalky appearance and does not look like old opalware. The metal lifting handle is shaped differently and is of heavier metal. This reproduction condiment was produced by the Fenton Art Glass Co. Also produced in opaque blue and yellow. 2⅝" tall; the old shakers are 2½" tall. Circa 1955-1956.

Versailles: Opaque white opalware; mold blown. Has concaved panels with an embossed pink colored rose. Also produced in blue and green opaque. 2¾" tall. Scarce. Circa 1900.

Swirl, Wide Diagonal: Pink opaque cased; mold blown. The motif consists of wide diagonal swirls that alternate from smooth to grooved. Known colors in opaque white, blue and custard. 2⅜" tall. Very scarce. Circa 1894-1896.

Wild Iris Condiment (Marsh Flower): White opaque opalware with applied gilt decoration; mold blown. The motif consists of continuous embossed reeds and Marsh Flowers protruding from a ¾" pillar base that allows for retention of each condiment dispenser within its matching glass base/holder. See page 96 of our first book which documents a pink and yellow color for this ware. Probably produced in other hand painted colors but we haven't observed any. Shakers are 3¼" tall. Rare as a complete condiment set. Circa 1898-1902.

The Dithridge Princess Swirl
Special Information

This pattern name was established by William Heacock in his custard glass book. (See No. 469, page 58.) While he made no special mention of the pattern, this illustration put in place the final piece of a pattern puzzle that we have been trying to solve for over twenty years.

First, a bit of relatively well known pattern information. Salt shaker collectors should be fairly familiar with the pattern name (established by Peterson) "Erie Twist"; in fact, we challenged the C.F. Monroe attribution and placed this pattern in the "Potpourri" section of our first book.

There was never any doubt in our minds that this pattern was originally design patented in 1892 by Carl V. Helmschmied who in turn, assigned the patent rights to C.F. Monroe Co.,which was strictly a glass decorating firm which did not manufacture glassware. So! Who manufactured this swirl pattern for them in the form of a blank?

We now know that this pattern was made by Dithridge under a contract agreement with the C.F. Monroe Co. of Meriden, Connecticut.

But this is not where the story ends!

Under their contract agreement, Dithridge did not just manufacture blanks for C.F. Monroe, they were also allowed to market this pattern on their own in the form of salt, peppers and condiment sets.

These salt/pepper shakers were produced by Dithridge in two height sizes: 2" and 2⅛".

The two inch shakers were reserved for use by C.F. Monroe on their "Wave Crest" decorated salt and pepper dispensers. It is a fact that these "Erie Twist" shakers appear in Monroe catalogues under the name "Wave Crest Salt." However, the "Erie Twist" pattern name is so well tied to the Monroe shakers, that we have no intention of trying to change it.

So! What about Bill Heacock's "Dithridge Princess Swirl?" Since "Wave Crest" is a special type of Monroe decoration, it is readily identifiable to today's collectors/dealers and it should continue to be known as "Erie Twist."

However, the taller 2⅛" shakers were manufactured and sold by Dithridge in a wide variety of colors, some of which are cased. The shakers and mustard used for their condiment sets all (that we have seen) have this same 2⅛" height but have a larger circumference and a slightly extended base protrusion for retention within the matching glass holder. These dimensional differences cause the swirl pattern to vary slightly in appearance, and if a collector happens to be fortunate enough to have both Dithridge and Monroe pieces available for physical comparisons, the chance of confusing an "Erie Twist" shaker with the Dithridge "Princess Swirl Pattern" is lessened considerably. However, only an advanced collector is likely to have such a luxury available to them. This scenario is directed to the average collector who is apt to purchase a Dithridge piece for a Monroe shaker or vice versa.

We have provided two photographs of the aforesaid Dithridge shakers. One is in lovely decorated Rubina; the second shows a pair of pink cased shakers. The shaker on the left is configured for insertion into a condiment set. The one on the right has a smaller circumference and top opening and was designed for individual salt and pepper usage.

Based upon the facts revealed relative to this swirl pattern, and coupled with the previously mentioned condiment set illustrated in Mr. Heacock's custard glass book; it seems appropriate that there should be a pattern differentiation between the Dithridge

and Monroe shakers. Therefore, we have adopted the pattern name "Dithridge Princess Swirl" that was established by William Heacock.

By way of further clarification, we are also illustrating a decorated C. F. Monroe "Erie Twist" opalware shaker.

The aforementioned scenario should help clarify the reasons that shakers in the "Erie Twist" pattern will be found in types of glassware that were never marketed by C.F. Monroe. Also there is the fact that the Fenton Art Glass company has produced similar shakers in this pattern starting in the 1950's.[1] As the reader can see, there is nothing very straightforward about this pattern that was such a perplexity to us for many years.

Authors' Collection

"Erie Twist" Reproduction
for L.G. Wright in opalware
with transfer decoration.

Author's Collection

"Erie Twist" Wave Crest Salt
C.F. Monroe decorated.

Authors' Collection

"Dithridge Princess Swirl" in
hand decorated Rubina Glass
with 2 piece metal top, 2⅛" tall
(not a condiment set shaker).

Authors' Collection

Dithridge Princess Swirl

Authors' Collection

"Dithridge Princess Swirl" in pink cased glass 2⅛"
tall. (Shaker at left configured for condiment sets). Has
larger opening under single piece metal top (shaker at
right is for individual salt and pepper usage).

George Duncan and Sons
Pittsburgh, Pennsylvania
(1866-1892)
George Duncan Sons Company
Washington, Pennsylvania
(1893-1955)

We many times get confused when we're involved with Duncan glassware patterns because both the Pittsburgh and Washington, Pennsylvania, factories were Duncan family owned. We suppose (as some do) one could say early Duncan or late Duncan; but that doesn't help much unless you realize the time demarcation period between the two glass houses.

The few glass shakers that we are illustrating are from the mid 1880's to the late 1890's; so technically speaking, both factories are involved. We will provide the reader with our estimated year(s) of first production and let you place the shaker in the factory location that first produced it. There have been many books and articles published about Duncan Glass.

Amberette: Clear amber stained pressed glass. This is a round shaped shaker containing two plain amber stained vertical panels; the remainer of the shaker body is completely covered with embossed daisy and buttons. A complete table service line was produced in this pattern and it has a high collectibility factor. Also produced in ruby-stained pressed glass with the pattern name changing to Ellrose. 2¾" tall. Rare. Circa 1885.

Block, Duncans: Clear ruby stained pressed glassware. The pattern consists of deep cut square blocks with the face of each block containing the ruby stain. Heacock reports later production by U.S. Glass. 2⅛" tall. Very Scarce. Circa 1887.

Button Panel (Diamond Crystal): Ruby stained crystal; pressed glass. As the pattern name implies the shaker is divided into vertical panels plain at the top with ruby staining; the remainder is covered with embossed buttons within large diamonds. Also produced in crystal. Pattern name by Peterson. 3" tall. Very scarce. Circa 1900.

Flowered Scroll: Clear amber stained crystal; mold blown and pressed. This pattern was reported by Mrs. Kamm (in Kamm 6) as Duncan's No. 2000. After staring at the pattern for quite awhile, we were at a loss to write a visual description of it, so we turned to see how Mrs. Kamm described it. Guess what? She too was at a loss, so she wrote no descriptive text. The shaker photograph we have furnished is quite clear and the reader should have no problem recognizing it. This was Duncan's first pattern made at their Washington, PA. factory and was design patented in 1893. The pattern was named by Metz. 2⅝" tall. Very scarce. Circa 1893.

71

George Duncan and Sons

Hat: Clear amber stained pressed glassware. This is a novelty shaker in the Daisy and Button pattern. Without a trade ad, placing the year of first production is difficult. This item does appear on page 144 of the Neila Bredehoft book *Early Duncan*. 1⅞" tall. Very scarce.

Zippered Block: Ruby stained crystal; mold blown and pressed. The pattern consists of wide bulging panels outlined by small embossed ribs very reminiscent of a zipper. Pattern name by Kamm. This was Duncan's No. 90 line. 2⅞" tall. Very scarce. Circa 1890-1897.

Three Face: Clear crystal and frosted pressed glass. This design was patented on June 18, 1878 by Mr. John E. Miller[1]. It was originally produced in clear crystal with frosted faces. Over the years this pattern has enjoyed extreme popularity; however, starting in the 1930's and for several decades thereafter, the pattern has been reproduced in a majority of the pieces it was originally produced in. This is particularly true in the goblets, lamps and salt shakers[1]. Over the years we have seen so many variations in terms of facial clarity, particularly around the eyes and nose, that we are no longer able to write a detailed description that will enable collectors to feel comfortable with their purchase. We are providing three illustrations: The completely frosted shaker is an L.G. Wright reproduction from the 1950's/1960's. **(RIGHT)** The other has a clear crystal base with the frosted face and comes the closest to what we feel may be an original. **(LEFT)** Our 3rd version is all in crystal and one of the earlier reproductions. **(CENTER)** Note the clarity of detail around the nose and eyes. Unless a collector is prepared to purchase several of the various versions that exist (and some are very high in price) you will probably never be 100% certain that you have an original old shaker. Our advice is "avoid this pattern" and save your money! Good luck. 2⅝" tall. Circa 1878-1885.

Eagle Glass & Manufacturing Company
Wellsburg, West Virginia
(1894-1937)

This glasshouse was founded by James, Joseph, H.W. and S.O. Paull in 1894. The factory specialized in opalware, globes and commercial drug bottles and containers. The factory produced their own glassware until around 1925. After that year, Eagle Glass resold glass that was obtained from the "Erskine Glass Mfg. Co." at Wellsburg.

Their most productive years, involving decorated opalware, was from around 1897 to 1906. After 1937, Eagle Glass became more commercial product oriented, producing such things as small metal containers for oil and gasoline, but the firm remained under the control of the Paull family and its subsequent generations.

Our personal experience, involving the collecting of Eagle Glass shakers and condiment sets, has shown that their hand colored decorative paints lack durability. It has always been difficult to obtain shakers that have retained reasonable hand painted decoration. Sometimes it has been necessary to settle for just the off-white opalware appearance in order to acquire one of their scarce patterns. They did a lot of Goofus decoration in red and gold paint, particularly on their salts. Our advice to a collector is that if an item is in reasonably good decorative condition and available for purchase, grab it! You have located a premium find.

Authors' Collection

Authors' Collection

Bow and Tassel: Opaque white opalware; mold blown. The pattern amounts to two large embossed tassles; one on each side of the shaker. The shaker surface contains a series of random, elongated bumps, somewhat reminiscent of tree bark. The bottom has an extended protrusion for the shaker to fit into some type of glass condiment holder. 3⅛" tall. Scarce. Circa 1899-1901.

McElderry Collection

Bow and Flower: Opaque white opalware with hand painted gilt coloring; mold blown. The principal motif consists of an embossed six petal flower and ribbon. The ribbon is tied to the flower in the form of a large bow. We have no additional color experience to report. 2¾" tall. Scarce. Circa 1901-1908.

Bulging Center: Opaque white opalware with embossed gilt painted flowers: mold blown & pressed. This is a footed shaker with the rim of the foot being beaded. 2¼" tall. Scarce. Circa 1899-1903.

Eagle Glass & Manufacturing Company

Butterfly: Opaque white opalware with red and gilt Goofus type decoration; mold blown. The pattern consists of four butterflies in raised relief. The shaker base has been configured for use in a condiment set. Also made in crystal with red and gilt Goofus decoration. 2¾" tall. Very Scarce in Goofus. Circa 1898-1902.

Dogwood Goofus: Crystal glass with red and gilt Goofus coloring; mold blown. The principal motif is a large embossed dogwood flower on each side of the shaker base. Also produced in opaque white with the same Goofus decoration. 3¼" tall. Very scarce. Circa 1901-1906.

Epaulette: Opaque white opalware with gilt painted motif; mold blown. This is a four lobed shaker with the top of each lobe containing a four leaf clover. 2⅛" tall. Scarce. Circa 1900-1905.

Cosmos Scroll Condiment: Opaque white opalware with yellow and blue hand painted cosmos flowers; mold blown and pressed. The condiments are bulbous shaped with each containing four Cosmos flowers in raised relief. Each flowered panel is separated by embossed yellow painted vertical scrolled columns. The matching glass tray is scallop shaped with a large yellow and blue cosmos in its center. There are recessed intaglio circles designed to hold the condiment dispensers in place on the tray rare as a complete set. Salt= 2¾", pepper= 2⅛", mustard= 1⅞" tall. Circa 1899-1906.

Fleur-de-lis Condiment: Opaque white opalware with gilt coloring; mold blown & pressed. The small matching tray is scallop shaped and contains edge scrolling with four fleur-de-lis symmetrically spaced around the area that holds the salt & pepper. salt= 3", pepper= 2⅛" tall. Very Scarce as a complete set. Circa 1899.

Fern Leaf: Opaque white opalware with gilt coloring; mold blown. The pattern consists of three large embossed vertical, fern-like leaves equally spaced around the shaker. The base contains twelve short embossed diagonal swirls. 3" tall. Scarce. Circa 1901-1907.

Flower, Open: Opaque white opalware; mold blown. The pattern consists of an elaborate large flower with associated foliage, in raised relief, on a tapered pillar. We have no additional color experience to report. 3⅛" tall. Scarce. Circa 1903-1908.

Floral Neck: Opaque white opalware with red and gilt Goofus coloring; mold blown and pressed. The principal motif consists of a sprig of embossed flowers on the front and back of the shaker neck. 3⅛" tall. Scarce. Circa 1899-1904.

Flower, Blooming: Opaque white opalware with gilt coloring; mold blown and pressed. The principal pattern consists of a series of flowers and leaves equally distributed around the top and bottom of the shaker. These shakers have been reproduced but the chalk-white coloring immediately flags them as not old. 4⅛" tall. Circa 1900-1907.

Eagle Glass & Manufacturing Company

Footed Six Panel: Opaque white opalware; mold blown & pressed. The pattern consists of six flat panels encircled by an embossed band of gilt colored diamonds. 2¾" tall. Scarce. Circa. 1903-1910.

Forget-me-not, Eagle's[1]: Opaque white opalware; mold blown. Has a small barrel shape but contains the same motif as the forget-me-not Peewee & companion condiment set. 2⅜" tall. Scarce. Circa 1901.

Forget-me-not Peewee & Companion: Opaque blue glass; mold blown and pressed. The pattern consists of an embossed daisy and vine sprig encircling each shaker body. The pressed glass tray's outer rim contains a continuous series of individual embossed beads. salt= 3", pepper= 2" tall; tray= 4⅛" long x 3⅛" wide. Very Scarce. Circa 1899.

Grape, Big: Opaque white opalware; mold blown and pressed. This was probably intended for use as a saloon condiment dispenser. The pattern consists of a large embossed bunch of grapes and leaves spread out over approximately two-thirds of the shaker body. The entire motif has been colored with the gilt type Goofus decoration. 4" tall. Scarce. Circa 1898-1905.

Grape, Four Leaf: Crystal glass decorated with red and gilt Goofus coloring; mold blown and pressed. The pattern consists of a large bunch of grapes containing four leaves equally distributed around the top of the shaker; all in raised relief. Also produced in opaque white with gilt coloring. 3½" tall. Very scarce. Circa 1899-1906.

Grape, Four Sided: Opaque white opalware; mold blown & pressed. This is a square-shaped shaker having a bunch of embossed grapes on each corner separated by a large leaf. Usually found with gilt coloring on the grapes and leaves. 3" tall. Circa 1900-1907.

Grape, Large: Opaque opalware with gilt colored paint; mold blown and pressed. The outside of this piece is completely smooth except for a large embossed bunch of grapes and leaves on the front and back. 3⅞" tall. Scarce. Circa 1900-1910.

Grape and Leaf, Footed: Opaque white opalware with gilt colored paint; mold blown and pressed. This shaker is decorated with a large sprig of grapes and leaves. Also produced in crystal with the red and gilt Goofus coloring. 3⅛" tall. Circa 1898.

Eagle Glass & Manufacturing Company

Grape Salt and Pepper Set: Opaque white opalware with gilt colored decoration; mold blown and pressed. These are four panel dispensers containing small bunches of grapes and leaves hanging from a long vine that completely encircles the center of each shaker. The tray contains a bunch of grapes and leaves, one on each side. All of the motifs are in raised relief. Salt= 2⅝", pepper= 2¼" tall; tray= 5½" long x 3⅛" wide. Very scarce as a complete set. Circa 1899-1906.

Grape and Vine: Opaque white opalware with a gilt painted motif; mold blown. A bulging shaker with a bunch of embossed grapes on the front and back. Probably part of a condiment set, although the trade ad portrays just the shaker. 2" tall. Scarce. Circa 1899-1902.

Lantern: Clear crystal; mold blown and pressed to accommodate a metal top & base that forms a small lantern. These shakers were designed to be used as a candy container and Mr. James Paull patented two of these types in 1904. Due to their perforated metal tops they were subsequently used as salt and pepper shakers by the public. Made in several sizes. 4" tall with a special wire handled metal top. Very scarce. Circa 1904.

Hen and Rabbit: Opaque opalware with gilt coloring applied over a blue background; mold blown. The motif is that of a large egg with a nesting hen on one side & a running rabbit on the other; all in raised relief. Also sold as a condiment set in a special silver plated holder. 2⅝" tall with a special dome-shaped metal top. Very scarce. Circa 1900-1910.

Rabbit, Four: Opaque white opalware with gilt coloring; mold blown. The pattern consists of four lop-eared rabbits, symmetrically spaced, hiding among tall grass or leafy foliage; all in raised relief. 2⅜" tall. Scarce. Circa 1900-1910.

Rabbit: Opaque opalware with hand painted gilt coloring; mold blown. The top is directly interchangeable with the "Hen and Rabbit" shaker previously described. This eggshaped shaker is the same except that it contains three embossed rabbits sitting upright. 2⅝" tall with a special dome-shaped metal top; Scarce. Circa 1900-1910.

Rib, Corner: Opaque white opalware with each of four panels outlined in gilt coloring; mold blown and pressed. This is a square-shaped footed shaker containing four smooth panels; two of the panels are undecorated; the other two contained a floral sprig which the ravages of time have all but obliterated. 2¼" tall. Circa 1906-1912.

Rose, Gaudy: Opaque homogeneous lavender; also bright red and shaded gilt Goofus decoration; mold blown and pressed; 3" tall with special metal tops that contain two small raised knobs that insert into special glass threading and then lock by a twisting motion. Tops containing regular threading will not work on this shaker. Very scarce. Circa 1904-1908.

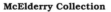

Eagle Glass & Manufacturing Company

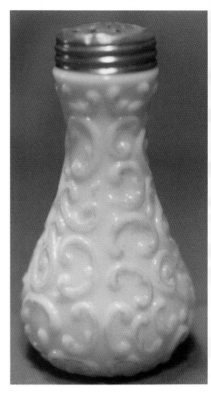

Scroll, Four Footed: Opaque white opalware; mold blown and pressed. As the pattern name implies, this shaker contains ornate scrolling on each of its four corners that form a supporting foot; all in raised relief. At one time the motifs were covered by gilt coloring which has been removed due to wear and tear. 3⅛" tall. Scarce. Circa 1899-1902.

Scroll, Mosaic: Opaque cream colored opalware; mold blown. The pattern consists of continuous artistic embossed scrolling which at one time was outlined with yellow paint. This is a tall, bulbous based shaker. 3" tall. Scarce. Circa 1899-1905.

Scroll, Gaudy: Opaque white opalware, mold blown. The pattern name given this shaker by Peterson pretty much says it. From top to bottom the motifs consist of various types of scrolling in all sizes. 2½" tall. Scarce. Circa 1900-1908.

Shell, Triple: Opaque white opalware with hand applied colors of pastel pink, green and yellow; mold blown. The pattern consists of three bulging shells, in raised relief, that are equally distributed around the shaker. Pattern name by Peterson. 1⅞" tall. Rare. Circa 1898.

Scroll, Twisted: Opaque white opalware over which hand painted colors of yellow and pink have been applied. The pink, which is present on the individual button-like flowers is a very delicate pastel. The uncolored white opalware can be clearly seen by looking at the shaker bottom. Mold blown and pressed. The pattern consists of three large scrolls each scroll is separated by a series of individual roses that diminish in size. Pattern name by Millard. 3¼" tall. Very scarce. Circa 1899-1904.

Top Heavy Variant: Opaque opalware with hand painted colors of pastel pink and green; mold blown. To look at it gives the impression that it is unbalanced (too heavy at the top); probably part of a condiment set. The surface of the shaker has small random scrolls covering the entire outside. 2⅛" tall. Scarce. Circa 1899-1905.

Top Heavy: Opaque white opalware with 98% of the gilt coloring worn off; mold blown and pressed. This is a footed shaker with two bulges; the larger one being at the top. The pattern name portrays a clear description of its overall physical appearance. Pattern name by Peterson. 3⅛" tall. Circa 1903-1910.

Swirl, Blossom: Opaque white opalware with gilt coloring; mold blown and pressed. The pattern consists of wide panelled swirls; each swirl contains two embossed flowers; the top and base of the shaker have intricate scolling. Pattern name by Warman. 3⅝" tall. Scarce. Circa 1898-1903.

Fenton Art Glass Company

Fenton Art Glass Company
Williamstown, West Virginia
(1905-Present)

The Fenton Art Glass Company was created by Frank L. and John W. Fenton. It began operations at Martins Ferry, Ohio during July, 1905, as a glass decorating shop after renting the old West Virginia Glass Company factory. Early Fenton production amounted to the purchasing of glass blanks from various glass companies, cutting their own design on the blanks and selling them. The operation proved to be profitable enough for the company to build their own glass factory and become an independent glass manufacturer. So, in November, 1906, the move to Williamstown, West Virginia began, with the new factory doors opening up in early January, 1907.

Early production of iridescent, chocolate and opalescent glassware resulted in a profitable operation. Aside from the talented Fentons, the company was able to acquire a nucleus of skilled glass workers from various nearby factories such as Jefferson, Heisey, etc. Also, the employment of Jacob Rosenthal as factory manager gave the Fenton factory an in-road to the manufacture of chocolate glass, which was pretty much an exclusive Rosenthal development. Early mold making support came from "The Hipkins Novelty Mold Shop" until the Fenton in-house mold shop became fully established.

As was the case with most of the American glass-houses from this time period, Fenton Art Glass Company had its business ups and downs. However, it stands today (1990) as an outstanding American glass factory with the capability of producing any type of high quality art glass or opalware.

The pattern names for the salt shakers that we are presenting have been taken from the three

Fenton Art Glass Company

Fenton glass books written by William Heacock, which were technically backed up by Mr. Frank M. Fenton. We feel that the pattern accuracy is unquestionable.

Mildred's personal love for Fenton glassware led her to collect as many of the Fenton salt shakers as possible. This ware has a high collectibility factor and is of outstanding quality. It was of great interest to us to find that there is only one Fenton salt shaker pattern listed in Mr. Heacock's first Fenton glass book that addresses the first 25 years of Fenton glassware production.

Blue Opalescent Hobnail: Clear blue with opalescent hobs; mold blown & pressed. The pattern consists of uniformly spaced hobs over the entire shaker body with a protruding opalescent bottom ring. 2¼" tall. Circa 1950-1954.

Block and Star: Opaque blue heavy pressed glass. This is homogeneous glass with the block and star motif having been intaglio impressed throughout the entire shaker; the bottom contains a small recessed circle. Listed as having been produced in opaque white, black and a **rare** rose. 2¼" tall. Circa 1955-1956.

Clear Over Cranberry: Clear over cranberry; mold blown. There is no mention of additional colors. To the uninitiated, this pattern could be mistaken for the old "Erie Twist" (Helmschmied Swirl) pattern. However, the top of this shaker has been ground down (polished out) and it has a larger circumference than the "Erie Twist" shaker. 2¼" tall with a 6⅛" circumference. Very scarce. Circa 1956-1959.

Cranberry Hobnail Opalescent: Clear cranberry opalescent; mold blown & pressed. The top of the shaker has been ground down smooth. The pattern consists of small rounded hobs covering the entire shaker body; only the hobs display opalescent. The bottom contains the original blue and silver colored Fenton paper label. 3⅛" tall with a 5⅛" circumference. Scarce. Circa 1955-1967.

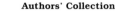

Swirl, Fenton: Opaque pastel pink; mold blown homogenous glass. The top of the shaker has been ground down smooth. The pattern consists of ten twisted vertical swirls similar to the old Hobbs Francesware pattern. Also made in opaque white, green and blue. If it weren't for the original chrome top, these shakers would look like late nineteenth century glass. 3⅛" tall with a 6" circumference. Scarce. Circa 1954.

Georgian: A deep royal blue (Fenton color name); mold blown and pressed. The top has been fire polished smooth. This is a footed honeycomb pattern...in fact A.G. Peterson assigned this pattern name to it in his 1970 book "Glass Salt Shakers" and he did not recognize it as a Fenton piece. We have also included a ruby colored shaker in our photographs. The metal tops shown are original. Also produced in crystal, jade, amber, green, rose, topaz and black. 3⅜" tall with 5½" circumference. Scarce. Circa 1931-1939.

Jacqueline: Opaque green cased glass; mold blown. The top has been fire polished smooth. This is a quality cased glass and when subjected to black light, gives forth a striking fluroesence. Also made in honey amber and wild rose (Fenton color names). This pattern appears in A.G. Peterson's book. 2⅞" tall with a 7⅞" circumference. Scarce. Circa 1961-1964.

Hobnail Opaque: Opaque homogeneous aqua colored; mold blown & pressed. The top has been fire polished smooth. The pattern consists of small hobs covering the entire shaker surface. Also made in opaque white and black. 2⅞" tall with a 5¼" circumference. Circa 1961.

Fenton Art Glass Company

Polka Dot: Clear cranberry opalescent; mold blown. The top has been ground smooth. This is a bulbous shaped sphere with uniform opalescent dots covering the entire shaker; just below the metal top there is a small protruding glass ring. No other color production is mentioned. This pattern has a high collectibility factor. 2⅜" tall with a 6⅞" circumference. Very scarce. Circa 1955.

Lamb's Tongue (Tulip, Footed): Opaque blue, mold blown. The top has been fire polished smooth. Analysis of the pattern leads us to the conclusion that "Footed Tulip", the name assigned by Peterson, is really more appropriate. The pattern looks like a large petaled flower growing upward from the shaker base. Also produced in opaque white. 2⅞" tall with a 7" circumference. Scarce. Circa 1954-1955.

Rose: Opaque white; mold blown and pressed. The top of the shaker has been fire polished and is smooth. The pattern consists of eight embossed roses; four at the top and four at the base. The footed base contains six scallops. Also produced in Colonial Amber & probably blue. The pattern has an interesting history; it was first produced by Tiffin in the late 1920's under the pattern name of "Queen Ann;" some of the Fenton yellow satinized glass pieces were uncovered by Bill Heacock prior to his involvement with the Fenton books and he named the pattern "Ruffles & Roses." 3⅜" tall. Scarce. Circa 1967.

Rib Optic: Clear cranberry opalescent; mold blown. The tops have been ground smooth. This is an absolutely unique and beautiful condiment pair. The ten white opalescent vertical stripes are uniformly spaced and are visible from top to bottom. Also produced in green opalescent. salt= 5", pepper= 4" tall. Very scarce. Circa 1953-1969.

Flower Panel (#6206 White Milk Glass):
Opaque white, mold blown. This a reproduction
of an old McKee pattern shown on page 42 of
our first book which Peterson called "Flower
Panel." The Fenton book states that this item
was also produced in Jamestown Blue
Transparent. 2¾" tall. Scarce. Circa 1957-1958.

Silver Crest: Opaque white, mold blown with a
crystal ruffled petticoat on the footed base. This is a
completely smooth undecorated shaker configured
along the lines of many of the so-called depression
glass shakers from the 1930's. No other colors are
mentioned in the Fenton books. 3¼" tall with a 5¼"
circumference. Very scarce. Circa 1956-1959.

Swirl: Opaque white; mold blown and pressed. This is the same
pattern that we described for the "Clear Over Cranberry" shaker and
all the comments that we previously stated apply to this shaker. It was
interesting to learn from the Fenton books that the pattern was
inspired by the purchase of a piece of "Wave Crest" ware by Frank M.
Fenton. Among antique glass collectors this Swirl is known as "Erie
Twist" or "Karl Helmschmied Swirl." Helmschmied patented the design
in 1892 and assigned the production rights to the C. F. Monroe Co.
who used this pattern on many pieces of their "Wave Crest" ware
during the 1890's. Also produced in opaque green and blue pastel. 2¼"
tall with a 6⅜" circumference. Circa 1954.

Illustration not shown. Teardrop Condiment: Opaque white; mold blown and pressed; 2⅝" tall (including the mustard). The reader is
referred to "Teardrop Bulging Reproduction Condiment" in the Dithridge & Co. section of this book.

The Fostoria Glass Company
Moundsville, West Virginia
(1887-1983)

Began factory operations on December 15, 1887 at Fostoria, Ohio with Lucien B. Martin as president. As a result of the continuing rise in fuel costs, the factory was moved to Moundsville, West Virginia, in 1891.

Over the years, much of the continuing success of this glass house must be credited to the hiring of W.A.B. Dalzell who joined the company in 1901 and was elected president in January 1902, a position in which he served until his death in 1928. Mr. Calvin B. Roe, Fostoria's vice president, became president and served until 1945, at which time William F.

Dalzell, son of W.A.B. Dalzell, took over as president until his retirement in 1958.

Fostoria reached its maximum size and production capability around 1950; having more than 900 employees and selling some 7,500,000 pieces of glassware involving approximately 5000 stores. After this period, this glass house slowly went downhill, primarily due to the competition from imports. The factory ceased production operations in 1983 and has never reopened. It is a tribute to this firm that it stayed in business manufacturing American glassware for almost 100 years.

Authors' Collection

Authors' Collection

Authors' Collection

Carmen: Clear crystal with partial amber staining; pressed glass. The pattern consists of eight vertical panels; each alternate panel is plain with the others each containing a single diamond that reaches from top to bottom. Each diamond is covered inside with hexagon-shaped blocks in raised relief. 3⅛" tall. Very scarce. Circa 1896.

Coin, Fostoria's: Clear ruby with a slight orange tint; mold blown and pressed. This is a rounded four panel shaker with each panel containing a simulated coin. One of the coins contains a spread-winged Eagle with an embossed date of 1887. The other coin depicts a flaming torch in front of a radiating sun. The glass is very high quality and quite heavy. This coin glass was first introduced in 1958 with additional glass pieces added to the line in the subsequent years. Also made in amber and blue. The ruby is highly collectible today. 2⅞" tall. Scarce due to high collectibility. Circa 1975-1980.

Clinging Vine: Opaque green homogeneous glass; mold blown. This is a tall long necked shaker with a bulbous base containing a large embossed flower and vine motif. Also made in opaque white with the motif hand painted. Pattern name by Peterson. 3¼" tall. Scarce. Circa 1901-1905.

Flower & Scroll: Opaque opalware with hand painted colors of pink and green flowers applied over a shaded blue to white background; mold blown & pressed. This is a bulbous shaped shaker containing two embossed pink and green floral bouquets (front and back); the neck contains eight scrolls in high raised relief. 3⅛" tall. Scarce. Circa 1897-1905.

Draped Beads: Opaque white opalware with painted pastel pink and tan coloring; mold blown. This is an octagon shaped shaker containing eight panels each of which is outlined by individual beads; every other panel has embossed tiny scrolls that have been highlighted by a pastel pink coloring. The plain panels have been painted in a pastel tan. 2¼" tall. Scarce. Circa 1898-1904.

Fostoria's Cameo: Opaque white opalware with red and yellow flowers & scrolls; mold blown. The pattern consists of a flared outward rib pattern containing an embossed floral sprig surrounded by random scrolls. Pattern name is OMN but slightly modified for clarity by Marilyn Lockwood. 3¼" tall. Very Scarce. Circa 1898.

Knobby: Opaque opalware with a pink flower & shaded turquoise blue background; mold blown & pressed. The pattern consists of ornate scrolling, in high raised relief, that encircles the top and bottom of the shaker. 3¼" tall. Scarce. Circa 1898-1904.

Fostoria Glass Company

Leaf, Cabbage: Opaque hand painted opalware with green shading; mold blown and pressed. The principal motif consists of three large cabbage leaves in high relief; the shaker neck contains a series of embossed scrolls. 3⅛" tall. Very scarce. Circa 1905-1911.

Leaf, Three Footed: Opaque white opalware from which all hand painting has disappeared; mold blown & pressed. The shaker stands on three feet that has been formed by three large bulging leaves. The top of the shaker is encircled with embossed scrolling; the body contains two flowering rose bouquets. 3⅛" tall. Circa 1900-1907.

Panelled Pansy: Opaque hand painted opalware with a shaded blue background; mold blown & pressed. The pattern consist of three decorated red and yellow pansies in raised relief. The shaker bulges at the top and tapers into a narrow pillared base that contains small embossed scrolls at the bottom edge. 3" tall. Very scarce. Circa 1904-1911.

Lobes, Bulging: Opaque opalware with hand applied brown paint; mold blown & pressed. The pattern consists of eight bulging base lobes; the top of the narrow neck has four embossed hanging leaves. 2⅞" tall. Very Scarce. Circa 1904-1910.

Pegleg, Tall: Opaque white opalware with somewhat worn red and yellow paint; mold blown and pressed. The pattern consists of six sharply defined protruding base ribs out of which are formed six peg-like legs. There is also a large embossed floral bouquet on the front of the shaker. 3⅛" tall. Very scarce. Circa 1899-1905.

Panelled Four Rib: Opaque white opalware with somewhat worn red and yellow paint; mold blown and pressed. The shaker contains four large curving panels separated by four vertical ribs in high raised relief. Each panel contains an embossed large flower, perhaps a pansy. 3⅛" tall. Circa 1903-1910.

Robin Hood: Clear crystal glassware; mold blown and pressed. The pattern consists of coin-like circles across the middle. Between each of the circles are three raised vertical spears that are pointed at each end; the outer two of each group are curved outward. 3⅛" tall. Very scarce. Circa 1898.

Scroll, Low-Bodied: Opaque hand painted opalware with blue coloring; mold blown. This is a short squatty shaker with a flattened lobe shape containing continuous intricate scrolling on the upper portion of its body. 1¾" tall. Very scarce. Circa 1905-1912.

Fostoria Glass Company

Tulip, Fostoria's: Opaque white opalware; mold blown. As shown in an 1898 Fostoria trade ad where it is listed as Fostoria's #1013, the patterns contains embossed petals very reminicent of a closed up tulip flower. Every other petal is hand painted yellow. Pattern name by Marilyn Lockwood. 2¼" tall. Very scarce. Circa 1898.

Victoria, Fostoria's: Clear and frosted thick crystal; mold blown and pressed. This is one of the early patterns that was produced by Fostoria and the pattern design was patented by Lucien B. Martin on July 15, 1890. The smooth glass surface around the crystal scrolls has been frosted which makes that portion of the design translucent. The pattern proved to be popular and was produced in a full line of tableware. 2⅝" tall. Rare. Circa 1890.

Wedding Bells: Clear cranberry stained glass; mold blown and pressed. Originally this was Fostoria's No. 789. Motif contains a series of swirled panels that alternate between smooth and embossed scrolling. The plain panels have been cranberry/rose stained. 2⅞" tall. Very scarce. Circa 1900.

Fostoria Shade and Lamp Company

Fostoria Shade and Lamp Company
Fostoria, Ohio
(1890-1894)

The Fostoria shade and Lamp Company was established in 1890 by Nicholas Kopp and Charles Etz. Both of these men had left the Hobbs Glass company. The financial backing involved several, foremost of which was Charles Foster (an ex-Ohio governor). A subsequent merger with Wallace & McAfee Co. of Pittsburgh resulted in an 1894 company name change to Consolidated Lamp and Glass Company of Fostoria, Ohio.

As a result of an 1896 fire, the factory was moved to Coraopolis, Pennsylvania. For more detail on Consolidated see our write up in the "Introduction" of this book.

Rose, Pink: Opaque pink satinized glass; mold blown with a two piece top. This shaker is a true piece of art glass that was designed and patented on March 10, 1891 by Nicholas Kopp. In his patent papers he referred to this shaker as a "closed vessel with perforated cover." The patent assignor was to the Fostoria Shade and Lamp Company located at Fostoria, Ohio. The patent that was issued to Kopp was for a term of 7 years. We are illustrating a copy of the original patent paper as copied at the U.S. Patent office in Washington, D.C. (see patent section). The pattern consists of a delicately designed individually petaled rose. Due to the fragile make-up of this shaker, it is extremely difficult to acquire one that is not chipped or cracked. Damaged shakers have very little value. Also produced in pink cased glass. A companion sugar shaker was also made in the same colors. 1⅝" tall. Rare. Circa 1891.

Gillinder and Sons
Philadelphia, Pennsylvania
(1861-1905)

The Franklin Flint Glass Company was started by William T. Gillinder in 1861 at Philadelphia, Pennsylvania. In 1863 he added Mr. Edwin Bennett as a partner and the company became known as "Gillinder and Bennet" until Mr. Bennett's departure from the firm in 1867. Mr. Gillinder's sons joined the factory and the name was changed to "Gillinder and Sons."

The company's Greensburg, Pennsylvania factory, was purchased by the U.S. Glass Company in 1891 and it began operations as U.S. Glass, Factory G. As a part of the sale contract, Gillinder and Sons agreed not to manufacture tableware for a period of twenty years.

Leaf, Four Sided: Opaque green homogeneous glass; mold blown. This is a concave shaped shaker containing four embossed leaves; one leaf on each corner. 2⅛" tall. Scarce. Circa 1890-1896; probable later production at Factory G.

Gargoyle: Opaque white opalware; mold blown. 2¼" tall. The pattern consists of a demon-like head surrounded by embossed intricate scrolling. Pattern name by Millard. Also produced in a sugar shaker. Scarce. Circa 1905.

Beaded Twist: Opaque white opalware; mold blown. This is a tall shaker consisting of nine bulging swirled vertical ribs; each rib is separated by a line of vertical beads. We have no additional color experience to report. 3¾" tall. Scarce. Circa 1890.

Melon, Ribbed: Opaque white opalware; mold blown. This is a plain melon-like ribbed pattern with no evidence that it had ever been hand decorated. However, we feel certain that some were produced with hand painted floral designs. There is a high probability that this ware was made in opaque colors. 2⅝" tall. Scarce. Circa 1890-1897.

Gillinder and Sons

Ribbed Melon, Six: Opaque white satinized opalware; mold blown. Similar in shape to the shaker that Peterson called Spangled Melon. The body contains hand painted floral sprigs. 2½" tall. Very Scarce. Circa 1888-1891.

Mellon, Gillinder: Opaque satinized opalware; mold blown. The pattern consists of six lobed vertical ribs with hand painted floral decoration over a pale blue background. Pattern name by Heacock.[1] Also made in a sugar shaker. 2⅝" tall. Scarce. Circa 1891-1897.

Rib, Scrolled: Opaque homogeneous blue glassware; mold blown. The pattern consists of twelve lobe shaped ribs. Every other rib contains small embossed scrolling. Pattern name by Warman. Also produced in opaque white and green. 2½" tall. Scarce. Circa 1891-1899.

Greensburg Glass Company Limited

Greensburg Glass Company Limited
Greensburg, Pennsylvania
(1892-1898)

The Greensburg Glass Company Limited was formed in 1892 with Mr. Julius Proeger as the chief executive officer. The glass patterns we are illustrating were introduced between 1894 and 1898, when the factory closed down. It was reopened by the National Glass conglomerate in 1899.

LEFT: Murano: Clear ruby stained mold blown and pressed glass. The principal pattern consists of three large leaves that are reminiscent of a shamrock. This motif is repeated three times around the center of the shaker. Murano is the original manufacturer name (OMN). 3" tall. Very scarce. Circa 1894.

CENTER: Sunk Honeycomb (Corona): Clear ruby stained pressed glass. The principal pattern consists of deep cut hexagon blocks side by side. Also produced in clear crystal. The illustrated shaker has ruby top staining. Pattern name by Kamm. 2⅞" tall. Scarce. Circa 1894.

RIGHT: Tacoma: Clear ruby stained crystal; mold blown and pressed glass. The pattern consists of large flat bevelled diamond blocks around the shaker center. Each diamond is ruby stained. The very top of the shaker is also ruby stained. Also produced in clear crystal. 3" tall. Very scarce. Circa 1894.

The A.H. Heisey Glass Company
Newark, Ohio
(1893-1957)

The company was established by Augustus H. Heisey in 1893, but production did not begin until 1896. It is significant to note that this glass house always remained under Heisey family control until its permanent closure in December, 1957.

The factory produced high quality glassware. much of which was marked by their famous "Diamond H" trademark. The salt shaker patterns presented here are primarily those of this factory's Victorian Era production years.

Of all of the glassware that was produced during that period, we would have to highlight their custard glass because of its outstanding color and quality. This ware has always enjoyed a high collectibility factor among glassware collectors.

Heisey also produced large quantities of ruby stained pieces, much of which was souvenired. Bill Heacock, in his volume on ruby stained glassware, reported that a large amount of the Heisey Factory's decoration was provided by the "Oriental Glass Company" of Pittsburgh, Pennsylvania via special contract orders.

There have been several publications that specifically address the glassware that this factory produced primarily from the 1920's until the firm went out of business. We include them in our "Bibliography" section.

Authors' Collection

Authors' Collection

Authors' Collection

Bead Swag: Opaque white opalware with rose decoration; also, clear ruby stained glass; mold blown & pressed. Shaped like a tall barrel with a continuous embossed scalloped swag containing small beads that encircles the center of the shaker. This pattern was also produced in emerald green but we have never seen any green salt shakers. 2⅞" tall. Very scarce in ruby stained; rare in rose decorated opal. Circa 1897-1908.

Ivorina Verde (Winged Scroll): Opaque custard glass with gold decoration; mold blown & pressed. This was the original name assigned to this ware by Heisey in the trade ads as it applies to their custard glass pieces. However, collectors like to use the pattern name "Winged Scroll" because this pattern was also made in crystal and emerald green. The pattern is nothing more than a small round cylinder containing three large tapering scrolls that usually contain hand applied gold paint. There was also a **Very Rare** bulbous custard shaker produced in this pattern; it is pictured on page 37 of Bill Heacock's custard glass book. We have never seen one of them in any of the major salt shaker collections. 2¾" tall. Rare. Circa 1901.

A.H. Heisey Glass Company

Locket on Chain: Clear ruby stained with heavy gold painting; pressed glass. The principal pattern consists of an embossed locket hanging from a chain. This motif is repeated four times around the shaker circumference. Now if you salt shaker collectors are looking for a challenge, here it is. A much sought after pattern in the ruby stained glass, and therefore has a high collectibility factor. 2⅝" tall. Rare. Circa 1897.

Pineapple and Fan: Clear ruby stained pressed glass. The upper part of the shaker is smooth and contains the ruby staining; there are deep slashed arches which receive deep cut fans with spreading tops that radiate upward from the base. Between each two fans are pineapples with bevelled edges that are filled with raised diamond point. Also made in crystal. 2⅞" tall. The ruby stained salt shakers are rare. Circa 1896-1897.

Punty Band: Opaque custard glass; mold blown and pressed. The basic pattern is that of a smooth cylinder containing a single row of vertical oval shaped puntys just above the base; the puntys are separated by a deep cut crease above and below the punty band. Also produced in crystal and clear ruby stained. 2⅞" tall. Very scarce. Circa 1896.

Tangerine, Orange Side: Clear shaded orange to red; pressed glass. Quality glass that results from labor intensive fire polishing/cutting. We have had a pair of these small individual place setting shakers since the early 1960's. The only reason we knew who made them was due to the presence of a small Heisey trademark paper label. In studying the Neila Bredehoft book *Heisey Glass, 1925-1938*, we were able to list this ware by the original Heisey name/color. Our other shaker would have to be called "Tangerine, Red Side" since it is a deep ruby color with little orange coloration. Apparently Heisey had continuing problems in controlling this color. 2" tall. Rare. Circa 1932-1935.

Ring Band: Opaque custard glass with gold decoration around the embossed bands; mold blown and pressed. The pattern consists of a slightly expanded pillar containing a single bulging lobe just above the footed base. The bottom of the shaker is concaved and contains the Heisey Diamond H trademark. Pattern name by Peterson. 2⅞" tall. Very scarce. Circa 1901.

The Helmschmied Manufacturing Company
Meriden, Connecticut
(1904-1907)

From a salt shaker collector's point of view, Carl V. Helmschmied is best known for his design patent of the "Erie Twist" (called "Wave Crest Salt" in the C. F. Monroe catalogues) which was issued on October 4, 1892, as a "Design For A Table Vessel."

As Monroe's head designer and plant superintendent, he assigned his patent rights to the Monroe firm. (See "Glassware Design Patents" section of this book).

During his early years in America it is known that Carl Helmschmied worked for such famous glass houses as the Smith Brothers, the Jesse Dean Decorating Company of Trenton, New Jersey and the Mt. Washington Glass Company.

During 1886 he went to work for the C. F. Monroe Company of Meriden, Connecticut. He remained at Monroe until 1903, at which time he left and opened his own business at Meriden. The corporation known as "The Helmschmied Manufacturing Company" was formally established on October 13, 1904. During this firm's functional years, it operated showrooms in New York City and Chicago, Illinois.

When the corporation closed, around 1907, Helmschmied continued to work alone; providing a variety of designer and decorative services. In fact, this talented man continued to perform his custom decorated glass and china crafts from a home workshop until he passed away on January 1, 1934.

We are highlighting salt shakers from one of his outstanding decorative lines that he sold under the name of "Bell Ware." According to Revi[1], this ware was named as a tribute to Mr. Helmschmied's sister-in-law, Mrs. Isabella Van Goerschen whom he affectionately called "Bella".

"Bell Ware" is always hand painted either in pink, blue, lavender or frosted effects. A majority of this ware will be found bottom signed. For an in-depth look at the "Bell Ware" line, the reader is referred to pages 185-194 plus Appendix D of *American Art Nouveau Glass* by A.C. Revi. This is a fine reference book obtainable at your local library.

Bulb, Footed: Opaque opalware, mold blown. This pattern amounts to an expanded bulbous body that is supported by a narrow round foot. The top portion of the shaker has been green painted and fired in a muffle to fix the color. Typical Helmschmied motif; i.e., a floral design with pink predominating on the white opalware background that is framed by a thick enamel painted line. The glass blank was furnished by Mt. Washington/Pairpoint. 2⅛" tall. Very scarce. This type of decorating technique is shown in the "Bell Ware" catalog. Circa 1905.

Lobe, Small: Opaque hand painted white opalware, mold blown. As the pattern name implies, the outside of the shaker is completely smooth and shaped in the form of a very small lobe. The top portion of the shaker has been painted with a delicate lavender and then fired in a muffle to fix the color. The pink floral motif has been applied to the shiny white opalware section and then framed by the application of a thick enamel painted line. 2" tall. Very scarce. Circa 1905-1907.

Helmschmied Manufacturing Company

Slender Neck, Helmschmied's: Opaque frosted opalware; mold blown. The pattern consists of a slender necked shaker with a bulging base. The base is decorated with a large pink floral spray. This ware was also produced in both satinized and shiny opalware. The "Bell Ware" line has a very high collectibility factor; especially in shakers with the so called "Frosty" finish. 3½" tall. Rare. Circa 1905-1907.

Hobbs, Brockunier & Company

Hobbs, Brockunier & Company
Wheeling, West Virginia
(1863-1891)

Formed in 1863, and operated until 1891. However, as a result of reorganization it became known as the Hobbs Glass Co. in 1888. Records show that Harry Northwood worked as this company's engraver from 1882 to 1884. Hobbs joined the giant U.S. Glass conglomerate during 1891 and thereafter operated as Factory H of U. S. Glass. Due to a strike of the glass workers, Factory H was closed in 1893. This Wheeling factory remained closed until it was reopened in 1902 by Harry Northwood after which it became known as H. Northwood & Co. with a subsequent name change in 1905 to H. Northwood Company.

Acorn: Black opaque; mold blown. This pattern was named by Peterson who felt that the physical configuration is reminiscent of an acorn. Known opaque colors in white, blue, and a variegated pink to white shading. The body of this black shaker is decorated with a large gold floral sprig. 2¾" tall. Rare in black. Circa 1889-1891.

LEFT: Barrel, Vasa Murrhina (Spangled-glass): Transparent Amber with imbedded pieces of gold mica flakes; mold blown. The pattern consists of a barrel shaped bulb that is smooth on the outside with small inverted thumbprints on the inside; accomplished by a dual mold process. 3⅛" tall with a two piece metal top. Rare. Circa 1885-1889.

RIGHT: Bubble (Bubble Lattice): Satinized cranberry opalescent; mold blown. This pattern was later produced and advertised by The Buckeye Glass Co. of Martin's Ferry, Ohio in 1889. The pattern consists of a simple barrel shape that tapers toward the bottom with a white opalescent lattice pattern formed over the cranberry glass. Pattern name by Peterson. 2⅞" tall. Very scarce. Circa 1885-1887.

Bulbous Base: Clear cranberry; mold blown. The pattern is comprised of a bulging based shaker with an extended short pillar at the bottom for insertion into a condiment set. We have no additional color experience to report. 3" tall. Very scarce. Circa 1889-1891.

Frances Ware Swirl: Frosted crystal with amber stain at the top; mold blown. A unique shaker containing a series of symmetrical swirls below an embossed ring neck. Also known production with no body frosting. 3⅜" tall. Rare. Circa 1885-1891.

Frances Ware Hobnail: Frosted with an amber band at the top; mold blown & pressed. The pattern consists of symmetrical hobs covering the major portion of the shaker; just below the metal top is an embossed ring. 2¾" tall. Very Rare. Circa 1885-1887.

Hobbs, Brockunier & Company

Opal Ribbon, Vertical: Crystal with opalescent vertical stripes; mold blown. A relatively small shaker containing 16 vertical opalescent stripes some of which partially carry over onto the shaker bottom. Pattern name by Peterson. 2½" tall. Scarce. Circa 1885-1890.

Leaf & Flower, Hobb's: Clear rose-stained crystal with a hand painted floral band encircling the shaker body; mold blown. Also produced in ruby and amber stained glass. 3¼" tall with a two piece metal top. Rare in rose color. Circa 1890-1892.

Opal Coin Spot: Translucent opalescent cranberry; mold blown. The pattern consists of white opalescent dots covering the complete shaker; on the bottom there are predominating circular white stripes covering the cranberry coloring. This is a tall, round pillar-shaped salt. Known color production in translucent green and blue. 3⅝" tall. Very scarce. Circa 1888-1891.

Polka Dot Swirl (Opalescent Windows): Cranberry opalescent; mold blown. The basic pattern shape appears to be a variation of the Francesware Swirl mold. Also made in white and blue opalescent. Pattern name by Peterson. 3¼" tall. Very scarce. Circa 1889-1890.

Pillar, Sixteen: Cranberry opalescent with a white lattice diamond configuration; mold blown. A pillar shaped pattern containing 16 embossed vertical ribs. Known colors in spatter; also blue and white opalescent. Pattern name by Peterson. 2⅞" tall. Circa 1885-1890.

Ring Neck: Translucent pink and white with scattered pieces of gold mica flakes; mold blown. The pattern is bulbous shaped with a large neck ring in raised relief. We have no additional color experience to report. This ware is often called "Spangled Glass" or "Vasa Murrhina." Pattern name by Peterson. 3" tall. Rare. Circa 1889-1890.

Ringed Panels: Translucent pink and white spatter; mold blown. This is a four sided shaker containing a series of narrow embossed rings from top to bottom. Known colors of opaque white, blue and pink. 2¾" tall. Rare in spatter glass. Circa 1888-1891.

Ring Neck Stripe: Cranberry opalescent; mold blown. This is a tubular-shaped pattern with an embossed ring surrounding the top of the shaker. The shaker contains 16 white vertical stripes; every other stripe overlaps onto the bottom. Also made in white, blue and vaseline opalescent. 3¾" tall. Very scarce. Circa 1888-1891.

Swirl, Opalescent: Blue/cranberry opalescent; mold blown. A tubular-shaped pattern with an embossed narrow ring just below the shaker top. The motif consists of a series of milky-white swirling stripes. Two shakers are illustrated. Also made in crystal/white opalescent glass. 3⅝" tall. Very scarce. Circa 1889-1893

Swirl, Opalescent Bulbous: Cranberry opalescent with swirling narrow stripes; mold blown. A small bulbous shaker with an extended short round pillar protruding from the bottom for insertion into a condiment set holder. Known production in opalescent blue and white. 2⅝" tall. Very scarce. Circa 1889-1892.

Hobbs, Brockunier & Company

Swirl, Ribbon: Vaseline opalescent; mold blown. The pattern consists of a round pillar containing embossed left to right swirls. The white diagonal stripes slant to the left. Also produced in opalescent blue and cranberry; some will be found in satinized glass. Pattern name by Peterson. 2¾" tall. Very scarce. Circa 1886-1890.

Swirl, Reverse: Apricot, pink-to-white satinized spatter glass; mold blown. The pattern consists of 15 embossed left-to-right swirls that add to the unusual shaded coloring. Also made in various other spatter type colors. Apparently later production of this pattern by the Buckeye Glass Company in various opalescent colors. 2⅜" tall. Rare. Circa 1885-1887.

Thumbprint, Concave: Cranberry Rubina shading from ruby to crystal; mold blown. This is a dual mold type shaker that is pinched inward in the center at four points; the inside contains a continuous series of thumbprints. We have no additional color experience to report. 3" tall with a two piece metal top. Rare. Circa 1886-1890.

Wheeling Peachblow (Coral): Cherry or fuchsia red in the upper portion of the shaker to a yellow gold at the base; mold blown. The more fuchsia red a piece has, the more desirable and valuable it is to the collector/dealer. This glass contains two layers, the inside lining is an opal glass. The shakers can be found in either a shiny or acid finish. The red colored shading is achieved by use of a heat sensitive glass that changes color when reheated at the Glory Hole. 2⅜" or 2¾" (two sizes made) tall with a two piece metal top. Both size shakers are considered to be rare, but for some reason the larger ones are more difficult to obtain. Good red coloring determines price and collectibility. Circa 1886.

The Imperial Glass Company
Bellaire, Ohio
(1904-1984)

The Imperial Glass Company was formed in 1901 by Mr. Edward Muhleman but did not start producing glass until January, 1904. Initial factory production consisted of jelly jars, tumblers, pressed glass goblets and glass lighting shades.

This is a quality glasshouse that during its total existence produced everything from art glass to reproductions. Yes, from time to time they did some quantity of contract work for what Mildred and I call "The House of Reproductions"; i.e., L.G. Wright.

Over the years, Imperial acquired the name rights and molds from Central Glass Company (1939); A.H. Heisey Glass Company (1958) and the Cambridge Glass Company (1960). Due to their tie-in to reproductions of the opaque white Atterbury Saloon Pepper "Johnny Bull" during the early 1950's, it

seemed to be a good idea to include some of the ware that this glass house produced.

Imperial became an unprofitable operation and was finally forced to close its doors in 1984. For those readers that would like a more detailed overview of this factory we recommend the book *Imperial* by Margaret and Douglas Archer published by Collector Books of Paducah, Kentucky.

Grape, Imperial's: Translucent red (pigeon blood); mold blown and pressed. The pattern has three bunches of embossed grapes; each bunch is separated by a leafy vine. Also made in opaque white and a rubigold carnival. 3⅜" tall. Circa 1965-1970.

Amberina Daisy & Button, Imperial's: Clear red to amber pressed glass. This is a late reproduction of an early Daisy & Button pressed Amberina glassware that was produced by Imperial for L.G. Wright. Overall quality is excellent. 2⅞" tall. Circa 1970-1980.

Diamond Ridge (Basket Caster Set): Clear vaseline; mold blown and pressed. The set comes with a matching glass handled basket[1] to hold the salt and pepper shakers, but was not available to us. The Imperial catalogue lists this ware as "Basket Caster Set." When exposed to black light radiation the shaker emits a striking fluorescence. Shakers = 1⅞" tall. Very scarce in vaseline. Circa 1925-1930.

Imperial Glass Company

Mary Bull & Johnny Bull, Imperial's: White opaque and rubigold translucent carnival glass; mold blown and pressed. We are illustrating two salt and pepper sets to enhance reader understanding. The "Mary Bull" shakers are a relatively new creation of Imperial Glass. The opaque white "Johnny Bull" shaker is a very close reproduction of the "Johnny Bull" saloon pepper that was produced by Atterbury & Co. around 1880. Of course, the Atterbury shakers were never originally produced in carnival glass. 5½" tall. This ware has a very high collectibility factor and the craftsmanship is of high quality. Peterson reported that he first saw the opaque white reproduction of the "Johnny Bull" shaker (by Imperial) in the early 1950's.

Poppy, Imperial's: Clear pink iridescent carnival glass; mold blown and pressed. The pattern consists of three large intaglio poppy flowers separated by large diamond shaped wedges. Very pretty in the unusual pink colored carnival. 3" tall. Circa 1975-1982.

Panelled Rosette: Clear red and gold colored crystal; pressed glass. Each shaker has the Imperial IG trademark impressed on the bottom. The principal pattern consists of four large embossed rosettes; each rosette is separated by a round pointed panel containing X-shaped crosses and hexagon shaped circles. One shaker is heavily decorated in gold. Excellent quality. 3¼" tall. Circa 1970-1980.

Sphinx: Clear crystal; mold blown and pressed. This is a very unique figural condiment configured in the form of an Egyptian image. During our 35+ years of collecting we have only observed four; these were in major collections. This is heavy glass and should have an excellent survival factor but it is a most difficult piece to collect. 2¾" tall. Rare. Circa 1910-1920.

Twelve Panelled Rib, Imperial's: Clear cobalt blue; mold blown and pressed. The pattern consists of twelve vertical panelled ribs; the pattern carries over onto the caster set glass base. Listed in an Imperial catalogue as their #200 Tall Caster Set[1]. Shakers - 2½"; handled glass base - 6¼" tall. Very scarce as a complete set.

The Indiana Tumbler & Goblet Company
Greentown, Indiana
(1894-1903)

The Indiana Tumbler and Goblet Company began operations in June, 1894 with D.C. Jenkins Jr. as President. The factory's production centered around plain and figured tumblers. This glasshouse enjoyed several major expansions and remained profitable throughout its independent existence. During July, 1899, this firm joined in the formation of the National Glass Company with D. C. Jenkins Jr. being both a stock holder and a member of the National Glass board of directors.

After the National Glass take over, Mr. Jenkins lost control of the Greentown factory operations; by June/July of 1900 he sold out his interest and left to form the Kokomo Glass Manufacturing company in Kokomo, Indiana. A number of the talented personnel, including his head designer Charles E. Beam, followed him to this new Kokomo glass factory.

To keep the Indiana Tumbler & Goblet Co. a viable operation, National Glass moved in William Barris as superintendent, Jacob Rosenthal as manager and Frank Jackson as head designer. Perhaps the greatest acquisition was the employment of Mr. Rosenthal who arrived at Greentown in September, 1900. With some thirty years of previous glass experience Rosenthal introduced the production of chocolate glass and a short while later Golden Agate (Holly Amber). These wares not only kept the factory profitable, but made it a famous one among American glass houses. On June 13, 1903 the factory was completely destroyed by fire and it was never rebuilt; thus ending nine years of existence.

There are a few of the so-called Greentown patterns that are a bit controversial. We say this because there is an honest difference of opinion as to whether they should be attributed to the Indiana Tumbler and Goblet Company or not. There are two past publications involved and we will list both of them in our bibliography. For example, it is our opinion as well as others, that the "Chrysanthemum Leaf" chocolate glass shaker was made by at least one of the National Glass Company factories. The way molds were moved around within this conglomerate of glass houses, it is impossible to tell without trade advertisement back-up data from the various publications that were used by glass factories to obtain consumer publicity. We invite those of our readers that are glass researchers to submit any valid evidence that proves that any of the following patterns were not produced by this Greentown factory.

Authors' Collection

Bruce Collection

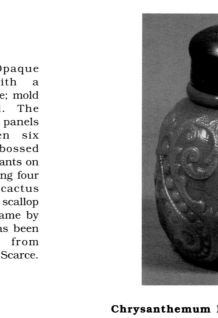

Caramel Cactus: Opaque chocolate glass with a Caramel-like appearance; mold blown and pressed. The pattern consists of six panels interspersed between six vertical ribs. The embossed motif has 2 three leaf plants on two panels; the remaining four contain a single leaf cactus plant. The base has six scallop shaped feet. Pattern name by Kamm. This pattern has been heavily reproduced from original molds. 2⅞" tall. Scarce. Circa 1902.

Chrysanthemum Leaf: Opaque chocolate glass; mold blown. This is a rather complex embossed leafy pattern with diminishing sized buttons in raised relief. The overall shape is that of a spheroid. Pattern name by Lee. 2⅝" tall. Very Rare. Circa 1901-1903.

Avery Collection

Authors' Collection

Lockwood Collection

Caramel Leaf Bracket: Opaque chocolate glass; mold blown and pressed. This shaker contains three feet; above each foot is a large embossed leaf. If the collector is lucky enough to find one of these shakers for sale, be sure and inspect each foot carefully because they are highly prone to annealing cracks. 2⅞" tall. Rare. Circa 1901.

Dewey: Clear green glass; mold blown and pressed. An embossed shaker containing medallions near the base and on each scalloped foot. Known production of shakers in chocolate glass which are quite rare. Pattern name by Kamm (see Kamm 1-84). 2⅞" tall. Very scarce. Circa 1900-1901.

Holly Amber (Golden Agate): Translucent variegated amber; mold blown and pressed. This ware has a remarkably warm color glow to it. While it is a pattern glass, such a limited quantity was originally produced it commands a high art glass type of pricing and is sought after by all antique glassware collectors. There have been no reproductions of the salt shakers but there are some darn good reproductions of the toothpick. Due to the processes involved, this ware is highly susceptible to annealing cracks so we advise the use of magnification prior to purchase. 3" tall. Very rare. Circa 1903.

Holly Clear: Clear crystal; mold blown & pressed. The pattern is identical to Holly Amber and quite difficult to obtain in crystal. It is interesting to note that Arthur Peterson rated the clear shakers with a higher scarcity factor than the "Holly Amber" in his 1970 salt shaker book. We certainly do not disagree with him. 3" tall. Very rare. Circa 1902-1903.

Shuttle: Clear crystal; mold blown & pressed. Also produced in Chocolate glass. The pattern consists of a series of diamond pointed oval panels each containing a small rosette. This is one of the earlier Greentown patterns. 2⅝" tall. Very scarce in crystal. Extremely rare in chocolate. Circa 1896.

Teardrop & Tassel: Clear crystal; mold blown and pressed. The best way to describe this pattern title; in terms of motif it is quite Busy! Busy! Busy! We have never seen a salt shaker in color. 2⅞" tall. Scarce. Circa 1900.

The Jefferson Glass Company
Steubenville, Ohio
(1901-1907)
Follansbee, West Virginia
(1907-1920's)

This factory was established in 1901 at Steubenville, Ohio. In 1907, the factory was moved to Follansbee, West Virginia. It produced quality blown and pressed colored glassware including opalescent patterns in various stripes, polka dots and floral designs, also a considerable quantity of custard glass. In 1913 Jefferson purchased the rights to the trademark name "Krys-Tol" from the Ohio Flint Glass Company. Jefferson also purchased and used a number of their molds, reissuing some of the patterns in a high quality crystal glass. By 1920, this factory ceased making colored glassware and concentrated on the manufacture of lighting fixtures. It ceased operations, and went out of business during the late 1920's.

Just Collection

Authors' Collection

Bead and Panel: Crystal to a translucent opalescent at the base; mold blown. This is a six panel shaker; each panel is outlined by individual beaded vertical ribs; the beads grow smaller as they progress toward the top of the shaker. Also produced in crystal. Pattern name by A.G. Peterson. 2¾" tall. Very scarce. Circa 1902.

Authors' Collection

Circle, Double (Jefferson No. 231): Clear green with a shiny iridescence; mold blown with a rough bottom pontil. Does not fluoresce when exposed to black light. The principal pattern consists of two intaglio circles; one directly above the other. Also produced in crystal and blue. Pattern name by Peterson who considered the green shaker to be rare in his 1970 book. 3⅛" tall. Rare. Circa 1902.

Diamond with Peg: Opaque custard glass; mold blown & pressed. This is a cylindrical shaped shaker with the pattern consisting of six diamonds, each containing a round peg that has been outlined with gold paint. All of this motif is in high raised relief. These shakers are usually found with some type of painted souvenir writing; however, our illustrated pair has been painted with a lovely pink rose sprig. Also produced in crystal and ruby-stained crystal. 3" tall. Very scarce with rose decoration! Circa 1907.

Ribbed Thumbprint: Clear ruby stained crystal; mold blown & pressed. The pattern consists of a smooth cylinder with eight large thumbprints around the base circumference. Also produced in crystal. 2⅞" tall. Scarce. Circa 1905-1907.

Iris With Meander (Iris): Crystal to a translucent opalescent at the base; mold blown with a polished out pontil. The principal motif amounts to four iris flowers equally disbursed around the shaker bottom. 3¼" tall. Rare in this color! Also made in green & crystal. Circa 1904.

Swag with Brackets: Clear amethyst with gold decoration; mold blown. The principal motif consists of a bulbous body that has been squared off at the bottom to form four individual feet. There is an embossed leaf on the base corner of each foot. Also made in crystal and blue; other colors in opalescent are very scarce and seldom available today. 3" tall. Rare in amethyst. Circa 1904.

Jefferson Optic: Opaque custard glass; mold blown. This is a plain shaker with no pattern motif. The base has been configured for insertion into a condiment set. Sometimes found with souvenir writing or in the case of the one we are illustrating, there is a picture of St. Mary's Abbey at Richardton N.D. that has been applied by the use of a transfer technique. This shaker was also produced in clear amethyst with a rather garish hand painted decoration. 2⅞" tall. Very scarce in custard or amethyst. Circa 1912.

Jefferson Glass Company

Scalloped Skirt: We are showing three different colors of clear blue, green and amethyst; mold blown. This is a bulbous shaped shaker that tapers at the bottom with the base consisting of a series of scallops. All that we have seen contain enamelled decoration. 3" tall. Scarce. Circa 1905.

Tokyo: Clear pale blue and green with slight base opalescence; mold blown. The pattern consists of three jeweled medallions equally spaced around the base; each medallion is separated by six vertial plumes that cover about three quarters of the shaker body. Also produced in white opalescent. 3¼" tall. Scarce. Circa 1904-1905.

Kanawha Glass Company
Dunbar, West Virginia
(1955-1988)

The Kanawha Glass Company was founded in 1955 by Mr. D. P. Merritt. Early factory production consisted of cut or etched crystal and opalware glass lighting fixtures.

Colored glass was introduced around 1960. From our point of view, this factory's most noted production, and what we think is a very worthwhile collectible, is their colored crackled ware.

We are illustrating the only shaker that we are aware of in this most ornate crackled glass line.

In 1988 the Kanawha name and factory was sold to the Raymond Dereume Glass Company of Punxsutawney, Pennsylvania. It is our understanding that the new owners are still producing glass under the Kanawha paper label.

Crackle, Bulbous Base: Clear Amberina shading with a crackle motif; mold blown. The shaker is completely smooth on the outside; the top edge (under the metal top) has been ground off smooth. The base has been configured so that it could be inseted into a glass or metal condiment holder. We are not aware of a condiment set, but there may very well have been one produced. 5⅝" tall. Circa 1965.

The Kokomo Glass Company
Kokomo, Indiana
(1900-1905)

This factory was built by Dr. David C. Jenkins in 1900 and began producing glass in February 1901. If the reader will peruse our write up about the Indiana Tumbler & Goblet Company, additional background relative to the talented Mr. Jenkins is provided.

The factory was destroyed by fire in September, 1905. Mr. Jenkins rebuilt it and reopened in 1906 as the "D. C. Jenkins Glass Company."

Panelled Grape: Clear crystal pressed glass with rose and green staining. The shaker consists of heavy thick hexagon shaped glass containing six wide panels. The motif is a grape vine from which is hanging a bunch of grapes, all in high raised relief. This was an outstanding pattern produced by this glasshouse. A.C. Revi[1] reported that the molds for this pattern had found their way to Westmoreland and various pieces were still being produced during the 1960's. Westmoreland acquired the molds from L.G. Wright and produced various pieces under the pattern name "Panel Grape" in opaque white and crystal. 2¾" tall. Stained pieces are very scarce. Circa 1903-1905.

The Lancaster Glass Works
Lancaster, Ohio
(1900-   )

A 1901 trade ad[1] shows the "Globule" pattern and indicates that this glasshouse was being operated by the National Glass Co. The factory produced mold & pressed glass in a wide variety of colors. We have been unable to establish an exact closing date for this firm.

Globule: Clear ruby glassware; mold blown. This pattern name was established by Warman and is a poor choice of words because it is truly a beautiful shaker. The pattern consists of eight long bulging lobes; perhaps reminiscent of water droplets or teardrops. Every other lobe contains embossed fancy scrolling. Also made in crystal, opaque white and red satin. 3⅛" tall. Very scarce. Circa 1901.

Flower Band: Translucent reddish orange (pigeon blood) satinized glass; mold blown. The pattern consists of a smooth bulbous based shaker with an embossed band of flowers encircling the shaker's base circumference. Also produced in crystal and clear ruby; perhaps other colors. 2⅝" tall. Very scarce in satinized pigeon blood. Circa 1901-1902.

Lobe, Six: Clear deep ruby glass; mold blown. The pattern consists of six bulging lobes and a beaded ring neck. We have no additional color experience to report. 2⅝" tall. Scarce. Circa 1910-1915.

W.L. Libbey and Sons Company
(1888-1892)
Libbey Glass Company
(1892-Present)

In order to obtain a better understanding of this company's history the reader should peruse our write up of the New England Glass Company.

There are three salt shaker patterns that we are presenting. They all are the result of special Joseph Locke patents. The patent office information for the Thimble and Single Dice are presented separately within the "Glassware Design" section of this book.

It should be noted that the two Libbey Company names were changes brought about by the board of directors in 1892. Libbey Glass remained at Toledo, Ohio.

There is a very comprehensive book entitled *Libbey Glass* by Carl U. Fauster that we highly recommend for those readers that would like a comprehensive overview of this factory's history and glassware production. We purchased our copy at The Chrysler Museum, Norfolk, Va.

Libbey Maize Art Glass Condiment
An Outstanding Rarity

The Maize shakers, as shown in today's art glass books, are bulbous in shape, widest through the middle, and taper towards both ends. All simulate an ear of corn with irregular foliage around the base that reaches approximately half-way up. The shakers may be found in white, green or pale-yellow opaque colors measuring 3¾" tall. The embossed leaves may be colored yellow, green or red.

It is established fact that first production of this ware began at New England Glass Company some months prior to the factory closure in 1888. Our research has concluded that the pale yellow (really more of a cream color) glass was made at the Cambridge, Mass. factory; the white colored Maize having been made at Toledo, Ohio.

What present art glass books don't show, is the existence of a four piece condiment set consisting of salt, pepper, mustard and glass base that contains an entirely different motif i.e.; the salt, pepper and mustard contain no irregular foliage (at all) upon their bases. Instead, a green leaf-like foliage is present only upon the outer rim of the condiment set glass base holder.

While Arthur Peterson disclosed the aforesaid configuration exceptions in his February and April, 1969 articles as published in *Hobbie Magazine*, it would be very difficult for a collector to understand the total impact of his revelation because of the lack of a Maize Condiment Set photo.

The No. 915 condiment set artist's rendition, shown in the Libbey trade ad, is unclear and in accurate (see Kamm 5, plate 22). Therefore, it is quite understandable why many collectors (particularly those looking for Maize) might ignore any shakers that have become separated from the

original condiment set. Even if such a type of shaker is purchased, there is high probability that the new owner will not realize that he/she has acquired a rare piece of Maize Art Glass.

With their single piece screw-on metal tops removed, the height measurements of the condiment set dispensers are: Salt & Pepper shakers - 3⅝"; Mustard - 2¾". The condiment set glass holder measured 6¼" in diameter (as measured across the base bottom). A complete Maize Art Glass Condiment set is **very rare**! In fact, our illustrated set is the only one that we have ever seen, and we have viewed most of the major antique salt shaker collections that exist in the U.S.A.

It is our opinion that these condiment sets were only made at the Libbey Glass factory in Toledo, Ohio. If any of our readers have been fortunate enough to acquire a Maize Art Glass Condiment Set, we would appreciate hearing from you. Circa 1889.

Authors' Collection

Authors' Collection

W. L. Libbey and Sons Company

Single Dice: Opaque white opalware with hand painted red, blue and white floral sprigs; mold blown. Design patented by Joseph Locke on December 3, 1889 as a "Condiment Holder." According to Mr. Locke's patent description "the leading features of my design are a cubical receptacle having on its faces any desired number of dots or depressions, an angular neck formed on the upper face, and a perforated cover fitted on said neck." 1¼" tall. Circa 1889.

Thimble, Ribbed: Clear crystal; mold blown. A review of the patent drawing shows that the Thimble could be made with or without ribbing. The principal difference is that an embossed band of small vertical ribs has been substituted since crystal does not lend itself well to hand painted floral decoration; particularly in the decorating space that would be available. 2⅜" tall. Very rare. Circa 1889-1890.

Thimble: Opaque white opalware with hand painted flowers encircling the shaker vase; mold blown. Design patented by Joseph Locke on December 3, 1889 as a "Condiment Holder." According to Locke's patent description "The leading feature of my design is a receptacle of the character specified in the form of a Thimble having a closed bottom and perforated top." 2⅜" tall. Very rare. Circa 1889.

Longwy Faience Company

Longwy Faience Company
Longwy, France
(1798-Present)

The Longwy Faience Company pottery was founded in 1789 at Longwy, France where it continues to operate today. Pronounced "lung-vee," this ware was imported from the pottery in France by Rogers, Smith & Company of Meriden, Connecticut. It was advertised in their 1882 catalogue.

Longwy Faience used a total of three pottery marks[1] which are stamped on the bottom of most of their shakers. This ware is highly ornate and hand decorated by the use of "Stanniferrous" enamelling.

All the shakers that we have seen come in two basic sizes: a large barrel shaped shaker 3¼" tall by 2" in diameter, and pillar-shaped salts 3½" by 2" diameter. Some of the shakers use a threaded top, while others require a two piece metal top. A sugar shaker was also produced.

From time to time, we have come across shakers that dealers were offering as oriental pottery; one enterprising dealer had his shakers ink marked with Chinese writing on the bottom. Unfortunately forged signatures are all too often present on antique glass and pottery/porcelain pieces that are offered for sale. Unless a collector is very knowledgeable, expensive items should never be purchased on the basis of a signature alone.

We are providing three photographs that should give the reader a good representation of the Longwy shakers that can be collected. The enamel paints that were applied to these pieces is very durable and can be readily hand washed without fear of the paint coming off. All of the shakers we are illustrating are circa 1870-1890.

112

McKee and Bros.
Jeanette, Pennsylvania
(1889-1899)

In 1850 James and Frederick McKee established a flint glass factory in Pittsburgh, Pennsylvania, using the name "J & F McKee." In 1853 the name became "McKee & Brother." Around 1865 another brother joined the Company and the name changed to "McKee & Brothers."

In 1889, the factory was moved to Jeanette, Pennsylvania. It is this Jeanette factory that produced the majority of the patterns that we are illustrating and addressing in this book.

In 1899, the McKee Factory joined and became a principal part of the National Glass Company's production. At times, pattern molds were pulled from other corporate member factory locations and produced at the Jeanette factory when it was deemed, by National Glass, to better meet the needs of the business. For example, National Glass established a glass staining department at the McKee factory. In the interest of efficiency and centralized control, glassware that was produced at other National Glass factories which required ruby or amber staining, was sent to McKee to be stained. In some instances, other factory molds would be moved to McKee for both production and staining. To today's American pattern glass authors and researchers this can create confusion in trying to establish factory attribution when trade catalogs from more than one glasshouse contain the same pattern.

By 1904, National Glass had discontinued the operation of the member factories under its corporate name. finally, this conglomerate went into receivership in 1908.

In 1910, the Mckee President, Mr. A.J. Smith, reorganized the factory under the name of "McKee Glass Co." It continued its production operation for many years before being purchased by the nearby "Jeanette Glass Co." Reports indicate that many of the old McKee molds were purchased during the early 1980's by "The Fenton Art Glass Company."

Clemantis & Scroll: Opaque blue homogeneous glass; mold blown and pressed. We are illustrating the salt and pepper, as a condiment set, in their matching glass holder. It was not too surprising to find this same pattern appearing in a "Cambridge Glass Co." catalogue; since Cambridge was built by National Glass Co. in 1901. Pattern name by Peterson. 2¾" tall. Rare as a complete condiment set. Circa 1895-1901 at McKee.

Eureka, National's: Ruby stained crystal; mold blown & pressed. This was always considered to be a National Glass pattern; McKee was selected to manufacture it. This is a busy pattern; the diamonds are filled with small embossed buttons and flat strips, outside the diamonds that encircle the center of the shaker, contain ruby staining as does the neck ring and area just below the metal top. 2⅞" tall. Highly collectible and Rare. Circa 1901-1904.

Croesus: Clear amethyst glass; mold blown & pressed. First produced by Riverside Glass Works in 1897 and advertised in a 1901 McKee trade catalogue. This is a well known pattern with a high collectibility factor despite the reproduction of some pieces; but not the salt shakers. 3¼" tall. Rare in amethyst. Circa 1901 at McKee.

Flower Panel McKee's: Opaque green; mold blown. See Fenton #6206 in this book for the same six panelled shaker with slightly different embossed motif. Pattern name by Warman. 2¾" tall. Circa 1904-1910.

Fancy Arch: Ruby stained pressed glass. This is really the same pattern name; Peterson liked to put the noun first and Heacock didn't. If you look for this in Peterson's Salt Shaker book, look under the A's. The main point of this pattern is at the base where the fancy arch is formed. The upper two-thirds of the shaker is ruby stained. Also produced in clear crystal. This shaker has a high collectibility factory in ruby stained coloring. 2⅞" tall. Very scarce. Circa 1901-1906.

Geneva: Opaque custard; mold blown. The pattern consists of three large embossed shell panels symmetrically spaced around the body of the shaker; just below the neck are three elaborate scrolls. The custard color is on the pale side but does fluoresce when illuminated by black light. Also produced in clear green and chocolate glass. 3" tall. Rare in green and custard; Very rare in chocolate. Circa 1901-1902.

McKee's No. 6 Variant: Ruby stained mold blown and pressed glassware. The pattern consists of a band of narrow vertical ribs at the top and base of the shaker. The middle is plain and smooth and contains the ruby staining. 3⅛" tall. Scarce. Circa 1903.

Siamese Twins: Clear crystal with curved vertical ribbing; mold blown. The pattern amounts to two separate shakers that have been joined/fused together. The design is such that two condiments are always available but can only be dispensed one at a time due to the left-right positioning of the opening. Pattern name by Peterson. 3¼" maximum height. Very scarce. Circa 1880.

Ovals, Interlocking: Clear blue glass; mold blown and pressed. The principal motif consists of six interlocking ovals that reach from the bottom to approximately ¾ of the way up to the shaker rim. The underside contains an elaborate recessed rosette. The base has been configured for insertion into a condiment holder. 1⅞" tall. Scarce. Circa 1891-1897.

Prism with Skylight (Naomi): Clear ruby stained crystal; mold blown and pressed. The top of the smaller has clear crystal prisms surrounded by ruby staining; the base contains short crystal vertical ribs. A 1901 McKee trade catalog shows that the OMN is "Naomi." The "Prism With Skylight" name was assigned by Peterson. There are two designs named "Naomi." Both are shown. 2¾" tall. Rare. Circa 1901.

McKee and Bros.

Scrolled Neck with Plume: Opaque white opalware; mold blown and pressed. There is no doubt that this item was produced in various hand painted colors; unfortunately our example no longer has its original decoration. The shaker center contains three embossed plumes; the neck is encircled with continuous scrolling. 3¼" tall. Scarce. Circa 1900-1908.

Swirl, Intaglio: Opaque white opalware; mold blown. The pattern consists of two sunken flowers between two embossed vines. Pattern name by Peterson. 3" tall. Circa 1908-1910.

The Prize: Clear crystal with ruby staining in the neck ring area; mold blown & pressed. The pattern consists of beaded coarse vertical bars. Peterson called this ware "an outstanding pattern of the early 1900's." Has a very high collectibility factor. 3⅛" tall. Very scarce. Circa 1900-1904.

Tiptoe (Ramona): Clear crystal glass; mold blown and pressed. Patented by O.K. Hogan, February 23, 1904. In the McKee catalog it is referred to as "Ramona." The details surrounding this particular pattern are related on page 179 of *Glass Patents & Patterns* by A. G. Peterson. 3⅛" tall.

Thistle and Fern: Frosted translucent crystal with hand painted red and gold goofus decoration over embossed thistle and fern leaves; mold blown. This is a very ornate pattern when the goofus paint is still intact. No mention of color is made in the McKee trade catalogue. Pattern name by Peterson. 2⅜" tall. Rare. Circa 1901-1906.

Wildrose with Bowknot: Frosted crystal with red and gilt Goofus type decoration; mold blown. The pattern consists of three wild roses and three elaborate chain/bow knots each of which is surrounded by frosted scrolls; all of the motifs are in raised relief. Also produced in clear green, and chocolate. There has always been controversy among past authors as to whether or not the chocolate shakers were made by the Indiana Tumbler and Goblet Company of Greentown, Indiana. This probably got started due to the influence of Dr. Ruth Herrick's book *Greentown Glass* which was first published in late 1959. A.G. Peterson references her book in his comments on this pattern. With the appearance of the 1901 McKee trade catalogue ad, this should dispel those past attributions. The chocolate shakers are highly susceptible to chips and annealing cracks so, if you are lucky enough to find one, use magnification before purchasing. 3" tall. Very scarce. Circa 1901.

Model Flint Glass Company

Model Flint Glass Company
Findlay, Ohio (1888-1893)
Albany, Indiana (1893-1903)

The Model Flint Glass Company of Findlay, Ohio, started glass production during October, 1888. The first company president was Mr. A. C. Heck; the factory manager was Mr. W.C. Walters. The first year of production was primarily crystal glassware. While this factory's production was always level loaded with crystal glassware, over all Model Flint made bar goods, lamps, and colored glassware. On October 25, 1893 the factory was sold to Model Flint Glass Company of Albany, Indiana; the plant at Findlay was closed and factory fixtures, etc. moved to the new Albany, Indiana plant.

We are able to illustrate one pattern example from each factory: The "Beveled Star" is a Findlay pattern; the beautiful "Ribbed Spiral" shaker was made at the Albany, Indiana factory[1].

For a comprehensive look at the Findlay, Ohio firm, we recommend the book *Findlay Glass* by James Measell and Don E. Smith.

Pride (Beveled Star): Clear crystal pressed glass. The pattern consists of a large beveled circle containing a large star in raised relief. The star has a flat octagonal central button. Pride is the OMN. Because Mrs. Kamm recognized that there were several other patterns by this name, she renamed it "Beveled Star." A. G. Peterson lists the pattern by the Kamm name. Kamm states that the pattern was produced in green and probably amber. 2" tall. Very scarce. Circa 1893.

Model Flint Glass Company

Reverse Swirl: Cranberry opalescent glass; mold blown. The pattern name describes the pattern. Also made in blue opalescent. 3¼" tall. Very Scarce. Circa 1901-1902.

Ribbed Spiral: Semi-translucent blue opalescent glass; mold blown. The pattern consists of embossed horizontal circular ribbing with a striking opalescence near the shaker base. Arthur Peterson refers to this item as "Albany Art Glass." This type of glassware has a high collectibility factor. 2¾" tall. Rare.

C. F. Monroe Company

C.F. Monroe Co., Meriden, Conneticut (1892-1916)

C. F. Monroe was primarily an elaborate opalware decorating firm that obtained its ware in the form of glass blanks supplied by both American and European glass manufacturers.

Among their principal suppliers was Mt. Washington/Pairpoint and Dithridge & Co. (see Dithridge Princess Swirl pattern). It is interesting to note that prior to the turn of the twentieth century a majority of their salt shakers were hand decorated. However, after 1900 outside competition seemed to dictate the use of various types of transfer decorative practices in order to achieve substantial labor cost savings. Sometimes shakers will be found that contain a combination of both hand and transfer decorative techniques. Naturally, both quality and type of decoration have a major influence upon each shakers retail value.

The three principal decoration categories are: Wave Crest, Nakara and Kelva. All are highly collectible and fall into the Very Scarce to Rare classifications. While it is a fact that Monroe marketed decorated crystal & cut glassware, very few are found in the form of salt & peppers. Their trade catalogues show minimal crystal shakers. As a result it is difficult to attribute crystal shakers to this decorating house.

Beaded Top & Bottom: Wave Crest white opalware; mold blown. This is a bulging based shaker containing a single ring of embossed beads at the bottom and top; the transfer type decoration consists of two red-headed birds sitting side-by-side among yellow and brown foliage. 2¼" tall. Rare. Circa 1901-1905.

C. F. Monroe Company

McElderry Collection

Authors' Collection

Creased Neck: Wave Crest white satinized opalware; mold blown. This is a uniform, tubular shaped shaker supporting a creased-like neck; the transfer type decoration depicts a large floral sprig. Pattern name by Peterson. 3½" tall. Very scarce. Circa 1898-1905

Chick On Pedestal: Opaque tan & brown shading over white opalware; mold blown. This shaker has never been formally attributed to any glass house, but we have always thought that it leaned in the direction of Mt. Washington/Pairpoint due to the similarity to the Chick Head shaker. However, a 1903 ad from Keystone (a jobber/distributor) indicates this shaker is a C.F. Monroe item. The trade ad was discovered by Wilfred Cohen.[1] 2½" tall with a special chick head metal top. Rare. Circa 1903.

Authors' Collection

Authors' Collection

Authors' Collection

Cube, Tall: White opaque opalware containing a Wave Crest trademark; mold blown. A square cube with a transfer type floral decoration essentially all on one panel. The back panel is blank. 2¾" tall. Very scarce. Circa 1903-1907.

Cube, Shortened: Creamy white opalware; mold blown. A shortened square cube containing a transfer type floral sprig primarily all on one panel. 2½" tall. Very scarce. Circa 1903-1907.

Creased Neck, Nakara: Tan shaded opalware; mold blown. Transfer type decoration showing an Indian with a full feathered head dress. See "Creased Neck" (above) for physical pattern description. 3½" tall. Exceptionally rare. Circa 1903-1906.

C. F. Monroe Company

Draped Column: Wave Crest opalware with fired on background coloring; mold blown. Pillar shaped with a bulging bottom below interspersed draped columns. The base contains a transfer type floral sprig. 2⅞" tall. Rare. Circa 1901-1906.

Cube, Rounded-Off: Creamy white opalware; mold blown. A square cube with the top corners rounded-off; transfer type floral sprig decoration. 2¼" tall. Very scarce. Circa 1903-1907.

Elongated Bulb: Wave Crest white opalware; mold blown. A tall bulbous-shaped shaker containing transfer type decoration that shows a brown, two story house surrounded by brown autumn foliage. 3¾" tall. Rare. Circa 1903-1907.

Erie Twist: Wave Crest red to white shaded satinized opalware; mold blown. This swirl shaped pattern was patented in 1892 by Carl V. Helmschmeid and assigned to C.F. Monroe Co. It was used on a wide variety of the Monroe Company's opalware products. The pattern name is by Peterson. The reader is referred to the "Dithridge Princess Swirl" pattern for some interesting facts about this pattern. All of the salt shakers that we have observed in this pattern have been hand painted/decorated. 2" tall with a two piece metal top. Scarce. Circa 1892-1900.

Foursquare Variant: Wave Crest off-white opalware; mold blown. Contains transfer type floral sprig decoration. The pattern appears to be a variation of the Foursquare configuration; accomplished, no doubt, by reworking one or more of the Foursquare molds by removing the bumps on each panel and outlining the decoration with scrolling. It should also be noted that single piece metal screw on tops are used on this later shaker design. 1½" tall. Rare. Circa 1899-1904.

Foursquare (Billow): Wave Crest white satinized opalware; mold blown. Hand decorated with a two piece metal top. This is a square shaped shaker containing small bumps and hand painted flowers. The Monroe trade catalogues list this pattern as "Billow," but the Foursquare name has been established by Peterson. The illustrated shakers are shown in their original silver plated stand/holder. 1¾" tall; Very rare as a complete condiment set. Circa 1895-1898.

Kelva, Small: Hand painted opalware with a single white lily painted over a mottled orange/red background; mold blown. A simple, bulbous base tapers upward toward the top of the shaker. 2½" tall. Very rare. Circa 1902-1906.

Kelva: Off-white opalware with hand painted pink and white Lilies over a mottled, batik-like background; mold blown. Very few Kelva patterns in salt shakers were produced by the Monroe factory. When located, the collector will find that their basic geometric shape is quite simple. This ware is most difficult to collect today. 3¼" tall. Very rare. Circa 1904-1906.

Panel, Tapered: Wave Crest opalware; mold blown. This is a good example of the application of both transfer and hand painted decoration. The basic floral sprig has been transfer applied and some of the flower centers contain hand painted enameling. The pattern design consists of a series of bulbous ribbed panels with a ring footed base. 2⅞" tall. Very scarce. Circa 1900-1903.

Necklace, Bulbous: Wave Crest white opalware; mold blown. Transfer decorated with an orange and brown bouquet. The pattern consists of an elaborate beaded and scrolled necklace just below the metal top; the footed base contains 16 small scallops. 2⅝" tall. Rare. Circa 1903-1907.

Pearl Wavecrest: Wave Crest opalware; mold blown. Transfer decorated with a large pink and green floral arrangement that has been applied over a yellow painted background to a Mt. Washington/Pairpoint glass blank. 3½" tall. Very scarce. Circa 1898-1903.

Pillar, Leaf Based: Wave Crest opalware; mold blown. Transfer decorated with a beautiful blue flowered bouquet. The pattern design consists of a tall pillar surrounded by large embossed leaves that flow upward from the base of the shaker. 3½" tall. Very rare. Circa 1899-1904.

Pillar, Leaf-Based Kelva: Kelva opalware with two hand painted Sun Flowers over a mottled brown background; mold blown. The basic geometric pattern is exactly the same as "Pillar, Leaf Based," although it is difficult to tell due to the heavy application of paint. 3½" tall. Very rare. Circa 1904-1907.

Pillar, Small Leaf-Based: Wave Crest white opalware with a hand painted single blue floral decoration; mold blown. The basic pattern consists of embossed leaves surrounding the base of a pillar. 3" tall. Rare. Circa 1896-1903.

Rib Base, Twenty-One: Wave Crest opalware with hand painted blue daisies; mold blown. The pattern consists of a tapered pillar containing 21 small base ribs. 3" tall. Very scarce. Circa 1896-1901.

C. F. Monroe Company

Shell, Two-Sided: Wave Crest opalware transfer and hand decorated with a pink and red floral sprig; mold blown. The pattern has a shell on two sides of a spheroid-shaped shaker. 2" tall with a two piece metal top. Rare. Circa 1895-1900.

Ring Neck, Wave Crest: Wave Crest white opalware having a large, hand painted single blue floral sprig; mold blown. This pattern has a wide base that tapers upward to a single protruding ring encircling the top. 2⅞" tall. Very scarce. Circa 1897-1900.

Sash: Wave Crest opalware with a hand painted floral sprig; mold blown. The pattern consists of a broad sash with florets and irregular nodular borders around the center of the shaker. 3" tall. Rare. Circa: 1896-1900.

Scrolled Panel: Wave Crest creamy white opalware hand painted with a blue floral bouquet; mold blown. The pattern has a series of embossed scrolls surrounding a plain vertical panel. 2⅞" tall. Very rare. Circa 1895-1900.

Scroll, Wave: Wave Crest opalware transfer decorated with an outstanding pink and red floral bouquet; mold blown. The pattern consists of two smooth panels surrounded by elaborate, embossed scrolling. 3⅝" tall. Rare. Circa 1896-1903.

Shasta Daisy, Single: Wave Crest satinized opalware from a Mt. Washington/Pairpoint blank; mold blown. This hand painted pattern has a large embossed daisy on its top surface; the bottom contains "Patented June 2, 1891." 1½" tall. Rare. Circa 1891-1896.

Swirl & Bulge: Wave Crest opalware transfer decorated with an extended floral sprig; mold blown. The pattern consists of a swirled neck above a bulging vase. 3⅛" tall. Rare. Circa 1901-1906.

Thumbprint, Wave Crest: Wave Crest opalware; mold blown. The pattern contains eight intaglio thumbprints below a single ringed neck. 2" tall. Rare. Circa 1902-1906.

Tulip: Wave Crest satinized opalware transfer and hand painted with a yellow breasted bird sitting among foliage; mold blown. The pattern has numerous interspersed embossed petals that are reminscent of a tulip. 2¼" tall. Very scarce. Circa 1894-1900.

Woven Neck, Wave Crest: Wave Crest opalware with transfer decorated red and yellow flowers; mold blown. The pattern consists of embossed, interwoven cane upon the shaker neck. 2⅞" tall. Rare. Circa 1906.

Moser Meierhofen Works

Moser Meierhofen Works
Karlsbad, Bohemia
(1895-1933)

Our detailed research indicates that the salt shakers that we are illustrating are a product of the Moser Meierhofen works which was founded by Ludwig Moser during 1895 at Karlsbad, Bohemia (Czechoslovakia). This glass house is famous for its outstanding hand painted decoration that has always enjoyed a very high collectibility factor among discriminating collectors.

Much credit must be given to Victor Buck of Upland, California for putting us on the proper investigation path which enabled us to further verify what he already knew. Victor is an extremely knowledgeable art glass collector and dealer of renowned reputation and experience, particularly in the Southern California area. We have enjoyed the benefit of his personal advice and guidance for over 25 years.

We are fortunate to be able to refer the reader to various color plates in a new 1988 book[1] that reveals many pieces of Ludwig Moser glassware. If you are interested in Moser Art Glass, this is a must book for a reference library.

There is a lot of confusing information that has been written relative to the relationship between Ludwig Moser, and L. Kolo Moser as it applies to Moser Glassware. In our opinion, as well as other authors, Kolo was a son of Ludwig. We earnestly solicit any relevant information that anyone has to the contrary.

The Moser Meierhofen works enjoyed many profitable years of operation but was ultimately acquired by the Bohemian Union Bank in 1933. The reader is referred to color plates 17, 127, and 57[1] in connection with the following shakers.

Barrel, Moser Tapered: Solid hand applied gold coloring over basic white opalware with elaborate heavy enamelled blue flowers and shaded green and pink vines and leaves; mold blown. The basic pattern is that of a tapered barrel. The busy floral motif creates the appearance of an embossed pattern due to the very liberal application of enamelling by the decorating artist, typical of the Moser capability to take very basic glass and turn it into a piece that reflects a very expensive look. We were fortunate enough to have this ware offered to us as a complete condiment set with its original intricately designed silver plated metal holding stand. The bottom of the condiment stand is stamped "Meriden B. Company" in the form of a circle. The "B" stands for Britannia. This silver company was established in 1879 and remained in business until it merged with Internation Silver Co. of Canada Ltd. around 1912. Our condiment stand is stamped "Quadruple Plate." Our research reference[2] states that this company ceased stamping their silver pieces with the words "Quadruple Plate" after 1896. 3⅜" tall with a two piece metal top. Rare as a complete set. Circa 1895-1896.

Fish Pond: Clear blue glass with hand applied glass fish and white enamel paint; mold blown. In the blue colored glass the pattern depicts a perfect fish and eel swimming scene entwined with this pillar shaped shaker. This same shaker can also be collected containing three embossed swimming fish with their bodies painted white and their heads colored red. Near the top of the shaker is a single embossed spotted eel with salmon colored stripes on its body. We have also seen this shaker with the fish and eel motif in a lovely cranberry. Pattern name established by Arthur G. Peterson. 3¾" tall with a two piece metal top. Rare in blue. Very rare in cranberry. Circa 1900-1910.

Mt. Washington/Pairpoint Corp.
New Bedford, Massachusetts
(1869-1938)

Formed in 1869 at New Bedford, Massachusetts but did not start operating as the Mt. Washington Glass Co. until 1876 with A. H. Seabury as president and Frederick S. Shirley as manager. In 1894 Mt. Washington merged into the Pairpoint Manufacturing Co. which in 1900 changed its name to Pairpoint Corporation and finally closed its doors in 1938. The reader is referred to our more detailed write up concerning these glasshouses in the "Introduction" section of this book.

Witt Collection

Authors' Collection

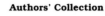

Apple, Little: Tan opaque satinized; mold blown. A sphere-shaped shaker that was named by Peterson. The motif is tan shaded with four multi-colored blue enamel dots. It is significant to note that an entire series of novelty items were produced by this glass house containing this same random blue dot decoration. We have personally observed a toothpick, cruet and sugar shaker and there are no doubt others. The Little Apple was also produced in decorated opaque white; some of them are satinized. 1⅞" tall. Very scarce with this type decoration. Circa 1890-1900.

McElderry Collection

Authors' Collection

Apple, Footed Little: Hand painted white opaque opalware; mold blown and pressed. This spheroid shaped shaker sits upon a ⅝" tall fan & scalloped pedestal. The shaker decoration contains a single blue and green floral sprig. Also produced in hand painted satinized glass with various floral decorations as well as the Palmer Cox Brownie elves. 2½" tall. Very scarce. Circa 1893-1902.

White Collection

Ball Swirl: White opaque satinized with hand painted flowers and leaves; mold blown. The pattern consists of a small sphere having a continuous series of diagonal swirls. Pattern name by Barbara White who brought this item to our attention. We have no additional color experience to report. 1⅜" tall with a two piece metal top. Rare. Circa 1894-1900.

RIGHT: Barrel, Baby Thumbprint: Clear cranberry with elaborate hand painted enamel floral sprigs; dual mold blown. This is a small barrel-shaped shaker; smooth on the outside with baby thumbprints on the inside. The small condiment set's ornate silver plated metal stand contains leaves, scrolling and a single ring lifting handle. The two end feet consist of a solid, molded bird that is reminiscent of a pelican with spread wings. The stand was made for Mt. Washington by Wilcox Silver Co. of Meriden, Connecticut. 2½" tall with a two piece metal top. Rare. Circa 1884-1888.

Authors' Collection

Authors' Collection

Authors' Collection

Not Royal Flemish Decorated

Royal Flemish Decorated

Bark Translucent: Translucent, veined glass with orange and white daisies; mold blown. The principal motif consists of vertically veined glass in the pattern that is used on the "Fig" shaker. This ware contained "Royal Flemish" decoration, and we entitled the pattern by this name in order to distinguish it from other Translucent Bark shakers that do not contain the Royal Flemish decoration. Generally speaking, Royal Flemish decoration consists of a mat finished (by acid roughing dip) crystal glass that is hand decorated in transparent enamel colors of brown, beige and sometimes gold. 2⅞" tall. Rare. Circa 1893-1897.

Mt. Washington/Pairpoint Corp.

Barrel, Bird-In-Flight: Clear blue with hand painted reed-like plants and a bird on the wing; dual mold blown. The basic pattern has a barrel shape that is smooth on the outside with baby thumbprints inside. Known production in decorated clear cranberry. 3¼" tall with a two piece metal top. Rare. Circa 1883-1889.

Barrel, Narrow Based: Opaque white opalware with hand painted brown floral decoration within two white panels (one on each side) mold blown. The pattern consists of a smooth barrel shape that tapers toward the bottom. Also produced in satinized opalware with various types of floral decorations. 2½" tall. Scarce. Circa 1893-1900.

Barrel, Ribbed Burmese: Opaque salmon pink shading to a pale yellow at the base with hand painted small floral sprigs; mold blown. This barrel shaped pattern contains 24 small embossed vertical ribs. This is a heat sensitive type glass that is highly fluorescent under black light illumination. 2¼" tall with the original two piece metal top. Very rare especially with hand applied decoration. Circa 1886-1890.

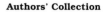

Barrel, Pseudo Overfired Burmese: Opaque white satinized glass hand painted to simulate Burmese glass that has been overfired by reheating at the Glory Hole; mold blown. The white glass can be seen by looking on the bottom or inside of each shaker. This ware does not fluoresce when subjected to black light illumination. True Burmese always does due to the Uranium salt content in the glass batch. These are truly beautiful shakers due to the addition of the hand applied enamelled floral sprigs. The metal tops are Pairpoint originals. 2½" tall. Rare. Circa 1894-1900.

Barrel, Ringed Neck: Opaque white opalware hand decorated with a flying insect (possibly a wasp); mold blown. The pattern consists of an embossed ring necked barrel that tapers toward the base of the shaker. Also made in various decorative opalware designs; some of them are satinized. 2⅞" tall. Scarce. Circa 1896-1904.

Barrel, Ribbed Mt. Washington Peachblow: Shaded pale gray-blue to a soft rose tint, this shaker is satinized homogeneous glass; mold blown. The pattern consists of 24 embossed vertical ribs (same pattern as the "Ribbed Burmese Barrel"). This is an extremely rare art glass that was produced by Mt. Washington in limited quantities due to the fact that it didn't sell very well. The coloring is achieved by the use of heat sensitive glass containing a small amount of cobalt or copper oxide as a colorant. This art glass was sold with paper labels containing the word "Peach Skin" or "Peach Blow"; both names being trademark protected by papers filed by Frederick S. Shirley. It is unlikely that any of these labels have survived the wear and tear of time since this glassware was produced during 1886. Most collectors will have to be content with either viewing this ware in a museum, private collection or a photograph. 2¾" tall. Extremely rare. Circa 1886.

Barrel, Ribbed Simulated Burmese: Satinized opaque white glass with hand painted colors simulating the classic pink-to-yellow Burmese coloring; mold blown. The pattern contains 24 embossed vertical ribs and is the same configuration as the "Ribbed Burmese Barrel" This item is in absolutely mint condition and the only way to ascertain that it is not Burmese glassware is to view it on the inside or on the shaker bottom. It does not fluoresce under black light illumination. 2¾" tall. Rare. Circa 1886-1890.

Barrel Tapered: Opaque white opalware containing hand painted multicolored floral sprigs encircling the shaker; mold blown. The pattern consists of a tapered barrel containing a large embossed ring just below the metal top. Also produced in satinized glass with various types of decoration. 3" tall. Circa 1897-1905.

Beaded Necklace: Opaque white opalware with a hand painted floral sprig on the embossed oval shaped beaded panels below what appears to be a necklace-like motif; mold blown. Also produced in satinized glass. 3½" tall. Very scarce. Circa 1894-1902.

Bird Arbor: Cased vaseline; mold blown. The basic pattern consists of a glass cylinder with an embossed ringed neck. The hand painted decoration reveals a bird sitting upon a branch containing two pieces of fruit in the form of two circles. This ware emits a brilliant fluorescence when exposed to a black light. Pattern name by Peterson. 3⅞" tall. Rare. Circa 1886-1891.

Bird Arbor Barrel: Cased vaseline with the same hand painted decoration as the Bird Arbor shaker; mold blown. This pattern forms a barrel shape very similar to the "Game Bird" type shakers. Gives off a striking fluorescence under black light. 3⅛" tall with a two piece metal top. Rare. Circa 1886-1890.

Brownie: Opaque pastel green; mold blown. The shaker has four slightly pinched-in beaded panels. Each panel contains a different embossed Palmer Cox Brownie elf. This item fluoresces when exposed to a black light. 2" tall. Rare. Circa 1894-1900.

Bulging Base: Opaque satinized yellow; mold blown. The pattern consists of a short cylinder having a bulging base that is configured for insertion into a condiment set. The shaker body contains very ornate hand painted floral sprigs. This ware gives off a striking fluorescence under black light exposure. 2½" tall with a two piece metal top. Rare. Circa 1889-1896.

Burmese, Ribbed Pillar: Opaque satinized shading from pink to a soft delicate yellow; mold blown. Burmese was patented on December 15, 1885, by Frederick F. Shirley. Pattern name established by A.G. Peterson. 3⅝" tall with the original two piece metal tops. Rare. Circa 1885.

Chick Head: Opaque beige painted opalware decorated with a large hand painted, reddish brown floral arrangement on the back part of the egg; mold blown. The basic pattern depicts a chick that is hatching from an egg. The molded metal top is special and consists of a chick head containing spring-like tapered fingers that can be pushed into the egg body opening. This type of top attachment was patented by Mt. Washington for use on their many different types of art glass condiment dispensers. Examples are: "Fig," "Cockle Shell," "Egg," "Flat End Variant," etc. The "Chick Head" was produced in various hand painted colors (usually floral) on opalware having pastel colored backgrounds. This ware has a very high collectibility factor today. 1¾" tall. Rare. Circa 1890.

Burmese, Glossy: Opaque glossy shading from pink to a soft yellow; mold blown. The basic pattern is the same as the "Ribbed Pillar" which was used for several types of art glass that was produced by this glasshouse. It is significant to note that the "Glossy Burmese" shakers are considerably more difficult to collect than the satinized type and therefore command a higher value. The value of all Burmese ware is determined by how much pink coloring is present; maximum pink shading is considered to be the more desirable by today's collectors/dealers. If this glassware has hand applied painted decoration, the monetary value goes still higher. This shaker has a striking fluorescence under black light exposure. 3⅝" tall with a two piece top. Very rare. Circa 1885-1887.

Mt. Washington/Pairpoint Corp.

Creased Neck, Bulbous: Opaque white opalware containing a creamy colored background; mold blown. Each shaker is hand decorated with a small cabin and an adjacent tree having bare branches with snow upon the ground. The pattern consists of a bulbous shaped body and an embossed creased neck. The bulging base is configured for insertion into a condiment set. 2¼" tall. Rare. Circa 1892-1900.

Cockle Shell Condiment: Opaque white satinized art glass with fired on pastel colorings to which hand painted floral designs have been applied; mold blown. As far as we have been able to determine, this is the first color photograph of the elusive silver plated metal holder that was designed to hold the delicate "Cockle Shell" shakers. The holder is 4¾" tall; the two oval loops (holding the shakers) have 3⅛" wide openings; the lifting ring is 1⅞" wide x 1¼" high and the holder base is 2⅜" in diameter. We are also illustrating a stand with dealer modified metal cups into which a pair of Cockle Shell shakers fits very nicely. Because of the money that a complete Cockle Shell set will bring, it is obvious as to why this deception was created. As viewed from the top, the real holding stand contains 4 five petaled daisies interspersed between 4 fleur-de-lis. Every collector/dealer is looking for one of these complete sets. We have viewed the majority of the major antique glass salt shaker collections in America and this is the only one that we know of, so the reader will understand when we classify it as a Museum piece that commands almost any price that a collector/dealer is willing to pay. If any of our readers have one of these sets we would appreciate hearing from you. 2⅝" tall with Sterling Silver spring fingered shell-shaped tops. Super! Super! Rare. Circa 1893. The photo on the left is the original. The photo on the right is the modified version.

Creased Neck, Coralene: Translucent blue satinized glass decorated with draped coralene glass beads; mold blown. Pattern name by Peterson. Generally speaking, the basic Coralene process consisted of the application of an enamel of a thick consistency to form the basic design and then adding/spreading small glass colored (or uncolored) beads so that when the glass was subjected to heat the enamel would become melted, thus causing the beads to adhere to the area being decorated. 3½" tall. Rare. Circa 1889-1894.

Dome: Opaque opalware with a large hand painted pink and yellow flower (probably a pansy) over a pastel green background; mold blown. The basic pattern is configured in the shape of a dome containing embossed equally spaced vertical ribs. Also produced in satinized glass and usually decorated with hand painted floral designs. 2⅛" tall. Very scarce. Circa 1890-1895.

Crown Milano: Opaque white satinized glass; mold blown. Crown Milano trademark papers were first issued to Mt. Washington on January 31, 1893 for this exotic name. It is a decorating technique that was accomplished by using a perforated corrugated stencil that was dusted with pulverized carbon to produce an outline for the decorator to follow while applying the floral ornamental patterns. The glass blank was first given a bisque finish using an acid roughing dip. The enamel colors most often found are shades of pink, beige and brown. It is rare to find a salt shaker trademarked with the blocked letter "C" and "M" arranged as a monogram in connection with the representation of a crown. Small items such as salts contained a paper label trademark with the crown ommited and displaying only the monogram "CM". The basic salt shaker pattern most often found is the "Ribbed Pillar" which our photograph shows. The "Crown Milano" decorations were the brain child of Frederick S. Shirley and Albert Steffin. 3⅝" tall. Rare. Circa 1893-1897.

Mt. Washington/Pairpoint Corp.

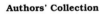

Egg, Palmer Cox Brownie: Opaque white satinized opalware; mold blown. This pattern is one of the many Flat End Egg variations that were produced for a number of years by Mt. Washington/Pairpoint. We are presenting two views (front & back) of hand painted Palmer Cox Brownie elves in the various action/comedy characterizations. The earlier Brownie eggs can be found with two piece metal top. This ware has both a high collectibility and scarcity factor; the Brownies have been sought after by collectors/dealers for many years. 2⅛" tall. Rare. Circa 1889-1900.

Egg in Blossom: Opaque white satin glass with a hand painted floral sprig; mold blown. In mint condition and shown with the original special top. Pattern name by Peterson who obviously viewed this pattern according to the name that he assigned to it. The bulging base lobes are in raised relief. 2" tall. Rare. Circa 1891.

Egg in Cup: Opaque white satinized glass hand decorated with sprigs of daisies; mold blown. The pattern consists of an egg that is nestled within a series of large base swirls. 2⅛" tall with an original special top. Rare. Circa 1889-1894.

Egg, Delft: Opaque white opalware with a hand painted blue Dutch Windmill and country scene; mold blown. The pattern consists of an egg shape. 2⅛" tall with an original special top. Rare. Circa 1889-1894.

Ellen: Clear blue glass; mold blown with hand painted flowers & double circle scenery using the same technique that is present on the "Bird Arbor" shaker. The quality of this piece is outstanding. 3⅛" tall. Rare. Circa 1886-1892.

Egg, Flat End Variant: Translucent red satin; mold blown; with a small spring-like top having tapering fingers that plug into the shaker opening. Very similar to the retention fingers used on the "Fig" shaker. An identical red satin sugar shaker, using this same type of top, was also produced. 2⅜" tall. Rare. Circa 1891-1894.

Egg, Floral Dome: Opaque white satinized with small hand painted daisy sprigs; mold blown; with the same spring-like top described in the "Flat End Variant Egg." We named this "Floral Dome" in our first book but it is really a spin-off variation of the "Flat End Egg" mold. 1⅞" tall. Very scarce. Circa 1892-1894.

Authors' Collection

Contains original paper label.

Bruce Collection

Over-Fired Burmese

McElderry Collection

Special Mt. Washington holder.

Bruce Collection

Undecorated Burmese

Authors' Collection

Decorated Burmese

Egg, Flat End: Opaque satinized opalware with hand painted pink and green flowers and leaves; mold blown with the original round Mt. Washington paper label present on the bottom which reads "PAT. DEC 31st 1889 MT.W.G. Co." This is the first egg design that was patented by Mr. Albert Steffin. We are also illustrating a pair of Flat End Eggs in a specially designed silver plated stand/holder for use as a salt and pepper condiment set and a very rare egg in undecorated Burmese. There were numerous mold variations of the Flat End Egg that were manufactured by Mt. Washington/Pairpoint; many of them are illustrated in this book. 2³⁄₁₆" tall. Very rare with paper label. Circa 1889.

Egg, Flat Side: Opaque white satinized with blue sunflowers; mold blown. This item was patented during April, 1893 by Alfred E. Smith. Numerous quantities were produced to a special order for the W.L. Libbey & Son Glass company of Toledo, Ohio for marketing as souvenirs at the 1893 Worlds Fair. These shakers were sold with a Libbey paper label attached to them, and embossed to read "Columbian Exhibition 1893." It is these souvenirs that are usually found by today's collectors. Flat side eggs with floral decorations are difficult to obtain. 1¾" tall. Very scarce. Circa 1893.

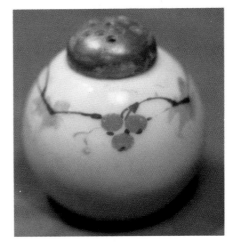

Egg-Like: Opaque white opalware with a hand painted sunflower applied over a pastel green background; mold blown. The basic pattern consists of a small, oblong shaped egg. 1⅞" tall. Scarce. Circa 1897-1905.

Egg, Pseudo Burmese: Opaque satinized opalware with hand painted yellow and white daisies; mold blown. This displays the outstanding artistic capabilities of the Mt. Washington decorating department. By the use of special fired on paints the artist has made this shaker to look exactly like a piece of Burmese glassware. However, when the top is removed it is apparent that this item is just a piece of white opalware. If the buying public could not afford the cost of Burmese shakers, Mt. Washington created a cheaper shaker by artistic means. An even quicker way to check for the presence of Burmese glass is by using a small portable black light. Burmese glass will always display a striking fluorescence when exposed to ultra violet light. 2³⁄₁₆" tall. Very scarce. Circa 1889-1894.

Mt. Washington/Pairpoint Corp.

Egg, Undeveloped Burmese: Same shape and size as the Flat End Egg. Has the appearance of a yellow-like custard glass but is really Burmese glass that has not been refired at the Glory Hole and therefore has no pink to yellow color shading. Gives off a striking fluoresence under black light. Found in both decorated and plain configurations. Very scarce. Circa 1889-1896.

Fidelity: Opaque blue cased glass; mold blown. A tall cylinder shaped shaker decorated with a hand painted dog in a sitting position. The word "Fidelity" is hand printed in a fancy red script just below the neck of the shaker. 3⅝" tall with a two piece top. Very rare. Circa 1890-1895.

Fig: Illustrated is a very rare "Fig" condiment set containing a pair of hand painted shakers, one in salmon pink and the other in a pale yellow. The silver plated stand has been specifically designed to hold these unusual shaped shakers in a secure manner. The shakers are mold blown, with special spring fingered tops that push into the opening of each shaker. The "Fig" was design patented by Albert Steffin in 1893 and is truly unique. This ware was produced in all colors including red translucent satin glass. All that we have seen over 35+ years are individually hand decorated. However, we have never seen a Fig in either Burmese or Mt. Washington Peachblow. We have seen them in a frosted crystal with Royal Flemish type decoration. 1¾" tall. Very rare as a complete condiment set. Circa 1893.

Fig, Disguised Stemmed: Translucent veined satin glass with hand painted flowers and leaves; mold blown; with a special design stemmed top containing the same spring loaded tapered fingers that are used on the "Fig" shaker. Here is a further example of an excellent artistic creation along with smart consumer marketing. We have been unable to locate any formal design patent being issued for this unique top. This top utilizes the basic Fig glass pattern and gives it a completely different look when used in place of the Fig top. We have provided two additional photos showing the appearance change when the stemmed top is moved from one Fig shaker base to the other. We wish to thank Stan McElderry for his assistance in consummating our study. 1¾" tall Rare. Circa 1893.

Floral Spray: Opaque white satinized glass containing hand painted floral sprigs; mold blown. This is a simple smooth bulging barrel shaped shaker. Known production in Burmese glass. 2⅜" tall. Very scarce. Circa 1885-1890.

Mt. Washington/Pairpoint Corp.

Flower & Rain: Opaque shaded red and pink, triple cased glass with a hand painted white floral band encircling the middle of the shaker; mold blown. A tall smooth cylindrical pillar with a two piece metal top. Pattern name by Peterson who stated "Coloration of inner layer resembles streaming rain on a window pane." Also made in blue and yellow cased glass. 3¾" tall. Rare. Circa 1885-1890.

Game Bird: Opaque vaseline, triple cased glass with two hand painted speckled brown birds feeding within a grassy area; mold blown. The basic pattern consists of a simple barrel shaped shaker that has a slight tapering towards the bottom. We have no other color experience to report. The quality of this shaker is outstanding and it has a very high collectibility factor. 3¼" tall with a two piece metal top. Rare. Circa 1884-1890.

Inverted Thumbprint Sphere: Clear amber with elaborate hand painted red/white daisies; mold blown. This is a dual molded pattern; smooth on the outside with tiny inverted thumbprints on the inside of each shaker. The shakers are shown in their original silver plated Pairpoint stand. No doubt produced in other colors but we haven't seen any. 1¾" tall with matching two piece metal tops. Rare as a complete set. Circa 1887-1890.

Game Bird, Tall: Opaque vaseline, triple cased glass with two hand painted speckled brown birds feeding within a marshland area; mold blown. The basic pattern consists of a cylindrical pillar taken from the "Bird Arbor" mold. We have only seen three of these shakers in 35+ years. No color experience to report. 3⅞" tall. Very Rare. Circa 1886-1890.

Leaf, Four Feet Berry: Opaque satinized opalware containing a large hand painted orange and green berry plant with a small berry sprig on the opposite side; mold blown. The basic pattern consists of an ornate flower and scrolled motif in raised relief encircling the top and base of the shakers. The bottom contains four small square feet. 2⅝" tall. Rare. Circa 1887-1894.

obe, Four: Opaque satinized opalware with hand ainted violet floral sprigs; mold blown. Can be found ith other colored floral decorations. The pattern onsists of four bulging lobes that narrow toward the p of the shaker. 2⅝" tall. Scarce. Circa 1891-1894.

Lobe, Six Mt. Washington's: Opaque satinized opalware with small pink/white floral sprigs; mold blown. The pattern has six bulging lobes each separated by small vertical ribs; every other panel contains dual hand painted decoration. We have no additional colors to report, but there is little doubt that this ware can be found with various colored floral paintings. 2⅝" tall. Very scarce. Circa 1888-1894.

Lobe, Eight: Opaque white opalware with a hand painted red and green floral sprig; mold blown. The motif consists of eight lobes. Also produced in white satinized glass containing various single floral decorations. We have seen one of these shakers containing a Pairpoint paper label. 2¼" tall. Very scarce. Circa 1897-1905.

Lobe, Five: Opaque satinized opalware artistically hand painted to look like decorated Burmese; the elaborate hand painted orange and green floral decorations are in mint condition; mold blown. Also produced in white opalware with floral sprig decoration. Some of the later versions do not have two piece tops. 2¼" tall with a two piece metal top. Very scarce. Circa 1886-1893.

Lobe, Squatty: Opaque white satinized opal glass with an interconnected series of hand painted pink floral bouquets; mold blown. The pattern is a variation of the "Tomato" shaker mold. The two piece metal top is original. 1¾" tall. Very scarce. Circa 1889-1894.

Loop and Daisy: Opaque salmon colored background with two ornate hand painted daisy sprigs; mold blown. The decoration is spread across six looping panels that are supported by six scallop-shaped feet. 2⅝" tall. Very scarce. Circa 1887-1894.

Authors' Collection

Mayfly: Opaque vaseline cased glass; mold blown. This basic shape is the same as the "Bird Arbor" shaker and is a variation of the same mold. The hand painted motif consists of in-flight mayflies among a grouping of daisy flowers. Name by Peterson who illustrated this item as a porcelain shaker. When exposed to black light illumination this ware displays striking fluorescence. 3⅞" tall with a two piece metal top. Rare. Circa 1886-1891.

Just Collection

Melon, Mother-of-Pearl Diamond: Opaque satinized blue cased glass with a diamond air trap pattern; mold blown. This is a small shaker and the shape of the lobes are reminiscent of a ripe melon; anyway, this is the way Peterson viewed this design. Mt. Washington/Pairpoint produced several different air trap pattern designs; some of them are in this book. Mother-of-Pearl (MOP) glass can always be associated with ware that has two or more layers of glass. It is highly collectible and rare in salt shakers. When found to contain hand painted decorations the value increases even more. 2½" tall. Rare. Circa 1886-1891.

McElderry Collection

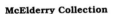

Mother-of-Pearl (MOP) Herringbone: Opaque satinized red-to-pink cased glass with a herringbone air trap pattern; mold blown. The bottom has been configured for insertion into a condiment set. This type of ware is also known as "Pearl Satinglass." The basic process was first patented in England by Benjamin Richardson in 1858 with subsequent improvements on February, 1881 by Messrs Dean & Peltier of Brooklyn, N.Y. Their patent was assigned to the Mt. Washington Glass Co. of New Bedford. Subsequently, Mt. Washington licensed Thos. Webb & Sons of Stourbridge, England to produce this type of glass. Due to some adjacent process patents by Joseph Webb of the Phoenix Glass Co. he began producing MOP glass which resulted in litigation between the two companies. Our research shows that limited quantites of MOP glass were produced by Phoenix. 3" tall with a two piece metal top. Rare. Circa 1882-1888.

Authors' Collection

MOP Decorated Diamond Quilt: Opaque satinized blue shaded decorated cased glass with a Diamond Quilt air trap pattern; mold blown. Contains white hand painted floral decoration; barrel shaped. 3¼" tall. Very rare. Circa 1886-1888.

Mt. Washington/Pairpoint Corp.

MOP Decorated Herringbone: Opaque satinized red-to-pink decorated cased glass with a Herringbone air trap pattern; mold blown. We removed this shaker from the condiment set (see right) so that the reader can better see the gold leaf and flower hand painted decoration. 3¼" tall with a two piece metal top. Very Rare. Circa 1882-1888.

MOP Decorated Herringbone Condiment: Opaque satinized red-to-pink decorated cased glass containing the Herringbone air trap pattern; mold blown. The set is complete and held within a special design silver plated stand which is stamped Meriden Company on the underside of its base. Overall stand height is 8¼". Shakers are 3¼" tall; mustard is 2⁹⁄₁₆" tall; the vinegar/oil bottle measured 3⅜" tall. Very rare. Circa 1882-1888.

MOP Decorated Large Raindrop: Opaque satin shaded apricot with a hand decorated floral spray & large air traps on the upper body portion; mold blown. This is a highly collectible color and a most difficult one to obtain. Over the years we have seen very few shakers in this color. 3¼" tall. Very rare. Circa 1884-1889.

MOP Diamond Quilted: Opaque satinized pink-to-white cased glass containing a Diamond Quilted air trap pattern; mold blown. The basic shape is that of a barrel. 3¼" tall with a two piece metal top. Rare. Circa 1885-1889.

MOP Decorated Raindrop Barrel: Opaque satinized rose-to-white shaded cased glass with large hand painted gold leaves and small red flowers. The physical pattern is that of a narrow shaped barrel containing air trapped raindrops. Rare. Circa 1885-1890.

MOP Diamond Spheroid: Opaque satinized blue-to-white cased glass containing a small Diamond air trap pattern; mold blown. The basic shape is that of tapered spheroid—most unusual for this type or ware. 3" tall with a two piece metal top. Rare. Circa 1883-1887.

MOP Diamond Barrel: Opaque satinized yellow-to-white shaded cased glass containing a Diamond pattern wherein the size of the diamonds get smaller as they progress toward the bottom of the shaker. This is another of those colors that is hard to obtain and is eagerly sought after by collectors. This is a mold blown shaker; 3¼" tall. Very rare. Circa 1884-1889.

MOP Raindrop Barrel: Opaque satinized blue-to-pale blue shaded cased glass containing a rather uniform sized Raindrop pattern; mold blown. The basic pattern is a barrel. 3¼" tall. Rare. Circa 1885-1890.

Narrow Based Bulb: Opaque white opalware decorated with a blue hand painted sailboat on a waterway in the manner of Pairpoint Blue Delft; mold blown. We believe that the pattern name provides an adequate geometric description of the shaker. 2½" tall. Very Scarce. Circa 1894-1895.

Pillar, Optic: Clear blue with heavy white hand painted enameling to create the cameo effect of a bird in flight; dual mold blown. This pillar shaped shaker is smooth on the outside with wide vertical ribbed panels on the inside. Mt. Washington engaged in a decorating practice (the 1880's) when a lot of their glassware contained various hand painted birds, ducks, etc. This shaker is an excellent example of quality decoration. 3½" tall. Rare. Circa 1885-1890.

Pillar, Ribbed (Mt. Washington Peachblow): Shiny opaque, shading from pale gray-blue to pink; the glass is homogeneous and mold blown. See "Barrel, Ribbed Mt. Washington Peachblow" for additional information relative to this extremely rare glass. We have provided two photos to give the reader additional information as to the differences in shading that can be expected. 3⅜" tall. Extremely Rare. Circa 1886.

Pillar, Tall: Opaque opalware with hand painted Palmer Cox Brownie elves; mold blown. The pattern consists of a double creased pillar with an expanded base that contains 10 small embossed ribs. We have learned over the years to not be surprised at the appearance of the Cox Brownies on any of the Mt. Washington/Pairpoint smooth opaque shaker patterns. Due to high collectibility they are a rarity. 2¾" tall. Rare. Circa 1889-1899.

Rafter Panel: Opaque opalware with hand painted pink and green leaves encircling the bulging portion of the shaker; mold blown. The pattern consists of eight ribbed panels standing upon a circular base. Known production in opaque decorated satin glass. 2½" tall. Scarce. Circa 1890-1895.

Pillar, Tapered: Clear cranberry with a large hand painted blue and white floral bouquet; dual mold blown. The pattern consists of a pillar that tapers downward toward the bottom; the glass is smooth on the outside with vertical ribbing inside. 3½" tall. Has two piece metal top. Very Scarce. Circa 1885-1890.

Pinched-In Sides: Opaque blue to white shaded glass with a hand painted floral sprig on two of the panels; mold blown. The pattern consists of two oval panels and two that have been pinched inward; the other shaker is identical except that it is a very clear deep blue with elaborate hand painted daisies and orange and white leaves. No doubt made in other colors. 1⅞" tall with a two piece metal top. Rare. Circa 1886-1891.

Authors' Collection

McElderry Collection

Cohen Collection

Rib & Scrolls, Vertical: Opaque white opalware with hand painted blue and green windmills (one on each shaker); mold blown. The pattern is a slight variation from the "Four Feet Berry Leaf" mold; Each shaker is decorated in the Pairpoint Delft style and due to having a high collectibility factor are difficult to obtain. 2⅝" tall. Very Scarce. Circa 1894-1895.

Authors' Collection

Rose Amber (Amberina): Clear deep ruby shading to a delicate amber color at the bottom; dual mold blown. This ware is in Avila's Pairpoint book. We are also showing the matching cruet bottle that appears in both Avila's and Dean L. Murray's books. The latter author has produced two books addressing art glass cruets. Since Amberina was first patented by Joseph Locke of the New England Glass Co. there was a big legal hassle over Mt. Washington also calling their glass Amberina. The litigation was finally settled by Mt. Washington changing the name of their ware to Rose Amber. The trademark papers were granted to Mt. Washington during May, 1886. but the name was used for at least one or two years prior to this. The pattern consists of Inverted Thumbprints. 3⅝" tall with an original two piece type top. The salt shaker is rare. The cruet very rare. Circa 1884-1888.

Sphere, Short: Opaque white hand painted opalware; mold blown. This is a smooth sphere with an slightly indented circular bottom. There is a single painted floral sprig that comprises the decorative motif. Known production in opaque white satinized glass with various hand applied decorations. 2" tall. Scarce. Circa 1895-1900.

Spheroid, Footed: Opaque white hand painted satinized opalware; mold blown. The principal pattern consists of a tapered sphere with a ⅜" pedestal/foot for support. The motif decoration consists of a single flower and leaf band encircling the shaker circumference. 2⅜" tall. Scarce. Circa 1894-1900.

Scroll and Bulge: Opaque white satinized opalware with hand painted pink floral sprigs on each panel; mold blown. This is a triangular shaped shaker containing three bulging panels; each panel is separated by red colored embossed scrolling. 2¼" tall. Scarce. Circa 1890-1895.

Mt. Washington/Pairpoint Corp.

Two Flower Sprig: Opaque blue homogenous glass with two hand painted flowers on a single branch containing brown leaves; mold blown. It has a basic spheroid shape; the glass has the same smoothness as Pearl ware (Mother-of-Pearl). We have also seen this shaker in opaque homogeneous pink glass with the same type of hand painted decoration on it. For those readers that have a copy of our first book, all you have to do is look on the back cover to see the shaker in enlarged form. The glass does not fluoresce under black light. 2½" tall with a two piece metal top. Rare. Circa 1885-1890.

Tomato: It has the same glass batch as Burmese but it has been subjected to what collectors today call "over-firing" in order to achieve the unusual red coloring. It contains beautiful hand painted daisies that were applied by the Smith brothers decorating artists at Mt. Washington. The so-called over-fired pieces have a high collectibility factor and are much sought after. Rare.

Thumbprint, Ball-Shape Inverted: One shaker is transparent cranberry and the other is blue; dual mold blown. The pattern design consists of a small round shape that is smooth on the outside with tiny inverted thumbprints on the inside. The hand painted floral decoration is in mint condition; the shakers are shown in their original silver plated Pairpoint holder. 2" tall with two piece metal tops. Rare as a complete condiment set. Circa 1884-1889.

Twelve Panel, Scrolled: Opaque white opalware with hand painted blue Pairpoint Delft windmills; mold blown: We called this shaker "Wreath, Twelve Panel" in our first book, but since the decoration varies from shaker to shaker we believe this name change is the proper thing to do. As we have previously mentioned, the Delft type decoration adds a very high collectibility factor. 2⅞" tall with original tops. Very scarce. Circa 1894-1905.

Mt. Washington/Pairpoint
Special Condiment Set Rarities

Burmese, Ribbed Pillar: Opaque satinized shading from pink to a soft delicate yellow; mold blown; with the original two piece metal tops. Burmese was patented on December 15, 1885 by Frederick F. Shirley. Pattern name established by A.G. Peterson. 3⅝" tall. Rare. Circa 1885-1890.

McElderry Collection

Cockle Shell Condiment: Opaque white satinized art glass with fired-on pastel colorings to which hand painted floral designs have been applied; mold blown; with sterling silver spring fingered shell-shaped tops. As far as we have been able to determine, this is the first color photograph of the elusive silver plated metal holder that was designed to hold the delicate "Cockle Shell" shakers. The holder is 4¾" tall; the two oval loops (holding the shakers) have 3⅜" wide openings; the lifting ring is 1⅞" wide x 1¼" high and the holder base is 2⅛" in diameter. As viewed from the top, the holding stand contains 4 five petaled daisies interspersed between 4 fleur-de-lis. Every collector/dealer is looking for one of these complete sets. We have viewed the majority of the major antique glass salt shaker collections in America and this is the only one that we know of, so the reader will understand when we classify it as a Museum piece that commands almost any price that a collector/dealer is willing to pay. If any of our readers have one of these sets we would appreciate hearing from you. 2⅝" tall. Stand marked Ⓟ Pairpoint. Extremely rare. Circa 1893. (See also page 134.)

McElderry Collection

Egg, Flat End Condiment Set: Stand marked Ⓟ Pairpoint. Note that lifting handle is same design as Cockle Shell condiment holder. (See also page 138.)

McElderry Collection

Egg, Flat End Condiment Set: Stand Marked "Pelton Bros & Co. St. Louis." Holder is 6⅞" tall 4½" long. Designed to hold smaller diameter egg than what was patented in 1889 by Albert Steffin. (See also page 138.)

Fig Condiment Set: Stand marked "Aurora S P MFG Co. #378 Quadruple Plate Warranted." (See also page 140.)

McElderry Collection

McElderry Collection

Authors' Collection

Bulging Four Lobes Condiment: Opaque white satinized opalware with hand painted floral sprays; mold blown. Stand marked "Homans Silver Plate Co." 93 quadruple plate. Holder is 5½" tall x 4⅞" long. The basic pattern shape consists of a rounded square with four bulging vertical lobes. 2⅝" tall with two piece metal tops. Rare. Circa 1889-1894.

Flower & Rain Variant: Opaque green condiment set; triple cased glass with hand painted floral sprays (simulating a cameo effect) encircling the middle of the shaker; mold blown. This cylindrical pillar is shorter and has a larger circumference than the taller "Flower & Rain" shaker. The stand is 4⅞" tall x 4⅜" long; quadruple plate and marked "James W. Tufts, Boston". 3⅛" tall. Very rare. Circa 1885-1890.

Tomato Condiment: Opaque undeveloped Burmese glass with hand painted decoration; mold blown. We collected almost 30 years before we came across this very special designed silver plated condiment set that was specifically made to hold the tomato shakers. While the photograph pretty much tells it all, the unique thing about the design is the presence of three vertical leaves on the outer rim of each circular shaped holder cup. When a shaker is placed within the cup, each leaf slips into the vertical grooves of the shaker thus retaining it securely. The stand is marked "Aurora S P MFG Co. 375" and the overall height to the top of the lifting handle is 6⅞"; total length as measured across the bottom is 5¾"; each vertical retaining leaf is 1¼" tall. 1⅝" tall. Rare as a complete set. Circa 1889-1895.

Rose Amber (Amberina) Condiment Set: Stand marked ⟨P⟩ Pairpoint MFG Co. Shakers 3⅝" tall. Very rare. Circa 1884-1888. (See also page 150.)

Creased Neck Country House Condiment: Opaque creamy white opalware; mold blown. Each shaker is hand decorated; one with a country house and the other has a windmill. The mustard has a large hand painted house has a sharp spire and a wooden gate. The three pieces sit within a silver plated stand/holder. The stand is 6¼" tall x 5¾" long (foot to foot). The stand base has a predominating leaf pair and is trademarked "Aurora S P MFG Co." quadruple plate warranted. Shakers are 3½" tall with two piece metal tops. Very scarce. Circa 1894-1900.

New England Glass Company
Cambridge, Massachusetts
(1818-1888)

The New England Glass Company was established and incorporated in 1818 by Deming Jarves & Associates who purchased the factory from the Boston Porcelain and Glass Company.

The beginning work force consisted of approximately 40 men. The plant's initial production was primarily plain and cut glassware.

In 1825 Mr. Jarves left the New England Glass Company and joined the Boston and Sandwich Glass Company at Cape Cod, Mass. Mr. Jarves position was succeeded by Henry Whitney.

In 1826, Thomas Leighton became factory superintendent, a position he occupied for more than twenty years.

In 1872, William L. Libbey came into the picture as Agent for New England Glass and two years later his son Edward D. Libbey joined the firm as an office clerk. By 1878, William Libbey had taken up the company lease and in 1880 the company name was changed to the "New England Glass Company, W. L. Libbey and Son, Proprietors."

After his father's death in 1883, young Edward inherited the company. It was under the leadership of Edward D. Libbey that the factory had its glory years which produced the highly profitable Art Glass types that are known as Amberina, Wild Rose New England Peachblow, Pomona, Plated Amberina and Agata. History shows that the Amberina glassware kept the company profitable during the 1880's until natural gas problems along with a series of glass worker strikes closed the factory in 1888.

During 1888 Mr. Libbey moved the glass works to Toledo, Ohio where the factory name became W.L. Libbey and Son Glass Company. In 1892 the board of directors changed the name to the Libbey Glass Company.

All of the aforesaid art glass was patented by Joseph Locke as follows:

Amberina July 24,1883
Pomona (1st grind) April 28, 1885
Pomona (2nd grind) June 15, 1886
New England Peachblow (Wild Rose) March 1, 1986
Plated Amberina June 15, 1886
Agata January 18, 1887

On September 10, 1889, a patent was granted for Maize Art Glass and Joseph Locke assigned the rights to W. L. Libbey and Son of Toledo Ohio.

Locke resigned from W.L. Libbey & Sons Co. in 1891 and he established the Locke Art Glass Company in Pittsburgh, Pennsylvania.

Today's antique glass salt shaker collectors all seek the aforementioned types of rare art glass. When available, this ware commands substantial prices in the antique glassware retail market. While there have been shipments of new Amberina glassware from Europe from time to time, particularly in the "Inverted Thumbprint" pattern, we have never seen any new Amberina salt & pepper shakers being offered for sale. We are not certain of the reason for this, but the Amberina salt shaker collectors appear to be relatively safe from the reproduction scourge. Let's hope that it continues this way.

Authors' Collection

Tapered Amberina Barrel: Clear Fuchsia-red that extends approximately two-thirds of the way downward and then subtly mixes into an amber yellow blend. The outside is hand decorated with a rather complex floral arrangement involving the colors green, blue, white and yellow. This pair is dual mold and free blown finished; very similar to the "Dual Mold Amberina Barrel" the principal differences are in height and circumference. 3¼" tall. Rare. Circa 1883-1885.

157

Lockwood Collection

Authors' Collection

Agata: Opaque shiny rose shading to off-white at the bottom; distinct mottled spots/splotches cover most, if not all, of the piece; mold and free blown finished; with an original two piece metal top. The decorating process, according to Locke's patent papers, amounts to first partially or completely covering the item to be decorated with a selected metallic stain or mineral coloring and then subjecting the portion so stained to either a spattered or directly applied volatile liquid such as Naptha, Benzene or Alcohol. The mottled surface is created by the random evaporation of the volatile liquid which is then fixed by placing the piece in a muffle. Over the years all the Agata decorated shakers that we have seen have been on New England Peachblow (Wild Rose) glassware. According to Revi "the mineral stains used on Agata were the same as Mr. Locke used to decorate his Pomona glassware." We are illustrating two Agata shakers so that the reader will get a pretty good idea of how the staining will usually appear after being in existence for over 100 years. The discriminating collector tries to obtain a shaker that has distinctive splotches. However, this ware was produced at New England Glass Co. for less than a year so we recommend that the collector keep our quality guidelines in mind but think twice before passing an Agata shaker by if you are fortunate enough to find one available for purchase. 3⅝" tall Very rare. Circa 1887.

Authors' Collection

LEFT TO RIGHT:
LEFT: Barrel, Dual Mold Amberina: Clear fuchsia-red that extends approximately one-half of the way downward and then shades into a soft yellow. The exterior is hand decorated with an elaborate floral arrangement. Dual mold & free blown finished. The pattern is barrel shaped, smooth on the outside with inverted thumbprints inside. Discriminating collectors consider the hand decorated Amberina pieces as being a top collecting priority. 3½" tall. Very rare. Circa: 1883-1885. **RIGHT: Bulb, Small Amberina:** Clear fuchsia-red to a soft yellow with elaborate hand painted pink and white floral decoration. Dual mold and free blown finished. The basic pattern is reminiscent of a small bulb which is smooth on the outside with small inverted thumbprints inside. 2⅝" tall. Very rare. Circa 1883-1885.

Lockwood Collection

Just Collection

Blossom Time: Clear fuchsia-red that extends approximately two-thirds of the way downward and then shades into a soft yellow to provide an outstanding Amberina coloring. Elaborately hand decorated with a marshland type of lily as shown in A.G. Peterson's book on page 155-L. Dual mold and free blown finished. 3⅛" tall. A barrel shaped pattern that is smooth on the outside and has a honeycomb inside. Very rare. Circa 1883-1885.

Blossom Time Variant: Clear fuchsia-red to a soft yellow, the red coloring extends approximately three fourths of the way downward before shading into a soft yellow coloring to provide a most striking Amberina coloring; elaborately hand decorated with a large floral spray; dual mold and free blown finished. A tapered barrel shaped pattern that is smooth on the outside with wide vertical ribbing inside. 3¼" tall with a two piece metal top. Very rare. Circa 1883-1885.

Krauss Collection

Curved Ribbing (Plated Amberina): Golden yellow at the base to a deep fuchsia-red at the top; mold blown and free blown finished; with an original two piece metal top. In our 35+ years of collecting, we have never seen a Plated Amberina shaker in this pattern which has thin vertical curved protruding ribs with a creamy opal lining. As far as we have been able to ascertain this will be a first time published revelation to antique glass salt shaker collectors. As was the case of the Mt. Washington Cockle Shell Condiment set, this is the only Plated Amberina shaker in this pattern that we are aware of so we must classify it as a Museum piece that can command almost any price that a collector/dealer is willing to pay. If any of our readers have one (or more) of these shakers, we would appreciate hearing from you. 1¹³⁄₁₆" tall Super! Super! Rare. Circa 1886.

New England Glass Company

Cylindrical Plated Amberina: Opaque golden yellow at the base to a deep fuchsia-red at the top; mold blown with thin vertical protruding ribs on the outer layer; has a creamy opal lining; A simple cylinder-shaped pattern with a small creased neck. To date we have seen a total of six shakers in this pattern. It goes without saying that the quality of all Plated Amberina shakers is outstanding and the collectibility factor is out of sight. This ware was produced at the New England Glass Works for a very short period of time. 3⅝" tall with the original two piece metal top. Extremely rare. Circa 1886.

New England Peachblow, Satinized: Opaque satinized (acid treated) rose shading to white at the bottom; mold and free blown finished. Advertised and sold by the name "Wild Rose." This ware was produced by combining an opal glass and a gold-ruby glass in the same pot. The sensitive glass mixture thus formed was reheated to produce color in the reheated portions of the shaker. For some reason the acid treated shakers are more difficult to find than the shiny ones. 3⅝" tall with two piece metal tops. Rare. Circa 1886.

Maize: Opaque creamy white (some call it pale yellow) opalware; mold blown; with embossed hand painted green and yellow husks at the base. This has become the classic Maize corn pattern that is so highly sought after by today's collectors and it appears in all of the current art glass books. The white Maize shakers without husks are pieces that have become separated from Maize condiments sets and generally are not recognized by a collector as being a Maize art glass form. In fact Arthur Peterson named one of the shakers "Corn, Bulging" on page 25M of his book "*Glass Salt Shakers*" before he recognized his mistake. It is not known why two types of salt shaker patterns were placed under the Maize Art Glass umbrella, but by highlighting it in this book both the record and future confusion should be pretty well alleviated. It should be noted that none of the Maize condiment dispensers fluoresce when exposed to black light illumination. 3⅞" tall. Rare. Circa 1888. (See also page 111.)

New England Peachblow, Miniature: Opaque satinized rose shading to white at the bottom; mold and free blown finished. This ware is beautifully hand decorated with blue and white enamelled flowers and stems with excellent matched Wild Rose coloring in a special designed silver plated stand that is marked "James W. Tufts. Boston Warranted Quadruple Plate." The stand measures 6⅞" tall x 4⅞" long. 2½" tall with a two piece top. In salt shakers decorated New England Peachblow is extremely rare. Circa 1886.

New England Peachblow Barrel: Opaque satinized rose, shading to pinkish white at the bottom, with a large hand decorated floral spray in green, white and yellow enameling; mold and free blown finished. Taken from one of the basic barrel-shaped molds used by this factory on their Amberina glass shakers. The overall condition of this shaker is mint, including the decoration. In our experience—and we have made many inquiries—this is the only hand decorated, barrel shaped, Wild Rose shaker currently in existence; hard for us to believe! We discussed this with Victor Buck, who is a seasoned veteran in art glass dealing and collecting, and he reported that he had never seen this pattern before in decorated New England Peachblow. If any of our readers have this piece we would certainly appreciate hearing from you. We have no pricing data base to compare with; Therefore, it is worth whatever a collector is willing to pay. 3⅛" tall with a two piece metal top. Extremely rare. Circa 1886.

Pomona, Cornflower Decorated; Translucent/frosted crystal; mold and free blown finished; with the original two piece metal tops. The illustrated shaker pair are "First Grind" which was accomplished by a very labor intensive technique as follows: After covering a piece with an acid resist wax, it was then hand etched with an enormous amount of concentric overlapping circles by utilizing a stylus needle. A subsequent acid bath removed the exposed surface resulting in the seeming appearance of frosted ice. Any outlined ornamentation was filled in with a colored mineral stain and the item was then placed in a muffle to assure a lasting quality. The staining colors used imparted delicate tints of amber, lavenders and pinks (sometimes used in combination). Due to high labor costs, this process was only used for about 1 year after which time Joseph Locke came up with a more cost effective procedure and received a patent for "Second Grind" Pomona on June 15, 1886. This latter method utilized the application of acid resist on the glass and applied acid was used to etch only the exposed surfaces which gave the final product a stippled ice-like appearance. The rarity factor associated with collecting this type of glassware is due to the limited amount of time that "First Grind" was produced plus the added fact that the total Pomona line was years ahead of its time in public acceptance. 3⅝" tall. Rare. Circa 1885.

New England Glass Company

McElderry Collection   **Just Collection**

Ribbed, Dual Mold Amberina: Clear Fuchsia-red that extends approximately one-third of the way downward and then shades into a delicate yellow; dual mold and free blown finished with a two piece metal top. A cylindrical shaped pattern with a ringed collar that is smooth on the outside with vertical ribbing inside. We have yet to come across one of these shakers with hand applied painted decoration. 3¼" tall. Very scarce. Circa 1884-1887.

New England Peachblow, Shiny: We are illustrating two glossy shakers shading from rose to a creamy off-white. This will give our readers a comparative overview of typical color differences & show how this ware can vary from one shaker to the other. Mold and free blown finished; with a two piece metal top. In salt shakers, this plain tubular shape seems to be what is available to collectors. 3⅝" tall. Rare. Circa 1886.

Authors' Collection

Authors' Collection

Pomona, Blueberry & Leaf Decorated: Translucent/frosted crystal; mold and free blown finished; with an original two piece metal top. As in the previously shown shaker, this is "First Grind" Pomona and all the comments previously discussed apply to this piece. The only difference is to illustrate to our readers another type of decoration motif. 3⅝" tall. Rare. Circa 1885.

Long Neck Barrel: Opaque deep rose shading to white with delicate gold flowers and leaves in outlined form; mold and free blown; with two piece metal tops. We are illustrating a shaker pair. This is a rare heat sensitive homogeneous glass that turns to rose when reheated at the Glory Hole. Our glass comparison studies show that this is New England Peachblow. The shakers are believed to have been a limited experimental hand production run; we know of only one other collection that has one of these shakers. 3¾" tall. Extremely rare. Circa 1885-1886.

The New Martinsville Glass Mfg. Co
New Martinsville, West Virginia
(1900-1944)

After incorporation on December 4, 1900, the factory began production in early 1901. This glass house produced both commercial and art/pattern glass. A perusal of their early catalog reveals they produced opaque colored ware that was called "Muranese." While there were ownership and corporate name changes, the company managed to remain in continuous operation. The cased art glass that was produced was without a doubt the direct result of the early-on employment of Mr. Joseph Webb, who came from the Phoenix Glass Company and remain at New Martinsville until March, 1905, at which time he left to take a position with the Byersville Glass Co., at Byersville, Ohio. The majority of the salt shakers we are illustrating come from the period 1901-1915. Since the 1940s there have been attempts by local New Martinsville antique dealers to label their early cased glass as "New Martinsville Peachblow." While the glass is beautiful and of high quality, the fact remains that the factory never marketed this ware as a peachblow type glass. However our listed opaque shakers were marketed as "Muranese Salts" which is an original manufacturer name.

In 1937 the factory was purchased by an investment group from Connecticut that changed the factory name to "The New Martinsville Glass Company." In 1944, as the result of a stock take over by Mr. G.R. Cummings, the name was again changed to the "Viking Glass Company." Although we haven't checked in the last two years, as far as we know the company is still functional as Viking Glass Company. Some of the contemporary salt shakers produced by Viking are of good quality and worth collecting.

Aster, Tall: Opaque blue homogeneous glass; mold blown. The pattern consists of three large embossed asters equally spaced around the center of the shaker; the base is encircled with various lengths of embossed leaves. Pattern name by Peterson. Also made in opaque pink, green and yellow. 3½" tall. Scarce. Circa 1902-1905.

Creased Waist: Opaque yellow homogeneous glass; mold blown. The pattern consists of four deeply embossed fancy scrolls both top and bottom with a large below center intaglio crease. Pattern name by Peterson. Also made in pink, blue and green. 3⅜" tall. Scarce. Circa 1902-1907.

New Martinsville Glass Mfg. Co.

Curly Locks: Opaque white opalware; mold blown. This unusual pattern has a long neck; short bulbous body and a narrow base. The neck is encircled with nine diagonal scrolls in raised relief. The base is encircled with 15 short hook-like embossed scrolls. Pattern name by Peterson. Also produced in opaque blue, pink, green and yellow. 2¾" tall. Scarce. Circa 1904-1910.

Leaf, Drooping: Opaque white opalware; mold blown. This is a bulbous shaped shaker. The pattern amounts to four large embossed leaves drooping from the neck ring; the rest of the piece is smooth and undecorated. Pattern name by Peterson. All that we have seen are in opaque white. Some will be found with a hand painted floral sprig both front and back. 3⅛" tall. Scarce. Circa 1904-1912.

Curved Body: Opaque white opalware; mold blown. The basic shape is that of a pillar that expands outward toward the bottom until it almost assumes a bell configuration. The salt & pepper we are illustrating is that of a Dutch boy and girl. Obviously one shaker is a companion to the other. The artistically drawn figures were accomplished by the use of a transfer technique with some subsequent color touch up by hand. Pattern name by Peterson. Usually found in opaque white with various floral decoration. 2⅞" tall. Very scarce with the Dutch boy and girl. Circa 1905-1911.

Many Petals: Opaque pink and green; mold blown. These shakers are sphere shaped with their outer surface being completely covered with embossed small flowers having seven petals. From a pattern standpoint, this item can be easily confused with Consolidated's "Periwinkle" pattern which has flowers with five petals and is a larger sized sphere. Also produced in opaque white, blue and yellow. 2½" tall. Very scarce. Circa 1902-1906.

Palmette Band: Opaque blue; mold blown. As the pattern name implies, the shaker contains a band of six embossed palmettes at the base and neck of the shaker. Pattern name by Peterson. Also produced in opaque white, green and pink. 2¾" tall. Scarce. Circa 1902-1906.

Pillar & Flower: Opaque white with embossed hand colored floral sprigs (one on each panel); mold blown. This is a four sided shaker with an extended base for insertion into a condiment holder. Also made in opaque pink, blue, green and yellow. 2⅜" tall. Scarce. Circa 1904-1910.

Radiance: Clear ruby glass; mold blown. The pattern consists of six bulging panels separated by an embossed vertical stem. This shaker also has a footed base. This is the original manufacturer's name (OMN). This ware has a high collectibility factor in the ruby color. The quality of the glass is excellent. 2½" tall. Scarce. Circa 1936-1939.

New Martinsville Glass Mfg. Co.

Rose Relievo: Opaque blue homogeneous glass; mold blown. This is a sphere shaped shaker containing two rose and leaf bouquets in high relief. Also produced in opaque white, pink and green. Pattern name by Peterson. 2¼" tall. Very scarce. Circa 1902-1907.

Rose, Viking's: Opaque pink cased glass; mold blown. While the shaker we are illustrating is an old one, this pattern was considered basic to the factory and periodically reissued over the years. Apparently the shaker that Peterson acquired was one of the newer reissues by New Martinsville or under the Viking factory name. This is a bulbous based shaker with two large embossed floral bouquets (one on each side). The base and neck are encircled with a short scalloped curtain in raised relief. Also produced in opaque white, blue, green and yellow (some of them cased). 3⅜" tall. Very Scarce. Circa 1903-1906.

Rib, Twenty: Clear dark ruby homogeneous pressed glass. This is quality glassware from the 1920's which today has a high collectibility factor in this color. The pattern consists of a footed tapered pillar containing 20 vertical ribs. We have no other color experience to report. 3⅜" tall. Very Scarce. Circa 1925-1929.

Scroll, Two Band: Opaque yellow homogeneous glass mold blown. An unusual colored yellow. Close inspection shows the color to be somewhat variegated. The pattern make-up is pretty well described by the pattern name which was assigned by Peterson. Also made in opaque white, blue, pink and green. 3" tall. Rare in yellow. Circa 1902-1905.

Vine with Flower: Opaque pink cased glass; mold blown. This is a heavy shaker due to the inside thick white opalware. The principal pattern consists of a long vine with a series of individual flowers in raised relief. The lower half of the shaker is bulbous. Other colors made are opaque white, blue, green and yellow. 3" tall. Very scarce. Circa 1902-1908.

Harry Northwood Glass Patterns
Various Factory Locations
(1887-1913)

When we published our first salt shaker book it was pointed out that Harry Northwood's glass career encompassed many glass houses/factories beginning with "The La Bell Glass Company" at Bridgeport, Ohio in 1887, where he was factory manager, and ending around 1920 at "The Harry Northwood Company" of Wheeling, W. Va. We believe that it is important that we again list those glass houses that Mr. Northwood was associated with during the aforementioned time frame.

La Bell Glass Company,
Bridgeport, Ohio 1887
Buckeye Glass Works,
Martins Ferry, Ohio 1887-1896
Northwood Glass Works,
Martins Ferry, Ohio 1888-1895
The Northwood Company,
Ellwood, Pa. 1895
The Northwood Company,
Indiana, Pa. 1897
Northwood Glass Works,
Indiana, Pa. 1898
National Glass Companies (merger),
Indiana, Pa 1900
The Harry Northwood Company,
Wheeling, W.Va. 1902-1920

Our purpose in highlighting this information is to have our readers keep in mind that Harry Northwood was often simultaneously involved with more than one glasshouse which also included the merger of his factory at Indiana, Pennsylvania into the huge National Glass Company conglomerate.

National Glass moved molds around between their various factories in an effort to realize production efficiencies and cost savings associated with over all corporate profits. The McKee plant at Jeanette, Pennsylvania was often used as a central production location for patterns that were previously produced by their other member factories when they were operating as an independent glass house.

To further emphasize our point, and by way of example, let's talk about the "Geneva" pattern:

Mr. William Heacock went through numerous published articles and five of his *Encyclopedia of Victorian Colored Pattern Glass* books in which he attributed the "Geneva" pattern to Northwood. Then along came his book six on oil cruets; on page 66 is a 1901 trade ad, that was brought to light by author/researcher Fred Bickenhouser, showing that the "Geneva" pattern line was produced by McKee Glass Company of Jeanette, Pennsylvania.

It may be true that "Geneva" was originally a Harry Northwood pattern, but in the final attribution analysis, the trade ad has to prevail.

With the above scenario in mind, we believe it is in the best interest of our readers to list and illustrate the patterns that are known to be Northwood, but we are not going to attempt an absolute attribution to each particular factory that Mr. Northwood either owned or was associated with. In the case of the Northwood/Dugan/Diamond situation...There is no way! The glass shards involved are interesting but still circumstantial evidence and subject to the many pitfalls associated therewith. We will leave it up to our readers, many of whom are most knowledgeable, to categorize where each Northwood pattern was first produced. In certain instances, we are sure that more than a single factory will be involved.

Authors' Collection

Alaska (Foggy Bottom): Clear blue shading to a white opalescent; dual mold blown. This is a bulging based pattern containing 16 vertical ribs inside and crystal and vaseline colors. 2⅜" tall. Very scarce. Circa 1897.

Harry Northwood Glass Patterns

Alaska Variant: Clear blue shading to a white opalescent; dual mold blown. The basic pattern is identical to Alaska except that the center is encircled with an embossed hand painted garland of flower and leaves. Also this shaker is ¼" taller. 2⅝" tall. Very scarce. Circa 1897.

Beaded Circle, Northwood's: Opaque custard with hand applied gold dots on the beaded motif; mold blown. As the pattern name implies, the shaker contains a large embossed beaded circle; the center of which is decorated with a hand painted floral sprig. This is a very difficult pattern to collect and has a high collectibility factor. 3⅛" tall. Rare. Circa 1902-1903.

Cactus, Northwood's: Clear cranberry opalescent; mold blown. This is the same pattern that Peterson lists as "Cactus." It is entirely different from the Caramel Cactus pattern of the Indiana Tumbler & Goblet Co. Attribution established by the Northwood trade ad on page 13 of Heacock and Gamble Book 9, published by Antique Publications in 1987. Also produced in a cased pale green and opaque white opalware. Finding this shaker in a rare cranberry opalescent glass was quite a surprise. 3⅛" tall. Rare. Circa 1895.

Argonaut: Opaque custard glass; mold blown and bottom signed with the Northwood script signature. Also referred to as "Argonaut Shell." This glassware does not fluoresce under black light exposure. Has a very high collectibility factor. 2⅞" tall. Rare. Circa 1900.

Apple Blossom (Cosmos, Short): Opaque white in hand painted pink and green; mold blown. The basic pattern consists of eight embossed netted swirls and three apple blossoms in high raised relief. The "Short Cosmos" name was given this ware by Peterson; but an 1896 Northwood trade ad shows the OMN to be "Apple Blossom". This is an outstanding opalware pattern and has a high collectibility factor. 2⅝" tall. Very scarce.

Daisy and Fern: Clear opalescent cranberry; mold blown. The pattern consists of eight swirls. The body of the shaker is decorated with three opalescent daisies surrounded by fern-like foliage. Also produced in opalescent crystal, blue and green. 2¾" tall. Very Scarce. Circa 1894-1905.

Chrysanthemum Sprig: We are illustrating two shakers, opaque custard and opaque blue with gilt decoration; mold blown. Each shaker contains two embossed chrysanthemum floral sprigs (front and back). There is really nothing special about the blue opaque glass to warrant the price that it brings in todays antique glassware market; however, the fact remains that it has a very high collectibility factor and is very much sought after by collectors. There has always been controversy among various authors as to the first year of factory production; some place it as early as the late 1880's. The custard shakers are very scarce. 3" tall. The opaque blue have always been considered rare. Circa 1898-1905.

Harry Northwood Glass Patterns

Circled Scroll: Clear green glass; mold blown. This is a bulbous item containing four large circles; each circle contains circular scrolling in high raised relief. When exposed to black light radiation it produces a striking fluorescence. Also produced in crystal and clear blue. 2⅞" tall. Rare. Circa 1902-1905.

Crocodile Tears: Opaque cased pastel green; mold blown. Has the same mold shape as "Royal Oak" pattern. The pattern consists of four oval shaped windows; each window contains what appears to be overlapping droplets in raised relief. Also produced in pink and blue cased colors. The pattern name was created by Peterson. 2⅝" tall. Very scarce. Circa 1902-1904.

Everglades: Translucent variegated lavender; mold blown. The principal motif consists of three large leaves equally spaced around the perimeter of the shaker. The configuration is reminiscent of floating lily pads. This is a rare, highly collectible color that is much sought after by todays collectors. Also produced in crystal and blue. 3¼" tall. Circa 1903-1906.

Grape and Leaf: Opaque white opalware; mold blown. The pattern consists of two large bunches of grapes and two large green leaves hanging downward from a vine; all are in high raised relief. This is quality opalware with a fire polished bottom. 3⅛" tall. Very scarce. Circa 1900-1905.

Intaglio: Clear green glass with hand applied gold decoration; mold blown. This is an eight lobe ribbed shaker containing two intaglio floral sprigs and two lengthy embossed leaves. The base has a short protruding ring which configures this ware for use as part of a condiment set. Normally sought after in custard, the green shakers are much more difficult to acquire. This pattern has a high collectibility factor. 3" tall. Rare in green. Very scarce in custard. Circa 1900-1903.

Leaf Umbrella: Opaque blue cased glass; mold blown. The principal motif comprises eight embossed leaves that completely encircle the shaker body. This is a bulbous based shaker that has been configured for insertion into a condiment set. Pattern name by Peterson. Also produced in all basic colors including a very lovely spatter. 2⅞" tall. Very scarce in blue. Circa 1899.

Jewel and Flower: Clear blue with an opalescent base; mold blown and pressed. The pattern consists of three embossed medallion ovals separated by three vertical leaves. The neck of the shaker contains circular threading. The base is configured for use as part of a condiment set; has the same mold shape as the Alaska shakers. Pattern name by Kamm. We have seen no more than half a dozen of these shakers in over 30 years. 2⅞" tall. Rare. Circa 1904-1906.

Flat Flower: Blue opaque; mold blown. This is a four sided shaker having two large flat panels; each containing a large, fully petaled flower with the center colored red. Also made in opaque white, pale green and custard. Pattern name by Peterson. 2¾" tall. Rare. Circa 1894-1896.

Harry Northwood Glass Patterns

Inverted Fan & Feather: We are illustrating two opaque shakers; one in pink slag and the other in custard. Mold blown. This is a very busy pattern, consisting of four embossed feather panels that are separated by four buttressed inverted fans that flow downward to form the supporting knobbed feet. It is very difficult to obtain one of these shakers in a chip/crack free condition. This ware has a very high collectibility factor. 3" tall. Rare in custard. Very rare in pink slag. Circa 1899-1900.

Louis XV: Opaque custard; mold blown. The pattern consists of two embossed gilt colored floral sprigs on the front and back of the shaker. Each flower is enclosed by three large embossed scrolls that are separated by a vertical vine. The pattern name is the OMN. This is another of those custard patterns with a very high collectibility factor. Also produced in green. 2⅞" tall. Very scarce. Circa 1898

Maple Leaf, Northwood's: Opaque custard glass; mold blown. The pattern consists of four applied handles with a large embossed maple leaf hanging from the lower part of each handle. Each maple leaf is decorated with gold paint. Each handle has a slight opalescent sheen. As with most of the Northwood custard shakers, this pattern is also highly collectible and if you are lucky enough to find one for sale the price will be high. 3⅛" tall. Very rare. Circa 1901-1904.

Leaf Mold (Rose): Deep cranberry; mold blown. The pattern consists of a series of entwining rose petals in raised relief that surround the entire shaker. Produced in opaque white, blue and pink; also pink and white spatter; cased Vasa Murrhina; frosted vaseline & pink spatter, and no doubt other experimental colors. Peterson named this pattern Rose but the pattern name Leaf Mold seems to be more accepted by today's collectors. 2¼" tall. Very scarce in cranberry. Circa 1889-1892.

Royal Oak: Clear cranberry rubina glass; mold blown. This is a four paneled shaker; each panel contains an embossed oak leaf. This is the same basic shaped mold that was used for the "Crocodile Tears" shaker. 2½" tall. Scarce. Circa 1888.

Opalescent Swirl: Illustrated are two shakers; one in opalescent cranberry and the other in cranberry rubina; mold blown. As the name implies the center of the shakers is a fairly wide swirled pattern; the base and neck of the shakers contain embossed threading; 2⅝" tall. Very scarce. Circa 1890.

Quilted Phlox: Translucent pastel green cased glass; mold blown. The pattern consists of two rows of bulging diamonds; each diamond is separated by an embossed flower. The base of the shaker has been configured for insertion into a condiment set glass holder/tray. Produced in all colors; some of which are cased. Also made in opaque white opalware with hand painted decoration. 3" tall. Most colors are scarce. Circa 1900-1905.

Harry Northwood Glass Patterns

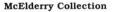

Scroll With Acanthus: Clear blue glass with gold decoration; mold blown. The pattern consists of a wide band of long ellipses that extend from the top to the base. The ellipses are broadly rounded at the top and fit into the upper scallops. A large heart shape is formed above each two ellipses. Produced in decorated crystal and apple green. Opalescent colors have been reported but we haven't seen any in salt shakers. 3" tall. Scarce. Circa 1895-1900.

Paneled Sprig: Clear cranberry; mold blown. The pattern consists of six ribbed lobes; three of the panels are plain; the other three contain a large long stemmed vine in raised relief. Pattern name by Heacock. The salt shakers have been reproduced but are easy to spot because the top of the shaker has been ground off smooth; the old shakers have been snapped off the pontil at the top and the glass will contain chipping. This was a normal production process used by Victorian era factories. 3¼" tall. Very scarce. Circa 1895-1900.

Royal Ivy: Frosted cranberry rubina glass; mold blown. The pattern consists of a basic swirl over which are embossed ivy leaves that completely encircle the center of the shaker. Also made in a variegated pink crackle glass which is rare. 2⅝" tall. Scarce. Circa 1889.

Shell: Clear blue with a stippled background; mold blown. The principal pattern consists of four embossed shells with gilded coloring. Also produced in crystal, apple green and opalescent colors; However, we have never seen any opalescent salt shakers. 1¾" tall. Very scarce. Circa 1900-1910.

Spanish Lace: Clear vaseline opalescent; mold blown. This a bulbous based shaker containing six opalescent base flowers; each flower is enclosed within a delicate vertical scrolled motif that extends from the top to the shaker base. The shaker gives off a striking fluorescence when exposed to black light radiation. 2⅞" tall. Very scarce. Circa 1895.

Spatter Glass Pleat: Pink and white translucent spatter glass; mold blown. This is a hexagon shaped shaker which consists of six panels of long narrow vertical ribbing very reminiscent of pleats. Pattern name by Peterson. Probably produced in other colors, but we have never seen any of them in salt shakers. 3⅜" tall. Very scarce. Circa 1888-1892.

S Repeat: Clear green with an iridescent sheen; mold blown and pressed; with a rough bottom pontil scar (not fire polished out). Somewhat barrel shaped, the principal motif is in consonance with it's pattern name; consisting of a large fancy scroll in the shape of a slanted S that is repeated eight times. Also produced in crystal, blue and amethyst. The pattern has been heavily reproduced by L.G. Wright; none of the reproductions will contain the bottom pontil scar, having been ground down and fire polished. When subjected to black light radiation our shaker gives off a very striking fluorescence. **The reproductions do not**. 3" tall. Scarce. Circa 1902.

Zippered Corner: Spangled cranberry (Vasa Murrhina); mold blown. A square shaped shaker with small embossed horizontal corner ribbing; reminiscent of a zipper. Pattern name by Peterson. 3⅜" tall. Very scarce. Circa 1888-1891.

The Paden City Glass Mfg Company
Paden City, West Virginia
(1916-1951)

The Paden City Glass Manufacturing Company began glass production on November 15, 1916. Mr. David Fisher, a former New Martinsville Glass Company manager, established this new glass-house and became the company's first president and chief executive officer. Mr. Fisher's glass background can be traced back to the Buckeye Glass Company.

All glassware produced by Paden City was handmade and the overall quality is excellent. They produced both mold blown and pressed glass which was primarily sold to wholesalers and jobbers. Butler Brothers did a lot of business with them.

When David Fisher passed away in 1933, he was succeeded by his son Samuel Fisher who took over as president until the factory was closed on September 21, 1951.

After Paden City closed, most of its molds were purchased by the Canton Glass Company, Marion, Indiana. Viking Glass Company, New Martinsville, West Virginia, is known to have purchased some of Paden City's "Georgian Line" tumbler molds.

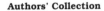

Aristocrat (Georgian Line): Translucent satinized reddish orange (pigeon blood); mold blown. This is a plain cylindrical shaped shaker except for the lower one-third which contains an embossed honeycomb pattern. The reader is looking at a Paden city rarity because of the color and satinized finish. The Georgian Line was made in all colors but the red and cobalt colors command the highest prices to today's collectors. 2⅞" tall. Rare. Circa 1929-1934.

Footed Four Panel: Clear ruby red; mold blown and pressed. The pattern consists of four curved tapering panels with a square supporting foot. We presume that this ware was made in other colors because of Paden City's color policies but we have no other color experience to report. 3⅛" tall. Rare. Circa 1928.

Party Line #191: Clear ruby red; mold blown. This is another of the Paden City plain patterns consisting of a series of round horizontal lobes that begin at the middle of the shaker and continue to its base. The metal top is of interest because it is counter weighted so that it opens up when the shaker is placed in the position for condiment dispensing. It should be noted that the Party Line was made in a wide range of colors and it was reintroduced periodically from the mid 1920's into the late 1940's. 3" tall. Scarce in red. Circa 1926-1933.

Phoenix Glass Company
Monaca, Pennsylvania
(1880-Present Time)

The Phoenix Glass Company was founded by Andrew Howard in 1880 at Phillipsburg, Pennsylvania. This town's name was changed to Monaca in 1892.

In 1883 the firm moved away from chimney and lamp shade production and began to manufacture art glass. Some glass historians state that this change was made possible by the hiring of Joesph Webb who was the nephew of Thomas Webb of English glassware fame.

Phoenix continued to manufacture art glass into the early 1890's and then entered into the cut glass market. By the turn of the century the factory was primarily concentrating on chimneys and lighting shades.

There were a couple of short time frames when Phoenix produced glass from molds they had acquired from other glass houses such as Co-Operative Flint and Consolidated Lamp & Glass. However, the factory has pretty much stuck to the lighting ware production categories. They operate today as a part of the Anchor Hocking Corporation.

McElderry Collection

Lockwood Collection

Leaf, Matted: Opaque hand painted shaded yellow to white opalware; mold blown. This shaker is the result of a special patent No. 27,132 that was awarded to Mr. Robert Hunter on June 1, 1897, (see patent section). The patent papers list this item as a "Design for a condiment Holder." The patent rights were assigned to the Phoenix Glass Company by Mr. Hunter. The pattern is a conventional representation of the chrysanthemum flower that comprises the bulbous body and base in raised relief. Pattern name by Warman. 2½" tall. Very scarce. Circa 1897.

Elk: Opaque blue satin glass with hand painted enamel to give a pseudo cameo-like effect; mold blown; with a two piece metal top. This barrel shaped shaker is in the configuration of a series of shakers that Bill Heacock named Coloratura[1] in his *Victorian Colored Pattern Glass Book III.* However in a 1986 publication[2], he changed his attribution from "Hobbs" to "Phoenix." Obviously this means that the entire Coloratura series of shakers should now have a Phoenix attribution. The Elk shaker should be listed as rare. 3" tall. Circa 1885-1889.

Pioneer Glass Company
Knoxville, Pennsylvania
(1892-1894)

Just Collection

The Pioneer Glass Company was formed in 1892 by the Werling brothers. It was located at Knoxville which, at that time, was a suburb of the City of Pittsburgh. This was a glass decoration factory that worked in ruby stained glassware, securing their glass blanks from various nearby glassware manufacturers. The trade periodicals and journals indicate that it was a flourishing business during the short time of Werling ownership.

Around mid-1894 Pioneer was purchased by Mr. L.J. Rogers who continued to operate the factory in conjunction with another one that he owned in the Pittsburgh area. Indications are that the factory operated under Mr. Rogers ownership well into the late 1890's. It is not clear if the factory name changed after the Rogers purchase. We have assumed that it did.

Beauty: Ruby stained crystal pressed glass. The pattern consists of vertical stained columns alternating with sunken crystal columns. Above and below them are horizontal rows of stained raised diamonds. Also sold in crystal. 3" tall. Very scarce. Circa 1892-1893.

Riverside Glass Works

Riverside Glass Works
Wellsburg, West Virginia
(1880-1908)

In 1880 the Riverside Glass Works was established by an experienced group of glass personnel that had left Hobbs, Brockunier and the Buckeye Glass Company. Over the ensuing years this factory became a producer of both ruby stained and quality emerald green glass patterns. In 1899 Riverside joined the National Glass conglomerate and lost control of many of their molds which were moved to other National Glass factories. With National's demise (around 1904), Riverside again began operating as an independent. However, despite management reorganizations/restructuring, etc., Riverside went into receivership in 1908.

Just Collection

Draped Top (Riverside's Victoria): Ruby stained crystal pressed glass. This is an elaborate swag pattern in raised relief containing beveled margins. The top portion resembles a ruby stained curtain. Also made in clear crystal. 2⅝" tall. Very scarce in ruby stained. Circa 1894-1895.

Petticoat: Clear vaseline pressed glass with gold decoration. The basic pattern consists of two rows of embossed diamonds above a scallop footed base that contains sunken daisies on each scallop. 3" tall. Very scarce. Circa 1902.

Empress: Clear emerald green pressed glass with gold decoration. The pattern consists of eight vertical scalloped panels rising out of an ornate scalloped base. This pattern has a high collectibility factor. 3¼" tall. Rare. Circa 1898-1899.

Ester: Clear emerald green pressed glass. This is a busy shaker; the base pattern consist of a group of intaglio daisies; there is also a small sunken daisy with a wide sloping outline. The sunk daisies contain hand painted gold decoration. This is a highly collectible pattern and considered to be rare in an emerald green shaker. 3" tall. Circa 1896.

Seed Pod: Clear emerald green pressed glass with gold decoration. The upper half of this shaker is plain, the lower half contains what appears to be a series of embossed vertical seed pods. Also produced in crystal. 3⅛" tall. Very scarce. Circa 1897-1900.

Winsome: Clear crystal pressed glass. The principal motif consists of six plain concave vertical panels. The base is flared with a leaf at the bottom of each panel edge. Riverside listed this as their No. 550 pattern. Pattern name by Heacock in his book *1000 Toothpicks.* 3⅛" tall. Scarce. Circa 1890-1896.

Riverside Glass Works

X-ray: Clear emerald green pressed glass with vertical gold trim decoration. The pattern consists of six vertical lobe panels that are supported by a round footed base. There is a high collectibility factor associated with this pattern. Arthur Peterson described how he traded off the only shaker that he ever acquired in this pattern because he didn't recognize it for what it was; he never saw another one that was for sale. 2¼" tall. Rare. Circa 1896-1899.

Robinson Glass Company

Robinson Glass Company
Zanesville, Ohio
(1893-1900)

There wasn't much information to be learned about this small independent company. It was established sometime in 1893. Very few glass patterns have been attributed to Robinson Glass. In 1899 the Robinson Glass Company was purchased by the National Glass conglomerate. The factory was closed and the molds were redistributed to other National Glass Company factories.

Josephine's Fan: Clear pressed crystal glass. Listed as Robinson's No. 129. Heacock saw the motif as a fan and added the word *Josephine's* in front of it. Heacock stated the molds eventually ended up at Cambridge. 2⅝" tall. Scarce. Circa 1896-1900.

Fagot: Clear ruby stained crystal pressed glassware. This was listed as Robinson's No. 1. Pattern name by Kamm. Mrs Kamm described this pattern as a large bundle of something tied together in the middle. The pattern also has a large diamond. It is very ornate with the ruby staining used to highlight the main motif. 2¾" tall. Rare in ruby stained. Circa 1893.

Zanesville: Frosted decorated crystal; mold blown and pressed. The glass surfaces of this shaker are completely smooth on the outside. It has a protruding neck ring and the motif consists of a large hand painted lavender, yellow and white floral spray. Arthur Peterson classified this as a rare shaker in his 1970 book *Glass Salt Shakers: 1000 Patterns.* 3" tall. Circa 1896.

L.E. Smith Glass Company
Mt. Pleasant, Pennsylvania
(1907- Present)

The L.E. Smith Glass Company was founded in 1907 by Mr. Lewis E. Smith with the idea of manufacturing glass mustard containers for a special mustard sauce that he had created. He obtained a nearby vacant factory to establish his glasshouse.

Naturally his first product line was mustard and fruit jars. But, he got caught up in the manufacturing of glassware and was soon into tableware lines, novelties, etc.

Mr. Smith left the company around 1911 and the new owners did not change the company name.

The 1920s and 1930s was devoted to colored glassware with an emphasis on black glass tableware and novelties. The majority of the glass ware produced by this firm is hand crafted. Many of their tableware lines are listed in Gene Florence's *Depression Glass* books published by Collector Books, at Paducah, Ky.

Snake Dance: Opaque black glass; mold blown and pressed. The pattern consists of a male flute player and three female dancers holding snakes. The Smith catalogue states this pattern was also made in cobalt blue, but, we have never seen any shakers in this color. Pattern name by Peterson who stated that the pattern is very difficult to photograph. We certainly agree with him! An entire set of tableware and novelties was made in this pattern[1]. 3⅜" tall. Rare. Circa 1928-1932.

Standard Manufacturing Company
Boston, Massachusetts

Some years ago we unearthed a trade advertisement from the *American Pottery and Glassware Reporter* dated Sept. 15, 1881. A wholesale jobber named the Standard Mfg. Company was advertising the latest novelty salt shaker named "Acme Salt." This is the shaker that today's salt shaker collectors know as "Coil Top," which was patented on July 26, 1881 by Thomas W. Brown of Belmont, Massachusetts as an "open cap for bottles."

We are including the aforementioned trade ad and a copy of the U.S. Patent Office data that clearly illustrates and describes this device's total intended use (see design patent section).

Today, these shakers are quite scarce. They were produced in two shapes and sizes; 2¼" and 2⅞" tall. To date, they have only been reported in crystal and opaque white. We are revealing the larger size "Coil Top" shaker in a rare cobalt blue color. This should stimulate some of the antique salt shaker collector's appetites and start them singing "A Hunting We Will Go!"

As a reliable vessel for dispensing table salt, the "Coil Top" left a lot to be desired. The wire coils corroded and became encrusted with salt. Also the air gaps between the coils allowed humid air to lump the inside salt into a nondispensable condition. However, the trade ad was correct they are a novelty.

"ACME SALT,"

(THE LATEST NOVELTY.)

PATENTED JULY 26, 1881.

The Cap and Pulverizer are made from one piece of plated steel wire.

The advantages claimed over all others are the simplicity of construction preventing any possibility of the salt clogging by its own action having a spring top, thus keeping itself clean.

Packed in boxes of one dozen, and ten gross in a case.

NO CHARGE FOR CASE.

Samples sent to the Trade free of charge with price, on application to the

STANDARD MFG. CO.,

131 Portland St., BOSTON.

Standard Manufacturing Company

LEFT: Coil Top: Clear crystal. Two sizes: 2¼" & 2⅞" Rare. Circa 1881.

RIGHT: Coil Top: Cobalt Blue; 2⅞" tall. Very rare. Circa 1881.

Steuben Glass Works

Steuben Glass Works
Corning, New York
(1903-Present)

The Steuben Glass Works began on March 2, 1904. The founders were Thomas G. Hawkes, Towsend deM Hawkes and Frederick Carder. The factory was named "Steuben" after the county in which the firm resides. The works was extremely productive and profitable under Mr. Carder's leadership. He officially left the firm by 1934, although he continued to work with his colored art glass as an independent from floor space within the factory.

Certainly of all the glassware made by Steuben, Aurene was the most popular. Various designs in both blue and gold Aurene were made from 1904 to 1930.[1]

The Aurene trade name was innovated by Frederick Carder from the Latin word Aureatus meaning "like gold in resplendence." The term "Aurene" was used for all of the Steuben lustred glass both blue and gold.

According to Revi[2] the Steuben catalogues differentiated by use of the terminology "Blue Aurene" or "Gold Aurene."

The "Blue Aurene" shaker that we are illustrating is very rare and a part of the Krauss collection. The only other known shaker like it is on display at the Rockwell Museum at Corning, New York.

In 1933, A.A. Houghton Jr. took over at Steuben. Under his management a high quality crystal clear glass has been, and still is, being produced. The bottom of this ware is signed by a craftsman utilizing a diamond point, and writing the word Steuben. It is a signature and not a trademark. The crystal shaker we are illustrating was signed in the aforesaid manner.

Blue Aurene: Opaque blue lustred glassware; mold and free blown finished. The appearance of the shaker is rather utilitarian with plain, undecorated panels. 2¹³⁄₁₆" tall with a base diameter of 1¼". Very rare. Circa 1912-1922.

Krauss Collection

Steuben, Crystal: Clear high quality crystal glass; free blown; with a two piece sterling silver top. The shaker has a rather flat bulging base and tapers upward into a very narrow neck. Diamond point signed with the word *Steuben*. 2⅜" tall. Rare. Circa 1934-1938.

Authors' Collection

Stevens and Williams Glass Works
Brierly Hill Staffordshire
England
(1847-Present)

This famous English glasshouse was established in 1847 as an outgrowth from the old "Brierly Hill Glass Works" which dated back into the mid-1700's.

In 1870 an updated factory was built on adjoining property. During 1949 the factory was again remodeled and modernized.

Stevens and Williams have always produced glassware to the highest quality standards, and over the years have supplied glassware to the Royal Family. Their Victorian Era art glass has always been among the best that could be obtained. Like their competitors, Thomas Webb and American glasshouses, they had their version of Peachblow Glassware that they referred to as "Peach Bloom," which in color appearance is very similar to Wheeling Peachblow (originally named "Coral").

This successful glass house continues to operate today, producing very high quality crystal.

Today's collectors/dealers simply call their Peachblow "Steven and Williams Peachblow." In terms of salt shakers we have never seen a different shape/style from that illustrated, due to a very high collectibility and rarity factor. We are unaware of any other major salt shaker collection, that we have viewed, containing this particular shaker.

Authors' Collection

Stevens & Williams Peachblow: Brick-red in the intense upper portion to a lightly tinged yellow; mold and free blown finished cased glassware. We owe our acquisition of this piece to Mr. Clarence Maier of *The Burmese Cruet* who brought its availability to our attention. We have not assigned it a pattern name, but for descriptive purposes, it consists of a rounded four sided shaker with a pinched-inward center on each side. There is an elaborate hand painted floral decoration primarily in the center of the shaker body. 2⅝" tall with a 1" base diameter. Very rare. Circa 1885-1889.

Tarentum Glass Company
Tarentum, Pennsylvania
(1894-1918)

The Tarentum Glass Company appeared in early 1894 as an outgrowth from Richards and Hartley Flint Glass Company, Factory E of the U.S. Glass Co. Mr. H.M. Brekenridge was President and Mr. L.R. Hartley, secretary.

This factory produced a considerable amount of pressed crystal glass tableware; much of which was ruby stained. Around 1903 Tarentum was into cut crystal glass, opalware and custard glass which some of the trade journals at the time referred to as "Tarentum's Pea Green" glass.

The factory continued into the production of tableware until around 1916 when the trade ads began to show that Tarentum was producing lighting fixtures. The firm was completely destroyed by fire in 1918 and never rebuilt.

Atlanta, Tarentum's (Diamond and Teardrop): Clear crystal pressed glass. This is an 1894 pattern of Tarentum. 3" tall. Very scarce.

Beaded Square: Opaque opalware glass, mold blown. This is a square shaped shaker containing four beaded panels with hand painted yellow and blue daisy sprigs; the bottom is round and also beaded. Also produced in custard and probably other opaque colors. 2" tall. Scarce. Circa 1898-1904.

Oregon, Tarentum's: Clear ruby stained pressed glass. The pattern appears on page 222 of the book *Tarentum Glass* by Robert Lucas. Also produced in crystal. 2⅞" tall. Very scarce. Circa 1900-1908.

Princeton: Clear crystal pressed glass. The principal pattern consists of four large embossed pointed ovals the center of which contains numerous small pointed triangular shapes. The top and base of the shaker are encircled with a single band of tiny beads. 2¾" tall. Scarce. Circa 1897-1905.

Georgia Gem: Opaque custard glass; mold blown. This is a round squatty shaker containing three bulging panels; each panel is separated by a vertical crease. The top and bottom are encircled by a single ring of small beads. Also produced in opaque white and green. Each panel is hand decorated with a blue and yellow daisy sprig. 2½" tall. Very Scarce. Circa 1900-1904.

Teardrop, Paneled: Opaque green cased glass; mold blown. The pattern consists of four teardrop panels and four smooth panels. This is a rare shaker in cased green glass. Pattern name by Peterson. Also made in opaque custard, white and green (uncased). This shaker has a high collectibility factor. 3⅛" tall. Very rare. Circa 1905-1908.

Thumbprint, Tarentum's: Opaque custard glass with a large hand painted red and pink floral sprig; mold blown and pressed. This is a very plain looking item having thick heavy glass that has concave walls. In order to see the pattern, the shaker must be tipped upside down which will then reveal a circular band of very small thumbprints on the outer rim and a large embossed star. Pattern name by Kamm. Also produced in opaque white and green 2⅝" tall. Rare in custard. Circa 1904.

Tarentum Glass Company

Victoria, Tarentum's: Opaque green glass; mold blown. It is supposed that almost every major glass house had to have a Victorian pattern; obviously Tarentum was no exception. This is a bell shaped shaker with a rather complex scroll pattern around the base rim. 2⅝" tall. Very scarce in opaque green. Circa 1896-1902.

Thompson Glass Company, LTD.

The Thompson Glass Company, LTD.
Uniontown, Pennsylvania
(1889-1895)

This is another of those obscure glasshouses that had a very short production life. The most detailed information we could obtain about this company was contained in a two-part article written by Arthur Peterson in the November & December 1962 issues of *Hobbies* magazine entitled "Glassware Patents by Julius Proeger."

Mr. Proeger joined the Thompson Glass Company in 1890, and in March of that year he obtained a design patent for the "Surface Ornamentation of Vessels." Mrs. Kamm subsequently named this pattern "Tile" (see Kamm 6, page 22). It is our opinion that Mr. Proeger's patents and talents gave this factory the sales boost that it needed. By late 1891, Mr. Proeger had moved on to Greensburg, Pennsylvania.

During this factory's production life, it produced lamps, bar goods, crystal, ruby-stained pressed glassware and novelties. The firm went out of business in 1895.

Tile: Clear crystal pressed glass. The pattern consists of a grouping of raised bands that are divided into sections or blocks that have two parallel and two converging edges. This design was patented on March 11, 1890, as design patent No. 19,694 by Julius Proeger and assigned to the Thompson Glass Company. Pattern name by Kamm. While we have no additional color experience to report, it would be of no surprise to find that ruby stained shakers exist. 3" tall. Rare. Circa 1890.

Summit, The: Clear ruby stained pressed glassware. The pattern forms a four leaf clover; each petal is sliced outside the triangle with the four parts meeting to form the flower. The ruby staining adds considerably to accentuating the overall motif. Heacock[1] states that there was additional production of this pattern by Cambridge Glass Company around 1903. 2⅝" tall. Rare. Circa 1895.

Tiffany Furnaces
Corona, Long Island, New York
(1893-1938)

This outstanding glass house produced glassware that is probably No. 1 in terms of collectibility. As we mentioned in the "Introduction" section of this book, very few salt shakers were made during this factory's lifetime. As far as we have been able to tell shakers were only made to fill special customer orders. In fact, the shaker we are illustrating contains the original owners initials "ESB" engraved upon the plug-in top.

The factory was operated by Arthur J. Nash on a shareholding basis for Louis Comfort Tiffany. However, almost all glassware designs were innovated and controlled/approved by Mr. Tiffany. The workers who actually made the glass objects were divided into five-man shops; each shop was headed by a "gaffer." It is interesting to note that throughout its entire history, Tiffany Furnaces employed only nine gaffers. As with all Tiffany pieces, the salt shaker we are illustrating is unique in both shape and design. Because of the special plug on type top, we are showing two photographic views. The Tiffany factory was using the name "Tiffany Studios" when it closed in 1938.

Krauss Collection

Krauss Collection

Krauss Collection

Tiffany: Iridescent gold, free blown and hand shaped with a special two-piece gold plated top and hand signed "L.C. Tiffany–Favrile"; the term *Favrile* was derived from the old English word *Fabrile*–meaning hand made. This shaker is classified as a single color, iridescent piece with ground pontil. This is the same shaker that is shown in the art glass plate of *Glass Salt Shakers; 1000 Patterns* by Arthur G. Peterson. 2⅝" tall with its push-on top removed. Extremely rare. Circa 1898-1905.

The United States Glass Company

The U.S. Glass Company was formed July 1, 1891 and it represented the merging of 18 independent glass houses. Daniel C. Ripley was elected as the corporation's first president.

A high percentage of their glass tableware that was produced consisted of old patterns that had been issued while their member factories were still independent.

The U.S. Glass factories were assigned alphabet letter designations, having lost their original, independent factory names. Since we will be referring to the aforesaid factories by their assigned letters, it seems appropriate to list them as they were entitled by this corporation beginning in 1891.

Adams & Company, Pittsburgh, PA.........Factory A
Bryce Brothers, Pittsburgh, PA...............Factory B
Challinor, Taylor & Co Ltd, Tarentum, PA..Factory C
George Duncan & Sons, Pittsburgh, PA..Factory D
Richards & Hartley, Tarentum, PA.........Factory E
Ripley & Company, Pittsburgh, PA..........Factory F
Gillinder & Sons, Greensburg, PA...........Factory G
Hobbs Glass Company, Wheeling, WV ....Factory H

Columbia Glass Co., Findlay, OH...........Factory J
King Glass Company, Pittsburgh, PA......Factory K
O'Hara Glass Company, Pittsburgh, PA...Factory L
Bellaire Goblet Company, Findlay, OH.....Factory M
Nickel Plate Glass Company, Fostoria, OH ....Factory N
Central Glass Company, Wheeling, WV...........Factory O
Doyle & Company, Pittsburgh, PA ....Factory P
A.J. Beatty & Sons, Tiffin, OH ....Factory R
A.J. Beatty & Sons, Steubenville, OH ....Factory S
Novelty Glass Company, Fostoria, OH ....Factory T

The two other glass factories that were built later by U.S. Glass were U at Gas City, Indiana and GP at Glassport, Pennsylvania.

Due to strikes, fires, closings and sell-off, there were only eight factories being operated after 1900. By 1904 this number had dropped to six.

It is worth noting that the individual state patterns that were created by U.S. Glass, started in 1897 and continued through 1903. Most of these state patterns are very difficult to acquire, and have always had a high collectibility factor.

Authors' Collection

Authors' Collection

Acorn, Little: Opaque blue homogeneous glass; mold blown. Very similar in appearance to the Acorn shaker produced by Hobbs which has a base circumference of 6⅞" and a much larger top opening for condiment dispensing. An 1891 trade ad shows that this shaker was produced at Factory C (Challinor). Also made in opaque white, green and pink. 2¾" tall, the base circumference is 6¾". Scarce. Circa 1891.

Alabama (Beaded Bull's Eye & Drape): Clear crystal; pressed glass. Also produced in clear ruby-stained and green. The top of the shaker is encircled with embossed bull's eyes each connected by a small horizontal bar. Projecting downward from each bull's eye is a beaded vertical buttress that forms support for the shaker. 2¾" tall. Very rare. Circa 1899.

Just Collection

Lockwood Collection

California (Beaded Grape): Clear green pressed glass. Also made in clear crystal. The pattern consists of a large woody spray of embossed foliage and fruit on each side of the shaker. 2¾" tall. Rare. Circa 1899 at Factories B and F.

Broken Column With Red Dots (Broken Column): Crystal with ruby stained dots; pressed glass. The pattern is primarily made up of notched ribs with ruby stained dots. Originally a Columbia Glass pattern, the majority of the red stained shakers appear to have been made while Columbia was operating as Factory J. Also produced in clear crystal in which case it should be called "Broken Column." The acquisition of the ruby stained shakers is very difficult due to this ware having such a high collectibility factor. 2⅞" tall. Rare in ruby stained. Circa 1891.

Lockwood Collection

Authors' Collection

Colorado: Clear emerald green with gold decoration; mold blown and pressed. The catalogue lists that the pattern was also produced in clear crystal, blue, ruby-stained, amber-stained and amethyst-flashed; however we have only seen the crystal, green and blue salts. The pattern was made at Factories E & K. 2⅝" tall. Peterson says that the shakers were made in two sizes. Very scarce. Circa 1898.

Carolina: Clear ruby stained glassware; mold blown. This is a tall shaker containing a bulging base that has ten ellipse shaped circles in raised relief. The rest of this item is smooth shaped with souvenired ruby staining. Listed as "states pattern No. 15083." Peterson lists this shaker but does not illustrate it. 3½" tall. Very scarce. Circa 1903.

United States Glass Company

Delaware (Four Petal Flower): Clear rose-flashed with gilded leaves; mold blown & pressed. Also made in crystal, emerald green, and custard at factories B and K. Highly collectible and most difficult to find. 2⅝" tall. Rare. Circa 1899.

Diamond & Sunburst Variant: Ruby stained pressed crystal glassware.The pattern consists of a series of intaglio sunbursts/stars completely encompassing the shaker; the upper part is ruby stained. Also produced in crystal. 2¼" tall. Scarce. Circa 1892.

Diamond Mat Band: Clear cranberry-flashed with hand painted floral decoration; mold blown & pressed. Pattern name by Peterson. This shaker is smooth on the upper portion with a series of embossed small pointed protrusions encircling the base. 3" tall. Very scarce. Circa 1900-1907.

Florida: Clear emerald green; pressed glass. The pattern consists of embossed herringbone designs on every other vertical panel. Manufactured at Factory B. 2⅝" tall. Very scarce. Circa 1898.

Galloway: Crystal with rose-flashing; pressed glass. Also made in crystal and ruby-stained. Peterson lists this pattern as Virginia which Heacock says is a misnomer. The pattern consists of a series of large oval panels. The rose-flashing is limited to the very top portion of the shaker. 3⅛" tall. Very scarce. Circa 1904.

Heavy Gothic: Ruby stained pressed crystal. The pattern consists of adjacent vertially divided Gothic Windows with pointed beveled arches. 2¾" tall. Rare. Circa 1892 at Factory K. Also made in crystal.

Just Collection

Authors' Collection

Lockwood Collection

Hexagon, Block: Crystal ruby-stained; pressed glass. This pattern consists of series of small intaglio blocks that begin in the middle and continue downward into the supporting foot. First produced at Hobbs around 1889, with continued production at factory H after 1891. Also made in crystal with amber staining. 2⅞" tall. Rare. Circa 1889-1893.

Hexagon, Six Panel: Black opaque homogeneous pressed glass. This is a simple six panel footed shaker; each panel flows downward onto the circular foot. 3⅝" tall. Very scarce. Circa 1929-1934.

King's No. 500: Blue translucent glass; mold blown and pressed. The shakers were made in two sizes. In appearance, the pattern is reminiscent of oval shaped panels separated by zippers. Produced at Factory GP. 2¾" tall. Scarce. Circa 1900.

Lockwood Collection

Authors' Collection

Iowa: Crystal with gold decoration; mold blown and pressed. The shakers were made in two sizes. In appearance, the pattern is reminiscent of oval shaped panels separated by zippers. Produced at Factory GP. 2¾" tall. Scarce. Circa 1900.

Maine (Stippled Panelled Flower): Clear decorated crystal. The pattern consists of vertical rows of beads separating base panels of embossed leaves and flowers. Also produced in crystal and emerald green 3" tall. Very scarce. Circa 1899.

United States Glass Company

Lacy Medallion (Jewel): Clear green with gilded base decoration; mold blown & pressed. The pattern consists of a cylinder shape with a beaded neck ring and an embossed button scallop-shaped base medallion. Also produced in ruby-stained, blue, crystal and a rare translucent camphor. 3" tall. Scarce. Circa 1904-1905.

Mario: Amber stained crystal; pressed glass; the upper one-third is amber stained with a floral design. This is a Hobbs pattern with continued production at Factory H. Also produced in crystal and ruby-stained. 2⅝" tall. Peterson classified this as a rare pattern in 1970...so imagine what it is today. Circa 1891.

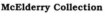

Michigan (Loop and Pillar): Ruby stained crystal; mold blown and pressed glass. Contains oval shaped jewels around the top; each jewel is surrounded with tiny beads. Also produced in crystal, decorated crystal, rose-flashed and green-flashed. 3" tall. Rare in the ruby stained and flashed colors. Circa 1902.

Millard (Fan and Flute): Ruby stained crystal; pressed glass. The principal pattern consists of embossed rounded triangles separated by spread out fans. Also made in crystal and amber stained. Shaker height is 2¾". Very scarce. Circa 1893 at Factory H.

Nail: Ruby stained crystal; mold blown. Has intaglio nail impressions on the shaker neck; contains four oval base panels; each oval is ruby stained. Another version of the shaker has acid etched leaves on each of the stained oval panels. Also made in crystal. 3" tall. Very scarce in ruby stained. Circa 1892.

United States Glass Company

Lockwood Collection

Lockwood Collection

Authors' Collection

Minnesota: Crystal pressed glass. Since this is Arthur Peterson's home state, we will use his pattern description "Has an octagonal button in an eight-pointed star." Also produced in ruby stained and green. 2¾" tall. Very scarce. Circa 1898.

Oregon (Beaded Loop): Clear crystal pressed glass. The principal motif consists of a series of interconnecting beaded loops. Apparently not produced in color. This is a most difficult pattern to obtain in a shaker; has a very high collectibility factor. 3½" tall. Rare. Circa 1901.

Lockwood Collection

McElderry Collection

Octagon Panel: Opaque black homogeneous pressed glass. This is a plain eight panel footed shaker that was designed to go with the U.S. Glass Octagon tableware. 3⅜" tall. Very scarce. Circa 1929-1934.

New Jersey (Loops & Drops): Crystal pressed glass. The pattern description is pretty well covered by the name "Loops & Drops." Also made in ruby stained. 2⅝" tall. Scarce. Rare in ruby stained. Circa 1900 at Factory D.

New Hampshire (Bent Buckle): Rose flashed crystal; pressed glass. The principal pattern is reminiscent of a large buckle that is bent under at the bottom. If a more detailed description is desired see Kamm 3-97. Also made in crystal and ruby stained. 3" tall. Rare in the rose flashed. Circa 1903.

Roman Rosette: Ruby stained crystal with red stained rosettes and neck ring; mold blown & pressed. The shaker contains six embossed rosettes on a stippled background. The top and base are encircled with short vertical ribs. Also produced in crystal and as a salt and pepper condiment set in a glass holder. 3" tall. Rare with ruby stained rosettes. Circa 1891.

Pennsylvania: (Balder): Clear pressed crystal glassware. The pattern consists of four bevelled diamonds containing a fine cut pattern; between the diamonds is a large splayed figure made up of four long pointed arms not meeting at a center, with two vertical pineapples between each with diamond point. Peterson reports that there are three types, so the pattern obviously various somewhat. Also produced in emerald green and ruby stained. 2¼" tall. Very scarce. Circa 1897.

Panelled Palm (Brilliant): Rose flashed crystal; mold blown. The pattern consists of a series of beaded arched panels; within each panel is an embossed palm leaf. Also produced in crystal. 3" tall. Rare in rose flashed. Circa 1906. Produced at Factory F.

Red Block: Ruby stained crystal with red colored blocks; pressed glass. We believe that the pattern name provides sufficient description. Also made in crystal and amber stained which changes the name to "Barreled Block." 2½" tall. Rare. Circa 1891 at Factory P.

Square Block: Amber stained crystal pressed glass. The pattern consists of a series of symmetrical spaced blocks in raised relief; the upper blocks are amber stained and etched with a single flower in the center of each. Also produced in crystal and ruby stained. 3" tall. Rare. Circa 1892-1897.

Swirl, Beaded (Swirl Column): Clear green pressed glass with gilded beads. The pattern consists of wide panelled swirls. Also produced in crystal. 2⅜" tall. Very scarce. Circa 1891 at Factory D.

Snail: Ruby stained crystal pressed glass. This is a most difficult pattern to acquire with the ruby staining due to its high collectibility factor. Made in two sizes. Also produced in crystal. 2⅞" tall. Rare in ruby stained. Circa 1891 at Factory P.

Texas: Clear crystal pressed glass. The pattern consists of a series of embossed loops containing stippled panels. Peterson states that this state pattern shaker comes in two sizes. Also reported in rose-flashed and ruby stained but we have not observed shakers in these latter two colors. 2¾" tall. Very scarce. Circa 1900.

Vermont: Opaque decorated ivory (custard), mold blown and pressed. The pattern contains buttresses down the body to form three scalloped and ribbed feet. The top is encircled by a series of five petalled flowers. Also produced in crystal, green and blue. 2⅜" tall. Very scarce. Circa 1899.

Wisconsin (Beaded Dewdrop): Clear crystal pressed glass. The pattern contains deep erect separated thumbprints encircling the shaker body; between each two ovals is a column of small teardrops, one above the other. Made in crystal only. 2¾" tall. Rare. Circa 1903.

Westmoreland Speciality Company
(1890-1924)
Westmoreland Glass Company
(1924-1984)

This glasshouse started as an outgrowth from the Speciality Glass Company of East Liverpool, Ohio, who sold out to the West Brothers that were financially backed by a Mr. Ira. A. Brainard of Pittsburgh. A new plant was constructed at Grapeville, Pennsylvania in the county of Westmoreland. Production started in 1890 at this location as the Westmoreland Speciality Company.

During the total existence of this company, their principal product line was opalware. During World War I, Westmoreland produced various candy containers (complete with candy) but the venture turned out to be unprofitable so production of this ware was discontinued.

During the 1920's and 30's, Westmoreland produced crystal, amber, green and blue glassware and (of course) opalware. In 1924, due to ownership problems, the company was restructured and the name was changed to the Westmoreland Glass Company.

From the 1950's into the 1970's Westmoreland did a lot of private contract manufacturing for the L.G. Wright Co. of New Martinsville, West Virginia. No doubt this was one of the reasons that Mr. A.C., Revi in his 1964 book *American Pressed Glass and Figure Bottles*, commented on the unmarked reproductions that were produced by this glass house. However, when one puts the situation in proper perspective, this helped to keep the factory doors open. After all Fenton did the same thing for the same reasons. It simply means that today's collectors must study and become more knowledgeable to avoid the reproduction pitfalls that currently exist.

Westmoreland was a very capable glasshouse that produced a wide variety of quality glassware. Therefore, due to the collectibility factor associated with this ware, we have included some of their recent contemporary shakers produced within the last five decades.

In 1981 Westmoreland was sold to Dave Gross Designs of St. Louis, Mo. Obviously the subsequent factory operations were not profitable because on October 14, 1984, the molds were sold on the open market to various currently existing glass manufactures such as "Viking," "Blenko," "Summit Art Glass" etc. So watch out! You will now have to deal with the recognition of reproductions of Westmoreland patterns. It seems like there is no end to the challenges a collector must face.

Daisy and Button, Westmoreland's: Clear amber pressed glass. The pattern name fits the motif; the shaker is completely covered with the daisy & buttons. 3" tall. Circa 1956-1965.

English Hobnail, Westmoreland's: Clear ruby pressed glass. This is a long established Westmoreland pattern that originally dates from the 1920's; however this color was not catalog listed among the early production. The ruby coloration contains some orange tint reminiscent of what many collectors call "Pigeon Blood." 3¼" tall. Circa 1961-1970.

Flute and Crown: Opaque opalware with a hand painted orange and green floral sprig on each side; mold blown and pressed. This is a unique pattern consisting of a square shaped shaker; each corner contains a vertical buttressed rib that forms into a supporting scrolled foot. Pattern name by Kamm. 3" tall. Very scarce. Circa 1896-1899.

Fruit Band: Clear ruby stained crystal; mold blown & pressed. The pattern consists of an embossed band of fruit and vines that encircle the center of the body. The flared glass foot contains two embossed groupings of what appear to be an apple, pear and two bunches of grapes stained red and purple. The OMN pattern is listed in the *Depression Glass Book II* written by Sandra Stout. The pattern name is "Della Robbia." This is a highly collectible pattern sought after by both Depression glass collectors and antique salt shaker collectors. 3⅝" tall. Very scarce. Circa 1938.

High Hob: Clear crystal pressed glass. This is a footed shaker with the principal pattern amounting to long double pointed oval with deep bevelled margins. Tiny hobnails cover the background which was Mrs. Kamm's basis for assigning the pattern name. Listed as the No. 550 pattern. Not listed or illustrated in Peterson's salt shaker book. 2¾" tall. Very scarce. Circa 1915.

Hundred Eye: Ruby stained crystal; mold blown and pressed. The pattern consists of twelve vertical rows of embossed eyes that produce a prism effect. Every other eye at the top of the shaker is ruby stained. The rest of the shaker is clear crystal. A Westmoreland catalog page calls the pattern their "1000 Eye Line." This is considered to be a Depression Glass collectible but was picked up in Peterson's salt shaker book. Has an above average collectibility factor. 3¼" tall. Very scarce. Circa 1934.

Westmoreland Glass Company

Marbleized Caramel: Translucent variegated caramel and white; mold blown and pressed. Quality glassware produced by Westmoreland beginning in the late 1960's, collectors have all pounced on this ware; we only see an occasional piece in the shops & flea markets. 3⅜" tall. Scarce. Circa 1967-1974.

Sterling: Clear crystal glass; mold blown and pressed. This is an early pattern of the Westmoreland Speciality Company, patented Nov. 17, 1891. It later appeared in their 1896 catalog. 3⅜" tall. Very scarce. Circa 1891-1896.

Star and Diamond: Opaque blue; mold blown and pressed glass. This is one of several similar contemporary patterns produced by Westmoreland. The pattern comprises an intaglio starred panel above a diamond shaped panel, the center of which contains a small embossed rosette button. 3⅞" tall. Circa 1970-1980.

West Virginia Glass Company

The West Virginia Glass Company
Martins Ferry, Ohio
(1894-1899)

The West Virginia Glass Company was an apparent spin-off from the "Elson Glass Company." Records indicate that the principal company officer was Mr. H.E. Waddel.

The factory produced pressed and blown glassware along with commercial bar goods. After joining the National Glass Company in 1899, the factory no longer appeared in the various glass trade journals.

Optic, West Virginia's: Clear cranberry; mold blown. The pattern consists of a bulbous based shaker containing 12 wide vertical ribs. The term *Optic* was used by glassware manufacturers to describe deep vertical grooves (inside or outside) on a plain body. Pattern name by Kamm. Also produced in crystal, emerald green, amethyst and cobalt blue. 2¾" tall. Rare in cranberry. Circa 1895.

Fandangle: Opaque green glass; mold blown. The pattern consists of series of embossed dangling fans that cover two thirds of the shaker body. Pattern name by Peterson. Also produced in opaque white (the most common), crystal and blue. 2⅝" tall. Very scarce in opaque green. Circa 1895-1898.

Blue Opal: Clear blue opalescent glass; mold blown. This is a very striking opalescent pattern, particularly in blue. The fern optical effect is created by use of a dual mold process causing the fern pattern to appear on the inside of the glass. This shaker has a bulging base that tapers toward the top of its ringed neck. An alternate name for this pattern is "Opalescent Fern." However, salt shaker collectors will find it listed in Kamm and Peterson as "Blue Opal." We are retaining the name to avoid collector confusion. 3⅜" tall. Rare. Circa 1894.

Optic, Nine Rib: Opaque white opalware; mold blown. This is a bulbous based shaker that tapers at the top. The motif consists of nine wide vertical ribs. The decoration amounts to a large blue flowered floral spray. No doubt made in a variety of colors but we haven't seen any other than the shaker being illustrated. 3⅛" tall. Very scarce. Circa 1895-1898.

IOU: Clear emerald green pressed glass. The pattern spells out the letters "IOU." The U is bordered on each side by a notched pillar and encloses a notched oval to form IOU. Listed as West Virginia's No. 219. The pattern has a very high collectibility factor. We have never found one that was for sale. 2¾" tall. Rare. Circa 1898.

West Virginia Glass Company

Medallion Sprig: We are illustrating two shakers to establish pattern clarity for the reader. Shaded amethyst to crystal and opaque white; mold blown. The shaded amethyst is one of the rare colors; opaque white being the more common. The pattern consists of an embossed base medallion with a leaf-like sprig suspended directly above it. William Heacock wrote an excellent article[1] on the color rarities associated with this pattern. 3⅛" tall. Rare in amethyst. Circa 1894.

Pillar, West Virginia's Tapered: Opaque white opalware; mold blown. This is a plain bodied shaker with a deep cut groove at the neck and base. The center contains a large blue and yellow floral spray. We have no additional color experience to report. The shaker is very light in weight for its size. 3⅝" tall. Very scarce. Circa 1895-1898.

Potpourri

Potpourri

This section contains a miscellany of glass salt shaker patterns that are available to collectors and dealers. Unfortunately, we lacked sufficient authoritative criteria to be able to say which glass house/manufacturer produced it. Therefore, we have placed these patterns in a category of what collectors usually call "Unknowns."

In our introductory remarks we detailed the many pluses associated with this type of documented approach. After careful research, those patterns that have not yet been named in previous antique glassware publications, (we hope!) have been assigned pattern names. It should be noted that a good percentage of the assigned pattern names have been created by the collective efforts of the Antique & Art Glass Salt Shaker Collectors Society membership at the club's annual conventions.

All of the pattern names have been arranged in alphabetical order.

To all the beginner and advanced collectors we would like to emphasize that there are still many more discoveries to be made and researched. So, Come On! Join in the fun and satisfaction that antique glass salt shaker collecting offers.

Ada: Clear cranberry pressed glass. This is a pattern of the Ohio Flint Glass Company, Dunkirk, Indiana. The reader is referred to Kamm 7, 199. It is reported by Peterson as being rare in red. 2⅞" tall. Circa 1898.

Amberina Sphere: Clear divided amberina, fuchsia-red on one half and amber on the other (most unusual); dual mold blown. This is a simple pattern, smooth on the outside with IVT on the inside. It appears to be identical in shape to the Mt. Washington/Pairpoint Little Apple but slightly smaller in size. 1⅞" tall with a two piece metal top. Rare. Circa 1886-1888.

Aztec Carnival: Translucent marigold Carnival pressed glass. This is a variation of the Aztec pattern but produced in a rare carnival color. Pattern name by Bob Bruce. 1¾" tall with a two piece top. Very rare. Circa 1890-1900.

Acorn, Footed: Opaque opalware; mold blown and pressed. The pattern is pretty well described by the pattern name. We have no color experience to report. 3⅛" tall. Very scarce. Circa 1897-1905.

Arched Oval: Clear pressed crystal glass; with an unusual type of rotary agitator that fits through a hole in the bottom of the shaker and requires manual operation by means of a rotating motion to dislodge coagulated salt. The glass pattern name is by Millard. 3" tall. Very scarce. Circa 1890-1900.

Banded Shere: Opaque white opalware with a yellow band beneath a hand painted floral sprig; mold blown. The pattern amounts to a small sphere. We have no other color experience to report. 1⅞" tall. Scarce. Circa 1905-1910.

Baby Thumbprint, Bulging: Clear Amberina coloring, a fuchsia-red to delicate amber; dual mold blown; with a two piece metal top. The pattern is unusual because of the sharp bulging center. The baby thumbprint motif is on the inside surface of the shaker. 2½" tall Rare. Circa 1885-1887.

Potpourri

Barrel, Custard: Opaque custard glass; mold blown. This is a completely smooth barreled shaped piece with an elaborate grape and vine hand painted decoration. It gives off a striking fluoresence when subjected to black light radiation. 3½" tall. Rare. Circa 1886-1890.

Barrel, Dual Molded: Clear cranberry glass; dual mold blown. As the pattern name implies, this is a barrel-shaped shaker. This is high quality art glass with a high collectibility factor. 2⅜" tall with a two piece metal top. Rare. Circa 1884-1889.

Barrel, English: Opaque coral cased glass with a hand painted fruit vine outlined in coin gold; mold and free blown finished. As the pattern name implies, this is a barrel-shaped shaker. This is high quality art glass with a high collectibility factor. 2⅜" tall with a two piece metal top. Rare. Circa 1884-1889.

Barrel, Flat Top: Clear cranberry with large hand painted white and green leaves; dual mold blown. The pattern consists of a flat shouldered barrel that is smooth outside with an inside honey comb pattern. 3⅛" tall with a two piece metal top. Very scarce. Circa 1886-1890.

Barrel, IVT: Clear cranberry with a large hand painted orange and white floral spray; dual mold blown. Barrel shaped with a smooth exterior and an inverted thumbprint (IVT) interior. Probably Mt. Washington/Pairpoint piece. 3¼" tall with a two piece metal top. Very scarce. Circa 1886-1891.

Barrel, Little: Clear cranberry; mold blown. This is a smooth surfaced shaker with a two piece metal top and a ringed glass base. 1⅞" tall. Scarce. Circa 1889-1893.

Barrel, Narrow: Translucent blue opalescent glass; mold blown; with a two piece metal top. The pattern name provides an adequate physical description. The principal motif is the presence of wide vertical opalescent stripes with enameled flowers. 3¼" tall. Rare. Circa 1886-1890.

Baseball Player: Crystal glass with red and gilt (Goofus) decoration; mold blown. Issued to honor Babe Ruth and sought after by bottle, candy container and salt shaker collectors. Has an extremely high collectibility factor. Purchased from Arthur Peterson by Carl Just. By the time this book is published it will have been auctioned off in New York City. 5" tall. Rare. Circa: 1921-1931.

Barrel, Opalescent: Translucent milky white opalescent glass with a large hand painted floral spray. Mold blown; with a two piece metal top that is too large for the size of the shaker; it is our opinion that the original two piece top was smaller in size. 2¾" tall. Very scarce. Circa 1887-1891.

Barrel, Ringed: Opaque white opalware; mold blown. This is an excellent replica of a small barrel with embossed staves and rings. 2½" tall. Scarce. Circa 1903-1910.

Bead Band: Clear crystal mold blown and pressed glass. The shaker contains a band of fancy beads encircling the top and base. Also produced in ruby-stained with chocolate glass a possibility. We believe this to be a McKee pattern. 2⅞" tall. Very scarce. Circa 1900-1904.

Barrel, Souvenir: Opaque green glass; mold blown. A smooth surfaced shaker with a thin embossed ring near the top. Ideal for souvenir stencils at fairs, carnivals, etc. 2⅞" tall. Scarce. Circa 1898-1906.

Beaded Diamond and Scroll: Opaque hand tinted opalware; mold blown. An unusual pear-shaped shaker containing embossed beads and scrolls. The tiny beads have been configured to form diamonds. The green-to-tan shading is accomplished by hand and then fixed by heating in a muffle. 3" tall. Very scarce. Circa 1900-1909.

Beaded Drape: Opaque white opalware; mold blown. The pattern consists of six vertical draped columns covering two-thirds of the shaker; each column is separated by columns of small beads. Believed to be an Eagle Glass Co. pattern. 3¼" tall. Scarce. Circa 1900-1905.

Beaded Panel, Concave: Opaque white hand painted opalware; mold blown. Each panel is outlined by small embossed individual beads; two of the four panels contain hand painted rose sprigs. Believed to be a Fostoria pattern. 3" tall. Very scarce. Circa 1900-1906.

Beaded Flower: Opaque tan painted opalware; mold blown and pressed. The pattern consists of an embossed daisy flower inside a beaded panel. Pattern name by Peterson. Believed to be a Fostoria product. 2⅜" tall. Circa 1896-1905.

Beaded Lattice and Frame: Opaque white opalware; mold blown. The shaker body is covered with tiny embossed beads and a lattice frame on each of the four sides. Listed in *American Canadian Goblets* by Unitt. 3½" tall. Scarce. Circa 1895-1900.

Bell, Fancy: Translucent blue opalescent glass with a hand painted gold floral band encircling the shaker; mold blown. The bottom appears to be configured for use in a condiment set. Very difficult to photograph, but it contains an embossed swirl pattern that terminates at the base in a series of diamonds. 3" tall with a two piece metal top. Rare. Circa 1886-1890.

Beaded Ring, Footed: Opaque opalware with hand painted floral sprays; mold blown and pressed. We believe this to be a product of the Eagle Glass Company. However it is listed on page 65 of *Early Canadian Glass*. Bill Heacock created a considerable cloud of doubt about the Gerald Stevens books[1] in a major chapter of his book *Collecting Glass, Volume 2.* We will leave it up to our readers to render their own decision about this and some other Canadian glass shakers we have referenced to Canadian manufacture. 3⅛" tall. Scarce. Circa 1902-1906.

Beaded Ovals in Sand: Clear blue glass; mold blown. Contains beaded concave panels with white enamel painted dots. See Heacock Book I, page 14. 2¾" tall. Very scarce. Circa 1894-1900.

Beaded Vertical: Opaque white opalware; mold blown. This is a six lobed shaker; each lobe is separated by an embossed vertical string of beads. 2⅞" tall. Scarce. Circa 1904-1909.

Potpourri

Authors' Collection

Authors' Collection

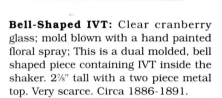

Witt Collection

Bell, Little: Clear deep amber glass; mold blown. As the pattern name implies, this piece is configured in the shape of a small bell. We believe this was a candy container that was configured for subsequent condiment dispenser use. No other color experience to report. 2⅛" tall. Circa 1912-1920.

Bell-Shaped IVT: Clear cranberry glass; mold blown with a hand painted floral spray; This is a dual molded, bell shaped piece containing IVT inside the shaker. 2⅞" tall with a two piece metal top. Very scarce. Circa 1886-1891.

McElderry' Collection

Beverly: Clear electric blue glass; dual mold blown. This is a smooth barrel-shaped shaker containing inside IVT. The hand applied enamel daisy flower decoration is outstanding. We believe this to be a Mt. Washington/Pairpoint product. 3⅛" tall with a two piece metal top. Very scarce. Circa 1888-1893.

Archer Museum Collection

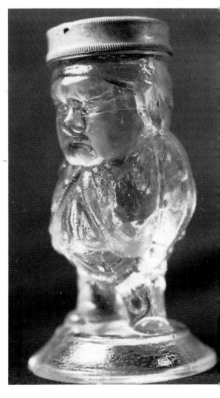

Benjamin Franklin: Clear pressed crystal glass. Sought after by figure bottle and salt shaker collectors; has an extremely high collectibility factor. The shaker we are illustrating is the only one that we have physically handled when we photographed it at the Archer Glass Museum at Kernersville, N.C. This is produced from a complicated mold with old Benjamin wearing an embossed powdered wig with the knotted braid showing at the back of his head. Trying to photograph this piece and get the facial features was a real challenge. 3¾" tall. Very rare. Circa 1875-1880.

Bell, Rubina: Clear deep red shading to crystal with elaborate hand painted floral sprays; mold and free blown finished. In its original silver plated stand, with high quality glass, the condiment set is in mint condition. The metal holder is 6½" tall and 5" long. The bottom is marked Aurora 336 Established 1869. 3" tall. Rare as a complete set. Circa 1883-1888

Bird: Translucent pressed glass in coral and pale green. This pair of birds was produced in Czcheckoslavkia in a variety of colors. They are cute little characters and have a high collectibility factor with their glass eyes and silver plated screw-on heads. The condiment dispensing holes are in the top of the heads. 2¾" tall. Scarce. Circa 1955-1963.

Billiken: Opaque opalware; mold blown. Again, you have a piece that is sought after by the bottle and salt collectors and the item has a very high collectibility factor. This item was patented on October 6, 1908 as a Design for an Image, by Florence Pretz of Kansas City, Mo. Patent No. 39603. 4" tall. Rare. Circa 1908.

Big Rib: Opaque white opalware; mold blown. The pattern consists of long, sharp, vertical ribs that separate plain panels. Occasionally found in chocolate[2] glass which is rare. 3¼" tall. Very scarce. Circa 1900-1904.

Bird Handled: Clear amber pressed glass. The principal pattern is that of an embossed bird (possibly a robin) in the center; a vertical distribution of beads that vary in size is present on each side of the shaker; each row of beads end in a scrolled projection at the top of the piece. This pattern was design patented on February 21, 1882 under patent No. 253,905. Produced in all colors some of which are opaque. 2⅞" tall. Very scarce. Circa 1882.

Potpourri

Bird, Paka: Clear crystal mold blown glass overlaid with English coin silver to form the body of a small bird (chick); the silver head plugs/pushes onto the body. The piece is engraved with the name "N Paka" which we have presumed to be the name of the designer. This is a real rarity and the craftsmanship is outstanding. It is our opinion that this a European produced piece. Rare. Circa 1895-1905.

Block Octagon: Opaque white opalware; mold blown and pressed. This is a wide squatty piece containing eight embossed square panels each containing a round button. This same base was also used for production on miniature oil lamps. Pattern name by Peterson. 2⅞" tall. Scarce. Circa 1903-1909.

Block Square: Opaque blue glass; mold blown. This is a square rounded shoulder shaped piece with outstanding detailed enamelling to create the illusion of a cameo cut shaker. The manufacturer succeeded because at a very short distance away it gives off the appearance of an expensive piece. It is our opinion that this was an early pepper dispenser. It has a two piece metal top and is the only shaker of this type that we have ever seen. 3⅜" tall. Rare. Circa 1870s.

Bristol: Opaque satinized opalware with excellent quality hand painted floral decoration that is outlined in heavy gold; mold blown. This shaker has a smooth glass exterior with a slightly bulging base. Decorated in the Thomas Webb technique and thought to be of English origin. 3" tall. Rare. Circa 1885-1890.

Bristol Bell: Opaque white satinized opalware; mold blown. The glass exterior is completely smooth & contains an elaborate hand painted floral spray with the flowers and leaves outlined in gold. Webb type decoration believed to be of European origin. The physical shape is described by the pattern name. We have provided two photos of this pattern, each decorated differently. 3½" tall. Rare. Circa 1885-1890.

Broken Rib: Opaque blue glassware; mold blown. The pattern consists of concave panels surrounded by large notched vertical ribs. A unique design. 2⅞" tall. Scarce. Circa 1897.

Bulb, Ringed Base: Clear cranberry glass with a hand painted blue and white floral band; mold blown; with a two piece metal top. This a small shaker containing two protruding base rings and an IVT pattern. 2¼" tall. Very scarce. Circa 1886-1891.

Bruce Lee: Clear cranberry glass; mold blown. The pattern consists of eight concave panels with a bulging base. Smooth homegenous glass; very utilitarian in appearance. 3¼" tall. Scarce. Circa 1897-1904.

Bristol, Ring Base: Translucent frosted Bristol glass mold blown. Old timer antique dealers called this glass "Clambroth." The shaker has a two piece metal top; we believe that the pattern name describes the physical configuration. There is an elaborate hand painted floral spray in the center. 3½" tall. Very scarce. Circa 1887-1895.

Potpourri

Bulbous Ribbed: Opaque chocolate glassware; mold blown. The pattern amounts to 18 protruding vertical ribs. The reader is referred to photo 206 of Measell's *Greentown Glass* for additional details. 3" tall. Rare. Circa 1900-1903.

Bulging Base, Tall: Clear blue glass with a hand painted floral sprig; mold blown. This a dual molded piece that has inside IVT. Also made in cranberry with hand decoration. The shaker is fitted with a two piece metal top. 2⅞" tall. Very scarce. Circa 1885-1891.

Bulging Cloud: Opaque blue glass; mold blown. This is a spheroid shaped shaker with an intricate embossed pattern that inspired Peterson to assign the unusual pattern name to the piece. It is our opinion that this is a Dithridge shaker. 3" tall. Scarce. Circa 1894-1900.

Bull's Eye & Daisy: Clear crystal with amber staining; mold blown and pressed. This is a unique as well as pretty piece; the condiment top is made of glass, which some of the factories manufactured in an effort to overcome the salt corrosion problems associated with metal tops after they had been in use for a while. The only problem with this was that the tops were soon broken due to table usage; they would not take any pounding to loosen up the congealed salt. This pattern is listed in Metz as her No. 2443 pattern. 3¼" tall. Very scarce. Circa 1897-1903.

Bungalow: Clear crystal pressed glass. The pattern consists of embossed rectangular blocks which are equally distributed around the shaker body. 3" tall. Scarce. Circa 1900-1903.

Buster Brown & Tige: Clear crystal glassware with minimal hand supplied paint; mold blown. This was an original candy container of the 1930's depicting the Comics character of Buster Brown with his dog Tige standing beneath his master's legs. Sought after by both the candy container collectors as well as the salt shaker collectors. The comic book characters have had a high collectibility factor for many years. The top is formed by Buster Brown's hat and contains the condiment dispensing holes. 2½" tall. Very scarce. Circa 1930-1935.

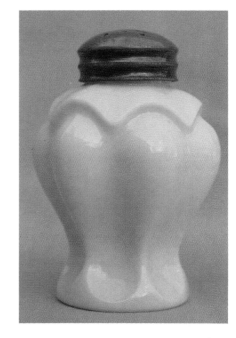

Buxom: Opaque off-white opalware; mold blown. The pattern contains an embossed scalloped curtain at the top with concave vertical panels that taper into a scalloped base. 2⅞" tall. Scarce. Circa 1899-1905.

Cameo: Translucent frosted free blown cameo glass with a two piece friction fit metal top. This piece has a bulb shape and contains blue leaves and gooseberries in raised relief. Considered to be English cameo art glass; shown in the colored art glass plate of Peterson's 1970 salt shaker book. Also made with the same motif having amber colored leaves & berries. 3¼" tall. Rare. Circa 1886-1894.

Cameo, Pseudo-Classic: The two shakers being shown (one in blue the other in red) are satinized homogeneous glass with outstanding hand painted decoration that gives the appearance of Cameo cut glass due to a 3D effect. They are mold blown with two piece metal tops. These are rectangular shaped pieces that contain no embossed pattern. 2⅝" tall. Rare. Circa: 1894-1900.

Potpourri

Candle, Small: Opaque white opalware with a sort of alabaster coloring; mold blown. Configured in the form of a small candle with a silver footed base. The tops are of sterling silver that push in by way of a guiding metal button and then lock by giving it a twist. 1¾" tall. Very scarce. Circa 1910-1920.

Cat, Contemporary: Translucent cranberry and pale green pressed glass. The two cats have silver plated heads and glass eyes. Made in most basic colors in Czechoslovakia. The heads unscrew for filling the condiment and the perforations are in the top of the head. These cuties have a high collectibility factor. 2¼" tall. Scarce. Circa 1955-1962.

Chevarie Pillar: Clear amber homogeneous glass; dual mold blown. with a two piece metal top. This is a round shaped pillar that is smooth on the outside with wide inside ribbing that creates an optic ribbing effect. The glass is of high quality with hand painted daisies and sunflowers We believe this to be a Mt. Washington/Pairpoint shaker. 3½" tall. Rare. Circa 1885-1890.

Carnival Corn: We are showing two identical shakers; one in peacock and the other in marigold carnival color. This is early carnival glass that is sought after by both figure bottle and salt shaker collectors. The peacock colored shaker was acquired from the Arthur Peterson collection by Carl Just; the marigold shaker is from the Bruce collection. These are mold and free blown finished pieces. The pattern is a tapered ear of corn with embossed husks. 4⅜" tall. Both are very rare and of equal value. Circa 1896-1905.

Chinese Lantern: Translucent opalescent glass; mold blown. The pattern consists of a continuous series of vertical concave lobed ribs that form a narrow circular base. Pattern name by Peterson who states that there are two types. We have only seen a half-a-dozen of these pieces in our 35+ years of collecting. 2½" tall. Rare. Circa 1887-1892.

Circle and Fan: We have provided a complete condiment set. Mold blown and pressed. Shakers - 2⅝" tall; condiment stand - 4⅛" tall. Very scarce. Circa 1898-1905.

Clover and Rosette: Opaque white opalware with worn base coloring; mold blown. Pillar shaped with a slightly bulged out base containing embossed clover and rosettes that alternate in their vertical distribution. 3⅜" tall. Scarce. Circa 1900-1910.

Column, Tiny: Opaque white opalware; mold blown with a hand painted floral spray over a tan colored background; 3" tall with a two piece metal top. This is a plain cylinder shape. Scarce. Circa 1890-1896.

Concave Bulb, Nakara: Opaque white opalware; mold blown with an Indian transfer motif over a tan colored background. This is Nakara type decoration[3]. The physical shape is identical to the Concave Bulb Niagara Falls shaker. Rare. Circa 1903-1906.

Columbus, Bearded: Opaque nile green; mold blown. Has the word "Columbus" embossed on the rounded base. Pattern name by Peterson. Outstanding detail & mold work. Sold at auction in 1990 for $1,200.00. 3½" tall. Very Rare. Circa 1892-1900.

Concave Bulb, Niagara Falls: Opaque white opalware; mold blown with a transfer scene of Niagara Falls applied over a tan painted background. We believe that this is C.F. Monroe Nakara decoration. 2⅝" tall. Rare. Circa 1903-1906.

Concave Crackle: Clear light green crackle glass with hand painted flowers and leaves; mold and free blown finished; with a two piece metal top. The shaker is rounded at the top but becomes square-shaped with concave panels in the center. 2¼" tall. Rare. Circa 1886-1891.

Concave Paneled: Opaque variegated opalware; mold blown. Has four concave panels that are rounded at the shaker base. This is an unusual mixture of white and chocolate glass coloring. Also made in opaque white; we have no other color experience to report. 2⅜" tall. Very scarce. Circa 1900-1908

Convex, Footed: Opaque jade green homogeneous glass; mold blown. The glass is of excellent quality & seldom seen in salt shakers. Thought to be a product of the Fenton Art Glass Company. 3¼" tall. Very scarce. Circa 1928-1936.

Convex Paneled: Opaque white opalware; mold blown. Has narrow convex panels with an embossed floral sprig; above each foot is series of embossed scrolls. Pattern name by Warman. 3¼" tall. Scarce. Circa 1899-1906.

Coquette: Clear rubina shading from red to crystal; mold blown. This is a barrel shaped piece with the exterior containing a slightly raised series of veins that can be felt both inside & outside. Most unusual. 3" tall. Rare. Circa 1886-1891.

Coquette Variant: Clear rubina with elaborate hand painted decoration of flowers, leaves and a diving gold colored bird. The shaker is slightly taller than "Coquette" but is of the same basic veined pattern. Pattern name by Shirley McElderry. Rare. Circa 1886-1891.

Coralene on Bristol: Blue opaque glass; mold blown; with a two piece metal top. This is a cylinder shaped shaker containing hand applied Coralene beads that form the petals of a flower. Probably an English piece. 2½" tall. Rare. Circa 1889-1895.

Coreopsis: Opaque white opalware with a hand painted daisylike red flower; mold blown. The pattern consists of a long necked shaker with a row of beads above & below its bulging base. Also made in red satin. 3⅜" tall. Very scarce. Circa 1900-1902.

Corn, Mustard: Opaque white opalware; mold blown. It may not look like a mustard to you, but it is. Some dealer put a salt shaker top on this Libbey Maize condiment set mustard. It fooled Peterson too because he named it "Corn, Bulging" until he later discovered that it was a part of the aforementioned condiment set and corrected the record in his 1970 salt shaker book. See our write up on the Libbey Glass Company for more information relative to this type of ware. 2¾" tall. Circa 1889.

Corn, Barrel: Opaque opalware; mold blown. The name of this shaker pretty much describes the pattern. The reader is referenced to page 175, Fig. 145 of *Glass In Canada* by Gerald Stevens. We believe that this is an American made shaker. Pattern name by Peterson who lists it as rare. 3" tall. Circa 1894-1900.

Potpourri

Cotton Candy: Translucent satinized glass shading from rose to a delicate pink; mold blown. This is a rounded bulging shaped piece with a rolled-lip base. Excellent quality glass and quite unique. No other color experience to report because this cutie is rare. 2⅝" tall. Circa 1887-1894.

Creased Neck, Burmese: Opaque satinized yellow homogeneous glass; mold blown with hand painted stemmed berries. Since this piece was not reheated at the Glory Hole to achieve the classic Burmese pink to yellow shading, it is considered to be an "Undeveloped Burmese" piece. The shaker has a striking fluorescence when subjected to black light illumination. We believe that this is a Mt. Washington/Pairpoint item. Rare. Circa 1886-1888.

Creased Neck, Cameo: Clear amber homogeneous glass; mold blown; with a two piece metal top. A smooth pillar shaped piece with heavy applied white, yellow and brown enamelling to produce a pseudo cameo effect. It is our opinion that this is a Mt. Washington/Pairpoint shaker. 3⅛" tall. Very scarce.

Creased Neck Column: Clear amber homogeneous glass; mold blown with a thick white enamel painted floral spray. The artistic decoration has been applied in such a manner that a cameo effect is produced. The glass quality is outstanding. Thought to be a Mt. Washington/Pairpoint shaker. 3⅞" tall with a two piece metal top. Rare. Circa 1886-1892.

Cosmos Band: Opaque blue glass with gilt outlining type decoration; mold blown. This is a squatty spheroid shaped shaker with an embossed group of interspersed flower petals covering the entire piece. Pattern name by Peterson who considered it to be rare. 1⅞" tall. Circa 1898-1905.

Creased Neck Pair: Opaque opalware glass with a pastel blue painted background containing a matched pair of decorated shakers. This style glass shape was extensively used by C.F. Monroe in their transfer type decorative practices. The reader is referred to page 88 of *Wave Crest Ware* by Elsa Grimmer which is a reprint of the No. 6 C.F. Monroe 1900-1901 catalog. Finding a matched pair is a rarity. Most of this style blank was acquired from the Mt. Washington/Pairpoint Glass house by Monroe. It is our opinion that this is Wave Crest ware. Circa 1900-1903.

Creased Neck, Floral: Clear amber homogeneous glass; mold blown; with a two piece metal top. This is a smooth cylinder shaped piece with hand painted flowers and leaves covering the shaker body. Thought to be Mt. Washington/Pairpoint. 3¾" tall. Very scarce. Circa 1886-1891.

Creased Neck, Tapered: Opaque opalware glass; mold blown. Smooth cylinder shaped with a two story hand painted country home[4] over an off-white painted background. The shaker has a two piece metal top. The creased neck pattern was widely used by Mt. Washington/Pairpoint, C.F. Monroe and the Smith Brothers for both hand painted and transfer types of decorations involving a variety of motifs. It is our opinion that this shaker is a Mt. Washington/Pairpoint piece. 3½" tall. Very scarce. Circa 1890-1894.

Crocus: Opaque white opalware; mold blown. This is a vertical panelled concavity with a band of intaglio pointed leaves surrounding the base. Also made in opaque blue, green and pink. 3⅛" tall. Circa 1903-1908.

Potpourri

Cuban: Opaque cased glass; mold blown. This is a bulbous nine panelled shaker with a beaded neck collar; each vertical panel is separated by four beads. A trade ad indicates that this ware was sold by "Ball and Crowl" of Wellsburg, West Virginia. Apparently they were some type of wholesale jobber/distributor. Also made in opaque white and crystal. 2¼" tall. Very scarce in cased glass. Circa 1900-1904.

Cross Swirl, Opalescent: Translucent opalescent canary yellow glass; mold blown. The pattern amounts to an intricate embossed cross swirled pattern. 2½" tall. Very scarce. Circa 1887-1891.

Crossroads, Double: Clear amber homogeneous glass; mold blown. This is a square shaped shaker with embossed crossing diagonal lines that apparently prompted Dr. Peterson to assign it the aforesaid pattern name. Also produced in crystal and blue. 3⅛" tall. Circa 1880-1890.

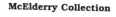

Cube, Black: Opaque black homogeneous glass; mold blown and pressed. Except for a slightly rounded shoulder, this is a perfect square shaped cube. The flowered motif has been hand painted with heavy enamelling. The inside of the shaker contained a patented Crossman Agitator (see book patent section). 3¾" tall. Rare. Circa 1872-1880.

Coat of Mail: Opaque white opalware; mold blown. The embossed pattern is reminiscent of a coat of mail which covers the lower half of the shaker. Also produced in other opaque colors some which are hand decorated. 2⅝" tall. Scarce. Circa 1904-1908.

Curl and Scroll: Opaque opalware; mold blown. This is a small spheroid shaker that contains three round windows that are formed by surrounding embossed scroll; the base has twelve small scrolls in raised relief. Pattern name by Peterson. 2⅝" tall. Scarce. Circa 1905.

Cohen Collection

Cylinder, Round Topped: Clear crystal to cranberry; sort of a reverse rubina; mold blown. Contains hand painted daisy flowers with orange colored vines. The shaker has a two piece metal top. 2" tall. Very scarce. Circa 1885-1892.

McElderry Collection

Cylinder, Short: Clear cranberry with hand decorated floral sprigs; mold blown; with a two piece metal top. Made of quality glass, this is a small pillar shaped shaker. 2" tall Very scarce. Circa 1884-1890.

Authors' Collection

Cylinder, Slender: Clear cranberry glass; mold blown with beautiful hand applied enamel decoration showing a pair of birds perched among branches and leaves. Rare. Circa 1884-1890.

Authors' Collection

Daisy & Button Barrel: Clear electric blue glass; mold blown with top & bottom glass threads. This is an unusual shaker because the bottom is threaded and a metal foot screws on it to form a base support. Every other panel contains the embossed daisy & button pattern. 3" tall. Very scarce. Circa 1878-1888.

Authors' Collection

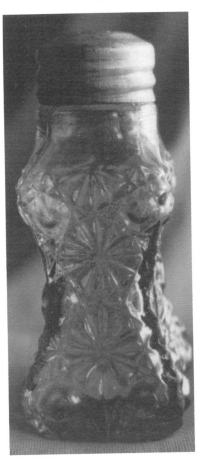

Daisy & Button, Plain: Clear amber homogeneous glass; mold blown. This shaker contains three large daisy & buttons on each of the four sides which represents the principal motif. Also made in crystal and blue. 3⅛" tall. Scarce. Circa 1878-1885.

Potpourri

Authors' Collection

Authors' Collection

Authors' Collection

Daisy & Button, Slender: Clear blue and amber pressed glass. Pattern name by Peterson. Each shaker has a peg hole in the bottom for retention in the glass condiment holder. It is most difficult to find a complete set that isn't chipped due to usage. The blue/amber shakers are the way these sets were originally sold. Shakers-2½"; glass holder-5⅞" tall. Rare as a complete set. Circa 1875-1885.

Daisy & Button, Square: Translucent blue glass; mold blown. This is a rectangular shape shaker; each side contains a row of three large buttons; the daisy flowers are bent in the middle at each sharp corner. The pattern is so heavily embossed and busy that it makes the glass translucent. 3¼" tall. Very scarce. Circa 1878-1887.

Daisy, Netted Panel: Opaque white opalware; mold blown. This is a very small piece with a ringed neck and a bulging base. The motif consists of an embossed daisy and leaf within a fine netted panel. 1⅞" tall. Circa 1901-1907.

McElderry Collection

Lockwood Collection

Daisy Sprig: Opaque satinized opalware; we illustrated the two larger shakers in our first book, since that time a still smaller one has been discovered making these shakers a family. It is interesting to note that they are always decorated with the hand painted daisy sprigs. All are mold blown. Two photos are shown; one protrays all three as a group; the other shows the small shaker by itself since it has never been published before. In our opinion, these are Mt. Washington/Pairpoint piece. Their sizes are: small-1⅞"; medium-2½"; large-3". Very scarce. Circa 1896-1902.

Daisy and Scroll: Opaque white opalware; mold blown. The pattern consists of daisy flowers interspersed with scrolls; all of which are embossed. We have no additional color experience to report. 2⅜" tall. Scarce. Circa 1901-1906.

Diamond Base: Opaque white opalware; mold blown. This is a bulbous base shaker with a large band of small embossed diamonds encircling the base. The upper part of the shaker contains a large hand painted floral spray. 3" tall. Scarce. Circa 1900-1907.

Diamond Point Corner: Opaque blue glass; mold blown. Has a rounded body that tapers into a square base. Each corner contains a series of small embossed diamonds within a rounded panel. Pattern name by. A.G. Peterson. 2½" tall. Scarce. Circa 1894-1901.

Diamond Panels: Opaque blue glass; mold blown. The principal pattern amounts to four large embossed diamonds encircling the shaker. For additional information the reader is referred to page 165, Fig. 131. of *Glass In Canada* by Gerald Stevens. This a rare shaker. 2¾" tall. Circa 1885-1890.

Diamond Point Discs: Clear crystal pressed glass. The principal pattern consists of circular discs uniformly filled in with diamond point. Pattern name by Kamm. 2¼" tall. Circa 1897-1904.

Dice, Double: Opaque white opalware; mold blown. The pattern is a replica of stacked dice with a mid-section twist. Has a very high collectibility factor. 3⅜" tall. Very rare. Circa 1890-1897.

Potpourri

Diamond Point and Punty: Clear crystal pressed glass. This is a tall shaker containing 24 sharp base ribs; the remainder of the shaker contains numerous embossed diamond points. Pattern name by Peterson. 3" tall. Very scarce. Circa 1890-1900.

Diving Bell: Opaque custard glass; mold blown. The pattern name is a good description of the embossed motif on this spheroid shaped shaker. 1⅞" tall. Rare. Circa 1899-1904.

Divided Panel: Opaque white opalware; mold blown. This is a small shaker with curved bulging panels accentuated by embossed vertical ribs. Pattern name by Warman. 2¼" tall. Scarce. Circa 1899-1907.

Dixie Belle: Clear crystal pressed glass. The principal motif is a large embossed flower within a diamond shaped panel. Pattern name by Millard. 2⅞" tall. Circa 1896-1903.

Domino: Opaque white opalware; mold blown. This piece looks like a stacked pair of dice that are bonded together. The odd thing about the dot configuration is that there are three fives on the dice. 3¼" tall. Very scarce. Circa 1894-1900.

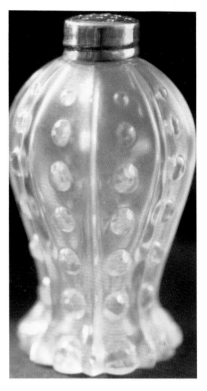

Doodler's Scroll: Opaque white opalware; mold blown. This is a busy pattern in which the primary motif lies within vertical recessed panels and consists of an intricate vertical scroll from the top to the base of the shaker. Pattern name by Warman. 3¼" tall. Scarce. Circa 1899-1906.

Dottie: Translucent canary yellow glass; mold blown. This is a lovely satinized piece with curved panels and embossed buttons. Also produced in opaque white. 3" tall. Scarce. Circa 1920.

Double Creased: Opaque red cased glass; mold blown with hand painted white flowers and leaves. With the exception of a deep double creased body this a smooth surfaced shaker. It also has an unusually large two piece metal top. It is our opinion that this piece is of European origin. 3¾" tall. Rare. Circa 1885-1891.

Draped Bow: Opaque white opalware; mold blown. The overall shape is that of a spheroid with a protruding neck ring; the principal motif is a large drooping ribbon bow in raised relief. 2⅜" tall. Scarce. Circa 1900-1907.

Dual Scroll: Opaque white opalware; mold blown with a hand painted floral sprig. The pattern consists of two bands of scrolls, one at the top and the other at the base of the shaker; both are in raised relief. 2¼" tall. Circa 1900-1906.

223

Potpourri

Egg, Tapered: Opaque white opalware; mold blown; with a tin screw-on metal top. The base appears to be configured for use with a condiment set. 1⅞" tall. Circa 1910-1916.

Egg, Pressure Top: Opaque white opalware; mold blown. This egg shaped shaker is unique because it contains a tensioned spring fingered metal top that snaps into place by use of hand pressure. It is functional, but rather awkward to operate. 2" tall. Scarce. Circa 1908-1915.

Egg-Shaped: Opaque opalware; mold blown. This is a round smooth surfaced piece containing an Indian on horseback. The decoration was achieved by use of a transfer technique that has been applied over a reddish brown back ground. This shaker appears to be C. F. Monroe using their Nakara type decoration. 2¼" tall. Rare. Circa 1901-1904.

Elephant Toes: Clear crystal pressed glass. Bill Heacock named this pattern and pictured it on page 28 of his Book 5 (U.S. Glass). Flashed colors are a good possibility, but we haven't seen any in salt shakers. 3½" tall. Very scarce. Circa 1905.

Ellen's Rubina: Clear rubina glassware with large hand painted daisies; mold blown; with a two piece metal top. This is a sharply defined vertical panelled piece with excellent coloring. It is our opinion that this is a Mt. Washington/Pairpoint shaker. 2⅝" tall. Rare. Circa 1885-1890.

Elongated Drops: Opaque white opalware; mold blown with hand painted floral sprigs interspersed throughout the shaker. The pattern amounts to various sized pointed lobes that are somewhat reminiscent of large water drops. Pattern name by Warman. 3⅛" tall. Scarce. Circa 1895-1902.

Elvira's Butterfly: Clear cranberry glass; dual mold blown with a pretty hand painted butterfly. The pattern consists of tiny IVT on the inside with the outside glass being a completely smooth surface. 2½" tall. Rare. Circa 1886-1891.

Enveloping Leaf; Clear green glass; mold blown. This is a short flat bulging shaker containing deeply embossed wide leaves. A most unique design. The overall glass quality is excellent. We believe this to be a Fostoria shaker. 2⅜" tall. Scarce. Circa 1896-1903.

Fancy Fans: Opaque white opalware with a hand painted floral band encircling the center of the shaker; mold blown. This is a bulging shaker with a band of embossed small fans at the top and base. Pattern name by Heacock. Known production in other colors, but we haven't seen them in shakers. 2⅝" tall. Scarce. Circa 1899-1905.

Fan, Beaded: Opaque white opalware, mold blown and pressed. Each side of this bulbous shaker contains an embossed fan. Pattern name by Warman. 2⅝" tall. Circa 1900-1906.

Fan Footed Scroll: Opaque white opalware; mold blown. The pattern name pretty much describes the piece. All the pattern is at the base. The center portion contains a handpainted floral sprig. 2" tall. Scarce. Circa 1898-1904.

Fan Tail: Translucent blue opalescent glass; mold blown. This piece contains four large embossed plumes or fans within a stippled background (sometimes called "Diamond Point"). For another opinion, see page 175, Fig. 144, *Glass In Canada* by Gerald Stevens. Pattern name by Peterson who lists this shaker as Rare. 2¾" tall. Circa 1894-1900.

Potpourri

Feather Panel: Opaque white opalware; mold blown with an embossed hand painted center that looks like a feather. With the exception of the center panel motif, this shaker has the same physical shape of the "Plume Panel" shaker. 2⅜" tall. Scarce. Circa 1900-1906.

Five Panel, Footed: Opaque white opalware; mold blown and pressed. The pattern amounts to five plain panels separated by a sharp vertical rib above a footed support base. We have no color experience to report. 2¾" tall. Circa 1904-1910.

Fern Condiment: Opaque opalware with hand painted red fern sprigs; mold blown and pressed. The condiment dispensers are plain except for a protruding neck ring. Shakers- 3¼"; mustard- 3" tall. The scalloped opalware base measured 5½" in diameter. Very scarce. Circa 1900-1907.

Flared Base, Wave Crest: Opaque opalware enhanced with a house and tree painted scene by use of a transfer technique; mold blown. This is "Wave Crest"[5] type decoration and in our opinion a product of C.F. Monroe. The overall pattern constitutes a smooth surface shaker with a protruding neck ring and a flared base. 2⅞" tall. Rare. Circa 1895-1896.

Flat Panel: Opaque white opalware; mold blown. The pattern consists of six flat panels outlined with embossed scrolls and five petaled flower. Pattern name by E.G. Warman. Probably an Eagle Glass Co. product. 2¼" tall. Scarce. Circa 1899-1905.

Fleur-De-Lis, Beaded: Opaque homogeneous blue glass; mold blown. Each scroll & bead outlined panel contains an embossed fleur-de-lis. Pattern name by Peterson. 2¼" tall. Scarce. Circa 1894-1900.

Flower, Footed: Opaque white opalware which no doubt was at one time hand painted; mold blown & pressed. The shaker body is entirely covered with embossed flowers above a footed base. Pattern name by Warman. 2⅝" tall. Scarce. Circa 1902-1910.

Flower on Globe: Opaque white opalware; mold blown. Contains a large embossed flower and vine. The color is suffering somewhat from the ravages of time. 2¾" tall. Circa 1904-1910.

Flower Sprig: Opaque green glass; mold blown. This is a spheroid shaped shaker containing an embossed large flower and vine in raised relief. Also made in opaque white and blue. 2¾" tall. Very scarce. Circa 1896-1900.

Fleur-De-Lis, Six: Two shakers are illustrated; one is opaque white; the other is translucent amber glass; mold blown. These are flat bulging based shakers each containing six fleur-de-lis in raised relief. The reader is referred to *Glass In Canada* by Gerald Stevens for his opinion. 3⅛" tall. Very scarce. Circa 1890.

Floral Complex: Opaque white opalware; mold blown. This embossed pattern is extremely complicated, consisting of a series of vertical vines and corner flowers. You will have no trouble in identifying this piece when it is seen. The mold designer of this shaker seems to have had a vivid imagination. 2¾" tall. Scarce. Circa 1901-1908.

Avery Collection

Authors' Collection

Authors' Collection

Flower with Cane: Clear pressed crystal glassware. This pattern was named by Bill Heacock and is listed in his book *1000 Toothpicks*. The principal motif is pretty much described by the pattern name. We have never seen this pattern before and do not know if it was made in opaque colors. 3⅜" tall. Very scarce. Circa 1895-1905.

Flower and Triangle: Opaque opalware; mold blown and pressed. This piece contains six concave vertical panels with an embossed flower upon a series of intaglio shaped base triangles. 3¼" tall. Scarce. Circa 1902-1908.

Flower Windows: Opaque frosted (clambroth) glass; mold blown and pressed. This is a tall, narrow pillar shaped piece containing an embossed stippled band at the top and base; the center contains small flowers in raised relief. Pattern name be Peterson. 3⅞" tall. Scarce. Circa 1890.

McElderry Collection

McElderry Collection

McElderry Collection

Flute: Opaque white opalware; mold blown & pressed. A bulging shaker with a footed base. The motif consists of a band of vertical flutes in raised relief. Pattern name by Peterson. 3⅛" tall. Circa 1899-1905.

Foliage: Opaque white opalware; mold blown & pressed. This is a bulbous footed shaker containing floral foliage in raised relief. No doubt made in other colors but we haven't seen any. 2¾" tall. Scarce. Circa 1906-1911.

Footed Six Lobe: Opaque white opalware; mold blown & pressed. The pattern consists of six lobes that are divided by three ribs on each side. No color experience to report. 3⅛" tall. Scarce. Circa 1902-1908.

Four Panels: Opaque white opalware; mold blown. A slightly bulging four panelled shaker that is formed by embossed wide scrolls that give the appearance of a handle. 3" tall. Circa 1901-1907.

Frisco: Clear crystal pressed glassware. This pattern appears in Bill Heacock's *1000 Toothpicks* and we presume that he named it. The principal pattern amounts to a continuous series of embossed bead outlined diamond shapes. No color experience to report. 3" tall. Scarce. Circa 1895-1905.

Frosted Rubina: Translucent rose to a frosted crystal with a hand decorated floral band; the foliage is outlined in gold paint; mold and free blown finished; with a two piece metal top. This is a bulb shaped shaker, believed to be a product of the New England Glass Company. 2⅝" tall. Rare. Circa 1884-1887.

Gibson Girl: Clear crystal pressed glass. The four medallions in high raised relief are supposed to be a copy of "The Gibson Girl"[6] that appeared in the form of ink sketches in Life Magazine around 1899 to 1905. Pattern name by Kamm. 3¼" tall. Rare. Circa 1900-1905.

Geranium: Opaque opalescent art glass; mold blown; with (as Peterson put it) "enamelled flora in colors" and a two piece metal top. Close examination of the basic shaker reveals that underneath all that fancy floral motif is milky-white opalescent glass. This is an unusually heavy shaker because the glass pillar has very thick walls. The bottom is undecorated and here is where you can see the opalescent translucent glass. All the decoration is hand applied and to top the whole thing off it is an extremely rare shaker. The over all quality is outstanding with the enamel paint in mint condition. This ware has a very high collectibility factor. Pattern name by Peterson. 3" tall. Extremely rare. Circa 1885-1890.

Bruce Collection

Avery Collection

Authors' Collection

Gold Nuggets: Opaque cobalt blue cased glass with gold flecks; mold blown; with a two piece metal top. This effect was created by using a spangled glass/Vasa Murrhina process. The physical characteristics are a slightly curved pillar with embossed pairs of rings. The outer glass layer is amber colored which enhances the appearance of the gold flecks. It is really a beautiful shaker and the picture doesn't pick up all the art glass characteristics. 3¼" tall. Rare. Circa 1888-1894.

Grand (Diamond Medallion): Clear pressed crystal glass. The principal motif is a large embossed diamond within a square panel. Kamm attributes this pattern to Bryce Higbee & Co. (See Kamm 8, 119). 3½" tall. Scarce. Circa 1877-1882.

Grape Concave: Opaque white opalware; mold blown. The pattern consists of two bands of grapes and leaves, one at the top and the other at the shaker base. Pattern name by Peterson. 2⅜" tall. Scarce. Circa 1900-1908.

McElderry Collection

Avery Collection

McEdlerry Collection

Grated Arch: Opaque white opalware; mold blown. The pattern consists of eight arches with depressed centers, separated by ridges. Pattern name by Peterson. 2⅝" tall. Scarce. Circa 1899-1905.

Grill & Scroll: Opaque white opalware; mold blown. This is a bulging vertical panelled piece with an embossed top scrolled motif forming a type of grill work. The body contains a hand painted floral spray. 3" tall. Circa turn of the twentieth century.

Hand With Ring (Beggars Hand): Clear amber mold blown and pressed glass. The basic stand is amber colored glass with two extended hands each holding a cup which holds a shaker. 7⅜" tall including metal handle. Each shaker measures 2⅝" tall. Rare. Circa 1875-1882.

Grecian Goddess: Opaque white opalware; mold blown & pressed. Patented March 30, 1937 by Robert Dorfman and Eugene Munk as a "Design for a Jar or Similar Container" (See patent section). This figural piece was shown in our first book on page 90. 3" tall. Very scarce. Circa 1937.

Haines: Clear crystal glass; mold blown. A simple bottle shape that contains inside stems or projections to break up lumpy salt as the bottle is shaken. Patented on June 4, 1878 as an "improvement in dredge bottles" by John W. Haines of Cambridge, Massachusetts (see patent section). Made in clear crystal only. 4" tall; also made in a 2⅝" tall size. Very rare. Circa 1878.

Hanging Lantern Condiment: Clear amber homogeneous glass; mold blown. The pattern name seems to convey a satisfactory description of this ware. This is a unique set with the companion pressed glass holding stand. 2¼" tall. Very scarce. Circa 1909-1917.

Heart Shaped: Opaque opalware with a very large hand painted floral spray over a red and beige background; mold blown and pressed. A completely smooth surfaced piece in the overall shape of a heart. Typical decorative practices of Fostoria on some of their lower priced pieces during this time frame. No doubt made in various colors over a basic opalware blank. 2⅝" tall. Very scarce. Circa 1902-1908;

Potpourri

Authors' Collection

Lockwood Collection Lockwood Collection

Heron and Lighthouse: Opaque white opalware; mold blown. This a rectangular shaped shaker containing an embossed heron and light house on opposite sides. Pattern name by Peterson. Obviously produced in hand painted colors over the basic white opalware. 3⅛" tall. Scarce. Circa 1900-1910.

Hexaglory: We are providing two photos that show the only two known colors that this ware was produced in; translucent frosted Rubina and Opaque custard both containing elaborate hand painted floral sprays; mold and free blown finished art glass. As the pattern name indicates, this is a six sided shaker in the form of an elongated hexagon as viewed from the bottom. The custard shakers give off a striking fluorescence when exposed to black light radiation. Pattern name by Marilyn Lockwood. Also produced in a special designed condiment set which is illustrated in our "Outstanding Rarities" group. The shakers by themselves are rare; as a complete condiment with special stand and a Rubina and Custard shaker, very rare. 2½" tall with two piece metal tops. Circa 1885-1890.

Authors' Collection

Authors' Collection

Hobnail, Sunk-in: Translucent cranberry opalescent glass; mold blown. The motif consists of opalescent hobs interspersed with the cranberry coloring. This type of ware was made by more than one glasshouse and would therefore necessitate multiple attribution. 3⅛" tall with a two piece metal top. Rare. Circa 1885-1891.

Hexagon, Paneled Rib: Clear lime green glass; mold & free blown finished. This is a six panelled piece that bulges outward toward the base and contains a base that has been configured for use within a condiment holder. Probably produced in crystal as well as other colors. 2⅞" tall with a two piece metal top. Scarce. Circa 1890.

Hobnail, Variant: Translucent blue pressed glass. A round pillar shaped shaker completely covered with small pointed hobs. It is our opinion that this is a reissued piece from an old mold. The original hobnail shakers were produced only in crystal. 2⅝" tall. Circa 1955-1965.

Honeycomb, Miniature: Translucent rose shading to frosted crystal; mold blown with a large hand painted floral spray.Has two fronts and back flat panels with narrow rounded sides. This is a very similar decorative technique to that of the "Hexaglory" shakers. 1¾" tall with two piece metal top. Rare. Circa 1880.

Honeycomb, Beehive: Clear blue glass; dual mold blown with hand painted white daisy flowers interconnected by narrow stems. This is a somewhat dome shaped piece; the honeycomb pattern stands out behind the enamelled floral decoration. 2⅛" tall with a two piece metal top. Very scarce. Circa 1882-1890.

Honeycomb, Rubina-Verde: Clear shaded rose to a pale green; dual mold blown. This is a cylindrical shaped piece that is smooth on the outside with a honeycomb pattern inside. 3⅝" tall. Very scarce. Circa 1889-1894.

Honeycomb, Small: Clear cranberry glass; dual mold blown. This piece has a slight spheroid shape; smooth on the outside with the honeycomb pattern on the inside. A band of hand painted flowers encircles the shaker. 2½" tall with a two piece metal top. Very scarce. Circa 1883-1890.

Authors' Collection

Just Collection

Authors' Collection

Horn: Clear cobalt blue pressed glass. Configured in the shape of the so-called "Horn of Plenty" pattern with a footed base. Also produced in clear crystal. 1⅛" tall. Rare in cobalt blue. Circa 1896-1900.

Irregular Pillars: Opaque white opalware; mold blown with a hand painted floral sprig. The pattern consists of a slightly expanded round pillar with varying sized vertical ribs at the top and bottom. Also produced in opaque blue and green and perhaps other colors. 2¾" tall. Scarce. Circa 1899-1904.

Honeycomb, Tall: Clear amber mold blown glass. This is a round pillar shaped shaker completely covered by a small honeycomb pattern. 3" tall. Circa 1883-1890.

McElderry Collection

Authors' Collection

Horseshoe, Little: Opaque blue and white opalware (two shakers shown); mold blown. Patented in 1900 via patent No. 32,307. The pattern is that of a horseshoe in high raised relief. Has a high collectibility factor; sought after by both bottle and salt shaker collectors. 3" tall. Rare. Circa 1900.

Horseshoe, Big: Clear amber glass; mold blown. Design patented 1900, comes in two sizes. The amber containers were used initially for marketing snuff[7]. 3¾" tall.

Authors' Collection

Just Collection

McElderry Collection

Hybrid, Covered: A clear glass tube with bottom threads onto which this elaborate silver plated cover screws. In our first book we illustrated other variations of this piece all of which were produced by the International Silver Co. in Meriden, Conn. We added this in hopes that it will complete the series. Circa 1898-1900.

Isabella: Opaque green glass; mold blown and pressed. This a companion to the "bearded Columbus" shaker and is embossed with the word "Isabella" on the footed base. Pattern name by Peterson. The mold work on this piece is outstanding with lots of detail. Has an extremely high collectibility factor. 3⅝" tall. Very rare. Circa 1892-1900.

IVT, Dainty: Clear amber homogeneous glass; dual mold and free blown finished. The outer glass surface is smooth; the inner surface contains tiny IVT. The shaker is covered by a heavy enamelled floral spray. 2¼" tall with a two piece metal top. Very scarce. Circa 1885-1891.

McElderry Collection

Authors' Collection

IVT Barrel Condiment: Clear fuchsia-red Amberina that extends approximately ¾ of the way downward on both shakers and then shades into a soft amber; dual mold blown. Each shaker is elaborately hand decorated with hand painted floral sprays; one shaker displays a dragonfly in flight. The silver plated condiment holder was made by Aurora S.P. Co. This ware is barrel shaped; smooth on the outer surface with IVT inside. 3⅛" tall with two piece metal tops. Rare. Circa 1884-1886.

IVT Pillar, Small: Clear cranberry glass; dual mold blown with a hand painted floral sprig. The pattern consists of a small round shaped pillar that is smooth on the outside and contains inverted thumbprints (IVT) on the inside. 2" tall. Very scarce. Circa 1885-1890.

Potpourri

IVT, Tiny: Clear cranberry glass; dual mold blown. The pattern has a smooth surface on the outside with a pattern of IVT on the inside. The shaker has a two piece metal top. The base has been configured for insertion into a condiment holder. 2¼" tall. Very scarce. Circa 1886-1891.

Kitty, Shirley's: Translucent frosted glass; mold blown & pressed; with a special silver plated top that is configured in the form of a kitty. The pattern amounts to a kitty sitting upon its rear haunches. The mold detail associated with the metal head is excellent. Pattern name by Stan McElderry. 2" tall. Rare. This an early shaker of the 1880's.

Ladder, Little: Clear blue glass; mold blown. Originally part of a condiment set, this piece has a peg hole in the bottom. Pattern name by Peterson. 2¾" tall. Circa 1880-1890.

Leaf Hanging: Opaque white opalware; mold blown. This is a tall shaker containing large embossed overlapping leaves that droop downward. Pattern name by Warman. Also produced in opaque blue and green. 4⅛" tall. Scarce. Circa 1894-1901.

Leaf Base: Opaque opalware glass mostly covered by red and green paint; mold blown. This is a ten lobed shaker with a deep embossed base leaf. Believed to be an Eagle Glass Co. piece. Sometimes these shakers can be found and they have only been painted with a single color. 2½" tall. Circa 1911-1915.

Leaf, Rosette: Clear crystal pressed glass. This is a heavy three footed shaker containing a band of embossed beads at the top. Pattern name by Kamm. 2¼" tall. Rare. Circa 1875-1880.

Leaf, Upright: Opaque white opalware; mold blown. Containing a hand painted floral spray, the pattern amounts to embossed leaves covering the sides and base of this piece. 3⅛" tall. Scarce. Circa 1900-1906.

Liberty Bell #2: Clear crystal glass; mold blown and pressed. This is a replica of the Liberty Bell. Pattern name by Peterson. 2⅞" tall. Very scarce. Circa 1876.

Lemon: Opaque yellow homogeneous glass; mold blown. The piece is configured in the form of a lemon; Pattern name by Millard. 2⅜" tall. Very rare. Circa 1890-1900.

Lemon, Flat End: Opaque yellow homogeneous glass; mold blown. Really this pattern is more egg shaped than anything else; utilizes a Mt. Washington/Pairpoint type top that is used on their "Flat End Egg"; has a very rough outer surface. Pattern name by Peterson. 3¼" tall. Rare. Circa 1889-1894.

Leaf and Rib: Clear blue glass; mold blown and pressed. The pattern amounts to three stippled leaves and three convex ribs. Pattern name by Peterson. 2⅝" tall. Rare. Circa 1885-1891.

Avery Collection

Avery Collection

Just Collection

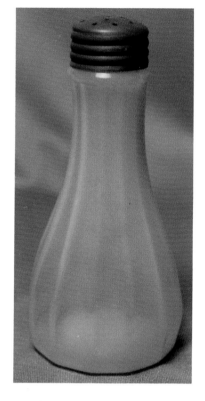

Little Scroller: Opaque variegated pink and white glass; mold blown. Contains embossed scrolls at the top with slightly protruding wide ribbed panels. Pattern name by Heacock in his *1000 Toothpicks*. 1⅞" tall. Rare. Circa 1880.

Lion with Cable: Clear crystal pressed glass. The pattern is a plain two-handled shaker with embossed diagonal ribs on the base. 2⅞" tall. Scarce. Circa 1878.

Long Neck: Translucent white opalescent glass; mold blown. This is a tall bulbous based shaker containing 12 vertical ridges in a rare color. Usually found in clear blue or opaque white. 4¼" tall. Rare in this opalescent color. Circa 1896-1900.

Just Collection

McElderry Collection

Lockwood Collection

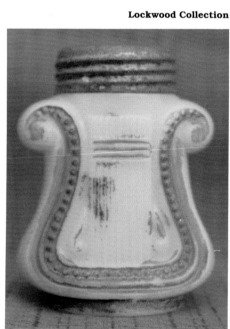

Martha's Thumbprint: clear cranberry glass with hand painted blue and green leaves; dual mold blown. Smooth on the outer surface with baby thumbprints on the inside. 2¼" tall. Very scarce. Circa 1884-1891.

Man with Hat: Clear crystal glass; mold blown. The pattern name describes this piece. We are not sure whether this should also be considered a figural bottle, but we have taken the position that it is; it may also have been an early candy container. Excellent mold detailing. Has a very high collectibility factor. 3⅛" tall. Very rare. Circa 1897-1908.

Lyre: Opaque white opalware with brown painted outlining over an embossed shape of a "Lyre" type musical instrument. Mold blown. 2⅞" tall. Very scarce. Circa 1898-1904.

Mae West: Clear cranberry glass; mold blown. This pattern was named by Bill Heacock presumably due to the "hour glass" shaped figure. The motif consists of segmented rows of hand painted enamelled dots. There is a large hand painted sunflower at the top and base. 3⅛" tall. Rare. Circa 1886-1891.

Matched Pillars Condiment: Opaque opalware with matched hand painted floral decoration over a pastel yellow painted background; mold blown; 3⅛" tall. This is a very ornate pair of shakers in a silver plated condiment holder. This type of shaker was produced by Mt. Washington/Pairpoint (see page 6 of *The Pairpoint Glass Story* by George C. Avila.) Very scarce. Circa 1889-1897.

Marilyn: Translucent amber speckled glass; mold blown. This is a sphere shaped piece that has been satinized and decorated with hand applied white enamel random dots. 2⅛" tall with a two piece metal top. Rare. Circa 1886-1891.

Mixup: Opaque variegated shades of brown bisque; mold formed. This is an early pepper shaker. It appears within the porcelain section of Peterson's salt shaker book. While this book is about glass shakers this is one of the few exceptions that deserves to be included. 2¾" tall. Rare. Circa 1870-1880.

Melonette (Bulbous Twenty-four Rib): Opaque blue glass; mold blown. The pattern consists of a bulbous sphere containing 24 bulging vertical ribs. Heacock has attributed this to the "Consolidated Lamp & Glass Company" and claims that it is a Kopp design. 2½" tall. Scarce. Circa 1894-1900.

Potpourri

Moon Mullins: Clear crystal glass; mold blown. This is a figural salt and pepper created as a likeness of the comic book character "Moon Mullins." Originally sold as a candy container but configured for subsequent use as salt and pepper shakers. 2⅝" tall. Very scarce. Circa 1935.

Owl's Head: Opaque lime green glass; mold blown. The pattern name pretty much describes this piece. The mold details are excellent. We believe that this shaker was produced by Challinor, Taylor. Pattern name by Peterson. Also produced in an opaque light blue. The reader may find it of interest to compare this green color to that of the "Bearded Columbus" & "Isabella" shakers; also the mold detail. 2½" tall. Rare. Circa 1890-1891.

Mop, Short Spheroid: Opaque red to pink air trapped satin glass; mold and free blown finished. An unusual diamond pattern that diminishes in size toward the base. We believe this is of European origin and probably English. 2½" tall. Rare. Circa 1885-1889.

Oval Panel: Opaque white opalware with a hand painted floral sprig; mold blown. The pattern consists of a narrow rectangular shape containing four oval shaped panels; the piece has rounded corners with emgbossed horizontal ribs. Also produced in cranberry opalescent and no doubt other opaque colors. 2¾" tall. Very scarce. Circa 1890-1900.

Ovals, Bulging: Opaque blue glass; mold blown. The pattern consists of a series of large bulging ovals. Each oval pair is connected to a small embossed daisy flower. Also produced in opaque white, green & pink. 2⅝" tall. Very scarce. Circa 1894-1902.

Opera Glasses: We are illustrating two colors, opaque white opalware and translucent red satin; both color versions are mold blown. This pattern was designed as a condiment set and the base has been configured accordingly. The pattern name was derived with the metal holding stand being present. The red satin colored shaker is attributable to Nicholas Kopp and many collectors refer to it as "Pigeon Blood." The total configuration was patented on November 20, 1883 by Daniel Bradley and the reader is referenced to page 400 of *American Pressed Glass and Figure Bottles* by A.C. Revi. The patent date does not seem to relate to the period that Kopp was active as a "Color Man" for Consolidated Lamp or the Pittsburgh firm that absorbed Dithridge & Co. around 1903. It was a surprise to see an Opera Glass shaker in the red satin color. However, if the reader studies Mr. Bradley's patent drawing, it can be readily seen that these shakers are configured somewhat differently. The Bradley patent was granted for a "flask or bottle." As you can see our approximated date of production for this ware is considerably later than the patent paper date. Glass manufacturers were notorious for making slight physical modifications to a piece in order to circumvent a patent. 3" tall. As a complete set this ware is very scarce, in the red satin color rare. Circa 1890-1903.

Panel and Leaf, Octagon: Opaque white opalware over which has been applied a pastel tan painted background; mold blown. This is an octagon shaped piece with vertical panels containing a hand painted floral spray. It is our opinion that this is a Fostoria Glass Co. shaker. 3" tall. Scarce. Circa 1885-1891.

Panel, Rubina Eight: Clear reverse rubina shaded coloring; mold blown. This is an eight vertical panelled piece containing hand painted daisy flowers. We have no additional color experience to report. 3" tall. Circa 1885-1891.

Potpourri

Panel and Star: Clear vaseline pressed crystal. Mrs. Kamm called this "Column block." The top and bottom shaped blocks contain a deep intaglio "X". Also produced in clear crystal. 3½" tall. Scarce. Circa 1890-1900.

Panel, Tall Vertical: Opaque blue glass; mold blown. The pattern consists of plain smooth vertical panels with no decoration; probably a pepper shaker. 3¾" tall. Scarce. Circa 1880-1885.

Panel, Fourteen: Opaque variegated blue glass; mold blown. This ware was design patented by Stewart McKee of Pittsburgh, Pa. on April 20, 1880 as a "Pepper-Cruet." This a very tall shaker containing 14 clearly defined vertical panels. The base has a large protruding ring and the dispenser has been configured for insertion into a condiment holder. It is our opinion that this shaker is a product of McKee & Bros. whose factory was located at Pittsburgh during the time that this pepper shaker was patented. 5¾" tall. Rare. Circa 1880 (see patent section).

Paneled Scroll, Four: Pink cased glass; mold blown. This is a four panelled shaker; each panel contains embossed double scrolls. The bottom has been configured for use with a condiment set holder. 2½" tall. Very scarce. Circa 1885-1891.

Pansy and Bud: Opaque white opalware that no doubt contained hand painted decoration at one time. A unique condiment set with a matching tray. The condiment dispensers are mold blown; the tray is pressed glass. These are slightly curved, four paneled shakers containing what appears to be an embossed pansy and bud. The shakers have been placed upon the trays so that the reader can see what the front and back motifs amount to. 2½" tall. Very scarce. Circa 1899-1905.

Panel Wrinkled: Opaque red and green paiunted opalware; mold blown. The pattern amounts to a four sided shaker with intaglio panels that are reminiscent of a large leaf. Pattern name by Peterson. 2⅝" tall. Scarce. Circa 1911-1916.

Parian Ruby: Translucent satinized glass; mold blown. This piece contains a lightly embossed swirl pattern with eight ribs. It is listed but not illustrated by Peterson. Pattern name by Kamm. 2⅝" tall. Rare. Circa 1889-1894.

Parker: Clear crystal mold blown and pressed glass. This combination salt and pepper was design patented by Lyman B. Parker of Chickasaw Nation, Indian territory (Oklahoma) on January 26, 1904 as a "Composite Condiment Holder." As designed, this combination salt and pepper was intended to improve upon a way for one shaker to hold several condiments and dispense only one at a time. This is accomplished by a moveable hinged cap that can be used to plug the dispensing holes of one compartment while the other is being used. 2½" tall. Very scarce. Circa 1904.

Potpourri

Peachbloom: Opaque heat sensitive cased glassware shading from a deep rose to a delicate pink; mold and free blown finished. The glass composite comprises a white inner lining with the heat sensitive color changing layer being clear layer covered on the outside. Over the years of our research we have seen two pieces of this glass in two different museums containing a Phoenix Glass Co. paper label. It is our opinion that this ware was produced while Joseph Webb was involved with art glass production at Phoenix. 3¼" tall. Rare. Circa 1884-1888.

Pearly Gates: Opaque putty colored homogeneous glass; mold blown. This represents a most unusual glass batch mixture in order to achieve such a unique coloring. The pattern name pretty well describes the physical make up of the piece. 2½" tall. Rare in this color. Circa 1898-1904.

Pearly: translucent shaded pink with a pearl sheen; mold blown. This is a smooth spheroid shaped shaker that is probably of European origin. The motif consists of a hand painted floral spray with matching twin leaves. 2½" tall with a two piece metal top.

Pearls and Scrolls: Opaque white opalware; mold blown. The pattern consists of an embossed beaded band encircling the top portion of the shaker. The center motif amounts to an elaborate pink and green floral spray; the base is covered with embossed scrolls. Named by Heacock. 2½" tall. Very scarce. Circa 1898-1905.

Pearls and Shells: Opaque white opalware; mold blown. The principal pattern amounts to an embossed, shell-shaped base with scrolling; the center portion of the shaker has a hand painted floral sprig. 2½" tall. Scarce. Circa 1898-1904.

Petals and Scrolls: Opaque tan painted opalware; mold blown. The pattern consists of plain center panels formed by intricate scrolling; the remainer of the shaker contains embossed vertical petals. 3⅜" tall. Very scarce. Circa 1897-1905.

Pillar, Pinched-In: Clear blue glass; mold blown with hand painted yellow and white flowers. The physical pattern amounts to a round, small shaped pillar with pinched-in sides. 2" tall. Very scarce. Circa 1889-1893.

Pillar, Curving: Opaque satinized opalware; mold blown. This piece has a plain body over which has been painted a floral sprig. We have no additional color experience to report. 3¼" tall. Scarce. Circa 1897-1902.

Petticoat Base: Clear ruby stained glass; mold blown and pressed. First patented on September 20, 1881 by Lewis W. Husk of Albany, New York, this is a dual purpose salt and pepper shaker that is mechanically operated for dispensing either salt or pepper. It is similar but not the same as "Ripley's Combination S&P Dredges" which are the recipient of a separate patent. The illustrated piece is a variant of the Husk patent. (See patent section). We have never seen a shaker just like this one before. 3⅛" tall. Very rare. Circa 1896-1904.

Pioneer Companion: Clear crystal glass; mold blown; containing a wooden rotary agitator. The words "patented September 15, 1863" are embossed upon the glass. While the overall glass quality is not the greatest this piece has a high collectibility factor. Peterson considers this to be a very rare shaker. 2½" tall

Pipe: Clear crystal glass; mold blown and pressed. A very fragile and (we think) impractical design for a condiment dispenser. Based upon over 35 years of looking, it is our belief that few have survived. This ware has a very high collectibility factor. The pattern name describes the item. 2⅛" tall. Rare. Circa 1895-1905.

Pig, Shirley's: Clear amber glass; mold blown. The glass is of good quality and the metal heads have outstanding detail. The condiment is dispensed from the top of the head; the facial expression is unusual. 2" tall with pewter tops. Rare. Circa 1898-1905.

Plain Band, Footed: Opaque opalware with hand painted pink and brown shading; mold blown. The pattern consists of a bulging spheroid with a wide smooth band encircling the center of the shaker. We believe that it is a product of the Eagle Glass Company. 2⅝" tall. Scarce. Circa 1902-1906.

Plain Salt: Opaque opalware with a pastel painted background; mold blown. The basic shape is that of a rounded bulging shoulder that tapers toward the base; contains a hand painted floral spray. Pattern name by E.G. Warman. 2⅜" tall. Scarce. Circa 1899-1906.

Plume Panel: Opaque white opalware with an off-white painted background; mold blown. Very similar to the Feather Panel shaker and made by the same company. The center panel contains an embossed blue painted plume. 2⅜" tall. Scarce. Circa 1900-1906.

Posey Patch: Opaque white opalware with an off-white painted background; mold blown. Very similar to the Feather Panel shaker and made by the same company. The center panel contains an embossed blue painted plume. 2⅜" tall. Scarce. Circa 1900-1906.

Lockwood Collection

Authors' Collection

Propeller: Clear crystal glass; mold blown. This is a unique special top with a suspended propeller device to break up lumpy salt. Comes in two sizes, 1⅝" and 1⅜" tall. Rare. Circa 1870.

Pyramid, Cut-Off: Opaque white opalware; mold blown. This is a four sided shaker configured in the form of a small pyramid cut off at the top; the piece has been hand decorated with random flowers and stems (somewhat worn). 2¾" tall. Rare. Circa 1898-1904.

Avery Collection

Bruce Collection

McElderry Collection

Quilted Pineapple: We are providing two photographs to show the differences in color technique. Opaque white opalware with hand painted floral sprigs; one with pink & white, the other with blue and yellow flowers, mold blown. It is interesting to note that one has a two piece metal top. The total pattern is configured in the form of a pineapple with embossed leaves at the top and base. 3½" tall. The pink leafed shaker is rare. Circa 1897-1902.

Rib Base, Sixteen: Clear ruby stained crystal; mold blown. This is a smooth, round-shaped cylinder piece with sixteen protruding base ribs. 2⅞" tall. Very scarce. Circa 1898-1905.

Rainbow, Bulbous Variant: Physically this pair is identical to our Rainbow, Bulbous, but contains a lesser quantity of the fused multi-colored vertical ribbons. Therefore, all of the aforementioned comments apply to this pair. Extremely rare. Circa 1920.

Rainbow, Bulbous: Opaque multi-colored vertical ribbons with a thin white inner lining; free blown and finished. We believe that the pattern name properly describes this ware. The only other shakers of this type known are in the McElderry collection and are also illustrated in this book. This ware appeared on the front cover of our first book, so it has been well publicized. This is quality Venetian Art Glass of the 1920s. Since we have no pricing baseline to compare against, our shaker pair is worth whatever a collector is willing to pay for it. 3⅛" tall. Extremely rare.

Ribs Below: Opaque white opalware; mold blown. The pattern consists of a flattened spheroid with a series of embossed base ribs. 2½" tall. Scarce. Circa 1901-1906.

Rib, Blair: Opaque variegated glass; mold blown. This is a bulbous ribbed pattern in brown and white marbleized glass. Pattern name by Warman. We believe this to be a Challinor, Taylor pattern. 3⅝" tall. Very scarce. Circa 1890-1891.

Rib, Double: Opaque white opalware; mold blown. The pattern amounts to a tall pillar with a band of embossed short vertical ribs at the top and base. 3⅞" tall. Very scarce. Circa 1895-1900.

Ribbed, Bottom and Top: Opaque custard glass; mold blown. The pattern name describes the motif. We are also illustrating an opalware piece with painted pink fleur-de-lis. 3⅛" tall. Scarce. Circa 1901-1907.

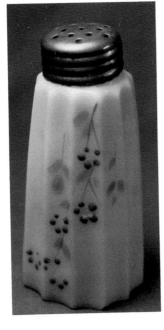

Ribbed, Shallow: Opaque blue glass; mold blown with 3 hand painted floral sprigs. The pattern amounts to a small bulbous shaker with shallow embossed vertical ribs. 2" tall. Scarce. Circa 1900-1905.

Ribbed, Sharp: Opaque white opalware with a pastel tan background; mold blown. The principal pattern consists of long sharp vertical ribs containing a large blue floral spray. 3⅝" tall. Scarce. Circa 1899-1905.

Rib, Short: Opaque white opalware with a hand painted pink and green floral sprig; mold blown. This is a relatively plain cylinder shaped piece with a bulging base that contains a band of embossed short vertical ribs. 2⅞" tall. Scarce. Circa 1898-1905.

Rib, Vertical Optic (Condiment Set): Clear Rubina crystal; dual mold blown with a pressed glass crystal base holder. All the condiment pieces are configured for insertion into the crystal base holder. This is a beautiful set and the condiment dispensers radiate a visual ribbed optic effect due to the dual mold pattern technique employed. Shakers - 4½"; mustard - 3½"; vinegar/oil - 4⅞" (less stopper) tall. The overall condiment set height is 9⅜" to the top of the metal lifting handle. Rare. Circa 1876-1882.

Ribbon Tie: Opaque white opalware with a somewhat worn hand painted floral sprig; mold blown. The physical pattern amounts to a large bulbous base and an embossed beaded neck band with a tied ribbon. The basic shape of this piece is identical to the "Spanish Lace" shaker which is a known Northwood pattern[8]. 2⅞" tall. Scarce. Circa 1895.

Ring Handled Basket: Opaque gray homogeneous glass; mold blown. The pattern consists of an embossed basket weave with a ring-shaped handle on the front an back of the shaker. Also produced in opaque white and pale blue opalescent. 2⅞" tall. Scarce. Circa 1905[9].

Ring, Double: Translucent cobalt blue with hand painted flowers at the base; mold blown. The pattern name provides an adequate physical description of the shaker. 2⅜" tall with a 2 piece metal top. Rare. Circa 1886-1893.

Ring Neck, Tapered: Clear amber glass; dual mold blown. The basic pattern consists of IVT inside and a smooth surface outside. The decorative motif consists of a hand painted yellow and blue feathered bird flying within a floral background. 2½" tall with a two piece metal top. Very scarce. Circa 1886-1891.

Ripley's Combination: Clear crystal glass; mold blown with a very special top (see illustration). This combination condiment dispenser was initially patented on September 2, 1873 with a reissue patent date of November 18, 1873 (see patent section) by Daniel C. Ripley of Pittsburgh, Pennsylvania,. Mr. Ripley patented this ware as an "Improvement In Salt and Pepper Dredges". The combination consists of two distinct and separate chambers that sift through the same top by rotation of a portion of the shaker top. This ware was made in two sizes—2¾" and 3¼" tall. Very Rare. Circa 1873.

Richardson: Clear crystal glass; mold blown; Patented Dec. 3, 1867 by George B. Richardson. The patent date is usually embossed on the shaker and relates to the individual agitator by itself.[10] These shakers were made in at least two sizes—2½" and 4¼" tall.Very scarce. Circa late 1860's.

Rooster's Head Condiment: Translucent blue, amber and crystal pressed glass. The pattern name describes the physical configuration. An original set will contain the aforesaid dispenser colors, with the mustard being crystal. However, this same set was also produced with all pieces in translucent crystal. We are also illustrating a Rooster's Head amber shaker so that the reader can better see the glass details. Pattern name created by Ruth Webb Lee. The survival factor on this pattern is very low due to the unusual configuration involved. The pieces are highly chip prone and should be carefully examined prior to purchase. All three condiments are 2⅞" tall. Very rare as a complete set. Circa 1875-1881.

Potpourri

Rosette Row: Clear blue pressed glass. The principal pattern consists of vertical rows of small embossed rosettes. Pattern name by Peterson. Also produced in crystal and green. 2⅞" tall. Very scarce. Circa 1890-1900.

Rose on Square: Translucent red (pigeon blood) glass; mold and free blown finished. This a sphere shaped piece containing a rose motif that was formed by hand cutting. It contains a two piece metal top. Believed to be of European origin. 1¾" tall. Rare. Circa 1884-1891.

Rubina Verde Honeycomb: Clear Rubina Verde glass shading from rose to greenish-yellow; mold blown. The principal pattern consists of a cylinder shaped piece having a large overhanging top collar. The motif is in the honeycomb pattern. 3½" tall with a two piece metal top. Very scarce. Circa 1886-1890.

Ribbed Abbie Ann: Opaque opalware; mold blown. This is a sharp vertical ribbed piece containing random hand painted red dots within a square. 3" tall. Very scarce. Circa 1897-1902.

Royal Oval: Opaque white opalware; mold blown. This is a plain, smooth surfaced shaker containing hand painted pink and green flowers and leaves. The top and base each contain a protruding ring. Pattern name by Warman. 3¼" tall. Very scarce. Circa 1898-1904.

Roman Key Base: Opaque white opalware; mold blown. The pattern consists of a beaded neck ring; the center is concaved with an embossed Roman Key pattern encircling the base. 3⅛" tall. Scarce. Circa 1900-1909.

Ruffled Neck: Opaque white opalware with hand painted daisy flowers; mold blown. This is a bulbous shaped shaker with a ruffled neck. 2¾" tall. Scarce. Circa 1901-1906.

Rubina Optic: Clear reverse Rubina glass with an elaborate hand painted floral spray; dual mold blown. The piece has a curved barrel shape that is smooth on the outer surface with vertical ribbed panels on the inside. This is really a gorgeous salt shaker. 2⅞" tall with a two piece metal top. Rare. Circa 1885-1890.

Rubina Verde, Footed: Clear Rubina Verde glass shading from a ruby red to a greenish yellow; dual mold blown. As with many dual molded shakers, the outer surface is smooth with the inside having an IVT pattern. This shaker has been hand decorated with an elaborate floral spray. 3" tall with a two piece metal top. Rare. Circa 1884-1891.

Sawtooth: Opaque yellow custard glass; mold blown. The pattern consists of a sphere shaped shaker covered with an embossed pointed diamond design often referred to as "Sawtooth." This piece gives off a striking fluorescence under black light radiation. 2⅜" tall. Very scarce. Circa 1898-1903.

Sawtooth, Bulbous: Clear blue glass; mold blown. This is an early shaker; the bottom has a pontil scar. The pattern name describes the physical configuration very well. Also produced in amber glass. 2¼" tall. Very scarce. Circa 1880-1890.

Potpourri

Scalloped Curtain: Opaque white opalware glass; mold blown and pressed. This is a footed shaker containing an embossed draped curtain that hangs down from the top. Probably made in other opaque colors. 2⅝" tall. Scarce. Circa 1899-1905.

Scalloped Neck: Opaque white opalwar[e] mold blown. The overall shape is a sma[ll] slightly concave cylinder with emboss[ed] scallops just below the top edge. The ba[se] has a band of flowers and tiny scrolls. Th[e] ware will sometimes be found decorated wi[th] gilt paint on the raised pattern surfaces. 2[?"] tall. Scarce. Circa 1900-1908.

Sawtooth and Thinline: Opaque white opalware; mold blown with hand painted pink and green floral sprigs. The upper portion of this piece has an embossed veined surface with the base containing sawtooth raised diamonds. Pattern name by Peterson. 3" tall. Scarce. Circa 1897-1903.

Scalloped Panels: Translucent dark ruby stained glass; mold blown. This piece has a completely smooth outer surface with slightly curved scalloped panels to which has been applied a liberal amount of red stain that causes the shaker to be translucent. 2⅞" tall. Circa 1900-1907.

Scroll and Chain: Opaque white opalware; mold blown. The pattern consists of ornate scrolling. The center of the shaker is encircled by a continuous embossed round linked chain. Pastel blue (somewhat worn) paint has been applied to the outer edge of the motifs. Pattern name by Peterson. 3⅜" tall. Scarce. Circa 1903-1905.

Scroll, Concave: Opaque opalware with a painted pale yellow surface; mold blown. This is a small concave shaped shaker containing embossed random scrolls and flowers. 2" tall. Scarce. Circa 1900-1907.

Scroll, Tapered: Opaque white opalware; mold blown with a hand painted pink and green floral sprig. This is a tapered cylinder shaped shaker containing embossed scrolls. Also produced in opaque pink and blue. Pattern name by Peterson. 3¼" tall. Scarce. Circa 1897-1904.

Scroll, Intricate: Clear crystal glass with gold decorated filigree; mold blown. The pattern name pretty much describes the pattern. Certainly different. 2⅝" tall. Scarce. Circa 1900-1905.

Shell, Footed: Opaque white opalware; mold blown and pressed. This a cylindrical shaped piece with three supporting feet. The center has a shell-shaped panel and a hand painted floral sprig. Pattern name by Warman. 3⅜" tall. Very scarce. Circa 1895-1905.

Shell and Scale: Translucent coral shaded glass; mold blown. The pattern amounts to a small footed piece with a bulging base that contains four shells in raised relief. The glass radiates a slightly opalescent sheen. Pattern name by Peterson. 2⅞" tall. Rare. Circa 1896-1900.

Potpourri

Shell, Three: Opaque white opalware; mold blown. The pattern consists of three embossed shells affixed to an egg-like shape. The top is the same type that is used on the Mt. Washington/Pairpoint "Flat End Egg" shakers. We believe this shaker is a product of Mt. Washington/Pairpoint. Pattern name by Peterson. 3⅜" tall. Very scarce. Circa 1894-1900.

Shirley: Translucent green glass; mold blown with hand painted daisy flower groups. This is a dual mold barrel shaped piece containing IVT on the inside and no outer surface pattern. This shaker was brought to our attention by Shirley McElderry. This is a rare color in green. Also produced in clear blue with the same hand painted motif. 2½" tall with a two piece metal top. Circa 1885-1891.

Soda Gold: Translucent carnival glass; mold blown. This is really a utilitarian plain paneled shaker with embossed interspersed vines. considered to be early carnival glass. The reader is referred to Kamm 7, 131 for additional details. 3" tall. Rare. Circa 1900.

Siamese Twin Variant: Clear crystal glass; free blown. Patented November 26, 1901 by Benjamin Crawford as "A Design For A Condiment Box" (see patent section). Intended to dispense salt from one side and pepper from the other. 2½" tall. Rare. Circa 1901.

Spatterglass, St. Clair's: Translucent blue and orange Spatterglass; mold blown. The pattern consists of a beaded arch and fern on six panels. Made in various colors. Pattern name by Peterson who considered this to be recent art glass and a product of the St. Clair Glass Co. 3" tall. Very scarce. Circa 1962-1968.

Sprig and Blossom: Opaque white opalware; mold blown. This is a cylinder shaped piece with a protruding neck ring and a large embossed flower and leaf sprig. Pattern name by Warman. 3⅜" tall. Very scarce. Circa 1898-1905.

Square Panel: Opaque white opalware; mold blown. This is a rectangular shaped shaker containing an orange and blue painted Dutch girl; the decoration was accomplished by using a transfer technique. Pattern name by Warman. 3¼" tall. Circa 1903-1910.

Starlet: Clear cranberry glass; dual mold blown with outstanding hand painted floral decoration. The quality of the glass is excellent with a smooth outer surface and an IVT pattern on the inside. It is our opinion that this is a Mt. Washington/Pairpoint shaker. 2⅝" tall with a two piece metal top. Very rare in decorated cranberry. Circa 1885-1891.

Spheroid, Tapered: Opaque white opalware; mold blown. This is a cylinder shaped piece with a protruding neck ring and a large embossed flower and leaf sprig. Pattern name by Warman. 3⅜" tall. Very scarce. Circa 1898-1905.

Squatty Lobes: Opaque white opalware; mold blown. This is a plain shaker containing six wide squatty lobes. No doubt produced in other colors but we haven't seen any. 2" tall. Scarce. Circa 1897-1903.

Strawberry Condiment, Inverted: Opaque red cased glass; mold blown. The pattern is reminiscent of an inverted strawberry. The illustrated ware is decorated with embossed flowers. The reader is looking at a salt shaker and mustard. We believe this to be a European condiment set. 2¾" tall in their original silver plated holder. Rare. Circa 1877-1883.

Potpourri

Stanley's Bluerina:[11] This type of glassware is seldom seen today. The color shades from a clear pale cranberry to blue.[11] The illustrated shaker is the only one that we have ever seen; although we have seen this same pattern in a lovely cranberry. The term *Bluerina*[12] is seldom used among today's collectors. The pattern consists of two rows of Bull's Eyes on the inside of the shaker; the outer surface is smooth. Very rare. Circa 1880-1887.

Stove: Clear blue and amber pressed glass; We are illustrating two shakers. Pattern name by C.W. Brown who no doubt viewed these pieces as being reminiscent of the old so-called "Pot Belly Stove." We have seen several over the years and they are almost always in a chipped condition; therefore, we urge the reader to look one over carefully prior to purchase. 4" tall. Rare. Circa 1877-1883.

Stump Condiment: Opaque opalware with hand painted floral sprigs on each of the condiment dispensers; mold blown and pressed. The pattern resembles a tree stump with embossed bumps representing sawed-off limbs. Also produced in clear crystal. 2¼" tall. Rare. Circa 1898-1905.

Stripe, Square: Translucent blue opalescent glass; mold blown. The pattern amounts to a four sided square shaped piece containing curving opalescent stripes. Also produced in a lovely cranberry opalescent color. 2⅞" tall. Rare. Circa 1885-1891.

Swirl and Band: Opaque off-white opalware; mold blown and pressed. Pattern name by Peterson. This is a tall shaker containing two wide plain bands with an embossed swirled base. Also produced in clear amber and crystal. 5¾" tall. Scarce. Circa 1899-1906.

Swirl, Opalescent Barrel: Translucent opalescent cranberry glass; dual mold blown. With a smooth outer surface, the inside is swirled and has opalescent stripes. Believed to be a Hobbs, Brockunier shaker. 2⅞" tall. Very scarce. Circa 1886-1890.

Swirl, Fine Threaded: Translucent opalescent cranberry glass; mold blown. This is a barrel shaped shaker containing continuous horizontal opalescent swirls. 3⅛" tall with a two piece metal top. Rare. Circa 1884-1891.

Swirl, Fifteen: Translucent spatter glass with the pink and brown colors predominating; mold blown. The pattern amounts to a bulbous shaped piece containing fifteen embossed swirls on the shaker body. 2½" tall. Very Scarce. Circa 1887-1891.

Potpourri

Swirl, Pillar: Opaque custard glass; mold blown. The pattern consists of twelve short vertical ribs and a plain base. 3⅛" tall. Rare. Circa 1899-1905.

Swirled Sphere: Clear cranberry glass; mold blown; 2⅝" tall with a two piece metal top. Very scarce. Circa 1883-1889.

Swirl Variant: Opaque white opalware; mold blown. This is an embossed swirl pattern. The center has small embossed diamonds. For additional information the reader is referred to Kamm 3, 49. 2¾" tall. Scarce. Circa 1900-1906.

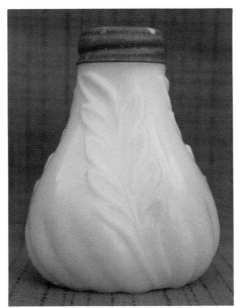

Teardrop and Leaf, Drooping: Opaque white opalware; mold blown. A bulbous based shaker; the principal motif consists of a band of embossed leaves that droop downward from a ring of beaded teardrops. 2⅝" tall. Scarce. Circa 1902-1907.

Tapered Shoulder Variant: Translucent dark amethyst glass; mold blown. The pattern amounts to a cylindrical shape with a slightly tapered shoulder containing outstanding hand painted floral decoration. 3⅝" tall with a two piece metal top. Rare. Circa 1885-1887.

Tapered Vine: Opaque white opalware; mold blown. This is a bulbous based shaker containing an embossed vine that tapers toward the top. Pattern name by Heacock who lists this pattern on page 31 of *Rare and Unlisted Toothpick Holders*. 3⅛" tall. Circa 1900-1907.

McElderry Collection

Avery Collection

Authors' Collection

Ten Rib, Optic: Clear blue with white enamel floral decoration; mold blown. This is a dual molded shaker that has a smooth outer surface and wide vertical inside ribbing. 3¾" tall with a two piece metal top. Very scarce. Circa 1885-1891.

Texas, Big: Clear pressed glass crystal. The reader is referred to Kamm 2, 58 for additional details concerning this ware. 3" tall. Scarce. Circa 1890-1900.

Thumbprint, Flared Base: Clear blue shading to crystal at the base; mold blown. Hand enamel decorated with two floral sprigs. The basic pattern consists of a flared-out base with embossed IVT that extends about half way upward. 3" tall with a two piece metal top. Rare. Circa 1886-1891.

Cohen Collection

Authors' Collection

Thumbprint Inside: Clear cranberry glass; dual mold blown. The outer surface of the shaker is completely smooth with thumbprints on the inside. 3" tall with a two piece metal top. Scarce. Circa 1887-1892.

Tiny Thumbprint Barrel: Clear cranberry with a hand painted floral band; dual mold blown. These little cuties are a matched pair; most difficult to acquire. The outer surface of the shakers is smooth and the inside contains tiny thumbprints. 2¼" tall with a two piece metal top. Rare. Circa 1893-1889.

Potpourri

Triangle, Pinched-In: Translucent variegated yellow and white cased glass; mold blown with a hand painted green and yellow floral sprig and a two piece metal top. This is a triangular shaped piece with four pinched-in panels. Rare. Circa 1884-1890.

Tortoise-Shell Bulb: Translucent multicolored in white and brown; mold blown. A process for producing this ware was patented on October 25, 1880 by a German chemist named Francis Pohl.[13] This is a rare type of art glass particularly in salt shakers. The pattern shape is that of an elongated bulb. 3⅛" tall with a two piece metal top. Rare. Circa 1881-1887.

Triangle: Clear blue pressed glass. As the pattern name implies, the shaker is configured in the form of a triangle. Pattern name by Peterson who states that this pattern has been reproduced. 3¼" tall. Scarce. Circa 1901-1903.

Tripod: Clear crystal pressed glass. This is a very plain shaker but of unique design. However, the way the early salt shakers were pounded on the table (due to coagulated salt) probably has had a major impact on the amount that are available today. 3⅛" tall. Very scarce. Circa 1905-1909.

Twins: Opaque custard and clear cranberry shakers with hand painted floral decoration; mold blown. The cranberry shaker is dual mold blown with inside baby thumbprints. Both shakers are from the same mold and believed to be Mt. Washington/Pairpoint. 2¾" tall with two piece metal tops. Very scarce. Circa 1886-1892.

Cohen Collection

McElderry Collection

Venetian, Bulbous: Shaded Rose to Amber satin glass; free blown sphere shaped. The shakers are identical to the "Bulbous Rainbow" shakers except that the piece is made from a heat sensitive glass that will change color in accordance with the reheating technique used at the Glory Hole. We have provided two photographs that clearly show the color shading differences that can be realized from the process. Our personal preference is the single shaker from the Cohen collection that has the more delicate shading. The other two shakers from the McElderry collection have a sharp color cut-off point. These are European pieces from the 1920s that were sold to the so-called "Carriage Trade." There are variances in the body size due to the free blown techniques involved. Since these are the only three shakers of this type we have ever seen, they have to be considered rare. 3⅛" tall with a two piece metal top.

Authors' Collection

Authors' Collection

Just Collection

Wide Band Base: Opaque black glass; mold blown. This pair of cuties has a wide band base with the remainder of the piece having a cylindrical shape. They are elaborately hand decorated with blue, pink and white flowers. 2¼" tall with a two-piece metal top. Rare. Circa 1884-1891.

Wide Band Stained: Clear ruby stained crystal; mold blown. This is a plain cylindrical piece with a protruding neck ring and ruby staining covering the preponderance of its body. 3¼" tall. Scarce. Circa 1900-1905.

Wings: Translucent variegated yellow and white cased glass; mold blown. The piece has been hand painted with black lily type leaves. This is a most unusual shaker produced in high quality glass. 2⅛" tall. Rare. Circa 1884-1891.

Potpourri

Winter Time: Opaque white opalware; mold blown. This is a small sphere shaped shaker containing a hand painted winter scene, very much along the lines of the type of painting that Barlow & Kaiser in their Sandwich Glass books attribute to Mary Gregory. 2" tall with a garish two piece metal top. Rare. Circa 1884-1887.

Wide Collar: Clear cranberry glass; mold blown with hand painted white floral sprigs. The pattern consists of a small bulbous body with a wide ringed collar protruding from the shaker neck. This is a dual molded piece with the inside containing small baby thumbprints. 1⅞" tall with a two piece metal top. Very scarce. Circa 1886-1891.

Window and Drape: Clear electric blue; mold blown. This is a square shaped piece containing a round top window that is outlined with embossed ellipses. Has "S.S. Co." embossed on the bottom. 3¼" tall. Circa 1902s.

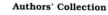

Zigzag: Clear pressed crystal glass. The pattern amounts to a series of embossed expanded Z's symmetrically spaced around the shaker. This is a U.S. Glass Co. pattern. Also produced in opaque white and amber. We are illustrating the complete glass condiment set and a single amber shaker. 3" tall. Very scarce. Circa 1900-1904.

T. B. ATTERBURY.

Salt and Pepper Dredges Combined.

No. 143,951. Patented Oct. 28, 1873.

Fig. 1
Fig. 2
SALT
Fig. 3
Fig. 4

Witnesses.
James Martin Jr.
J. N. Campbell

Inventor.
Thos. B. Atterbury
by
Mason, Fenwick & Lawrence.

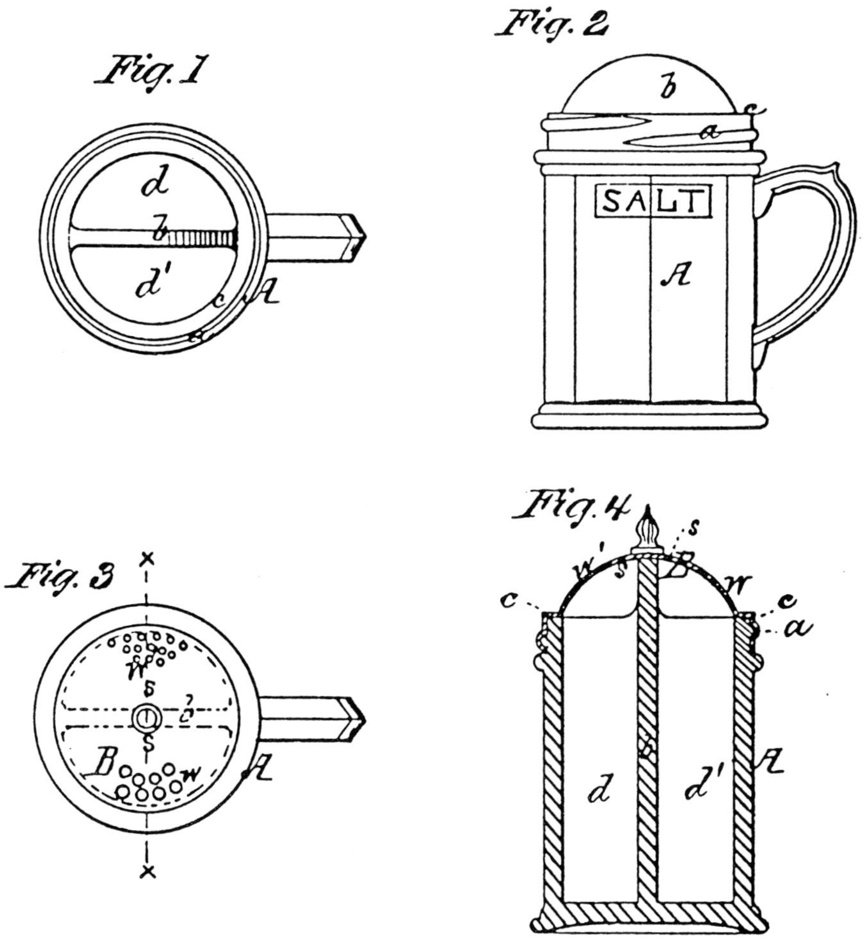

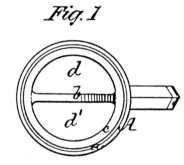

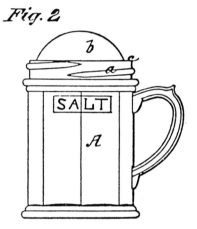

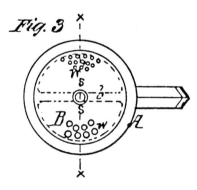

UNITED STATES PATENT OFFICE.

THOMAS B. ATTERBURY, OF PITTSBURG, PENNSYLVANIA, ASSIGNOR TO JAMES S. ATTERBURY AND THOMAS B. ATTERBURY, OF SAME PLACE.

IMPROVEMENT IN SALT AND PEPPER DREDGES COMBINED.

Specification forming part of Letters Patent No. **143,951**, dated October 28, 1873; application filed October 3, 1873.

To all whom it may concern:

Be it known that I, THOMAS B. ATTERBURY, of Pittsburg, in the county of Allegheny and State of Pennsylvania, have invented a new and Improved Combined Salt and Pepper Dredge; and I do hereby declare that the following is a full, clear, and exact description thereof, reference being had to the accompanying drawing forming part of this specification, in which—

Figure 1 is a top view of the dredge with the cover removed. Fig. 2 is a side view of the same. Fig. 3 is a top view of the dredge with the cover in place. Fig. 4 is a vertical section of the same in the line *x x* of Fig. 3.

Similar letters of reference indicate corresponding parts in the several figures.

The nature of my invention consists in a double-chambered salt and pepper dredge with the partition thereof extended up above its upper rim in form of a segment of a circle or other form which will form a closing partition between the salt and pepper apertures in the cover of the dredge, and with the salt and pepper discharging perforations in its cover for the respective chambers located some distance outside of the vertical axis of the chambers, the construction of the dredge and its cover being such in the particulars stated and in other respects that the two condiments cannot become mixed; nor can they respectively work down between the screw-rim of the cover and the screw-fastening of the dredge; nor can the salt apertures be screwed round to the pepper-chamber, and vice versa; neither will the pepper be discharged while the salt is being discharged, and vice versa, notwithstanding the dredge is constructed to operate without a valve for closing the respective sets of apertures.

In the accompanying drawings, A represents the salt and pepper dredge, made of glass or porcelain, with a handle, and of a circular form internally and of a hexagon form externally. Its base, which is slightly larger than its body, is circular and beaded. At its upper edge it is circular and enlarged and beaded. Above this latter bead a short rim with a screw-thread, *a*, cut upon it is formed, said screw-thread beginning on one side and running entirely round and terminating on the same side, as shown. Centrally on this dredge a narrow web or partition, *b*, rises, commencing at the bottom and extending up to the top of the screw-thread, and from said point continuing in form of a segment of a circle a distance equal to the depth of the cover which is used upon the dredge. There is a horizontal shoulder, *c*, formed all round between the extending portion of the partition and the screw thread. B is the cover or top of the dredge, made of sheet metal, and screw-threaded to match the screw-thread of the dredge. This cover is, in cross-section, internally the same in form and depth as the extended portion of the partition. Near the base of the cover and on the outer side of the vertical axis of each of the chambers *d d'*, formed by the partition, perforations W W' are formed in the cover, the perforations W being larger than those, W', and serving for salt, while the perforations W' serve for pepper.

It will be seen that a blank surface, *s*, for pepper to rise against when salt is being discharged, and a similar surface for salt to rise against when pepper is being discharged, is left above the perforations, and therefore two kinds of condiments cannot, under ordinary use of the dredge, be discharged at the same time. Further, it will be seen that the extended portion of the partition separates the two sets of holes of the cover by reason of the cover packing tight upon it. And further, the horizontal shoulder at the top of the screw prevents the insinuation of the condiments between the screw of the cover and of the dredge, while the screw, terminating always on the side it started from, prevents the perforations getting in the wrong position.

The shape and form of the dredge shown may be varied to suit fancy and taste without departing from my invention.

I am aware that a dredge with two or more compartments and with a regulating discharge-

113,951

valve is a common thing, and, therefore, I do not broadly claim such contrivance; but

What I do claim as my invention, and desire to secure by Letters Patent, is—

The within-described combined salt and pepper dredge with a partition, *b*, extended up beyond its screw-fastening, in combination with the cover or top which is perforated on two sides of its vertical axis, and fits snugly down upon said partition, substantially as and for the purpose described.

THOS. B. ATTERBURY.

Witnesses:
E. G. KREHAN,
J. ALEX. KNOX.

H. J. WHITE.
Table Salt-Bottle

No. 198,554.   Patented Dec. 25, 1877.

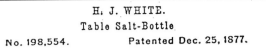

Fig. 1.   Fig. 2.

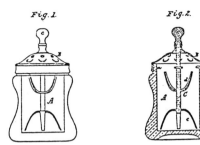

Fig. 3.

Witnesses
S. N. Piper.
L. W. Miller

Inventor
Hiram J. White.
by his attorney.
R. H. Eddy.

UNITED STATES PATENT OFFICE.

HIRAM J. WHITE, OF BOSTON, MASSACHUSETTS, ASSIGNOR TO DANA K. ALDEN, OF SAME PLACE.

IMPROVEMENT IN TABLE SALT BOTTLES.

Specification forming part of Letters Patent No. **198,554**, dated December 25, 1877; application filed December 11, 1877.

To all whom it may concern:

Be it known that I, HIRAM J. WHITE, of Boston, of the county of Suffolk and State of Massachusetts, have invented a new and useful Improvement in Table Salt Bottles; and do hereby declare the same to be described in the following specification and represented in the accompanying drawings, of which—

Figure 1 is a side view, and Fig. 2 a vertical section, of a salt-bottle provided with my invention. Fig. 3 is a perspective view of the agitator, to be hereinafter described.

It is well known that table-salt is liable to deliquesce and become hard or cake when in an open bottle or other vessel.

My invention is for the purpose of stirring or breaking up the salt, in order to prevent it from caking in the body as well as in the perforated cover of the bottle. Such invention is also to break up the salt when caked, either in the body or the cover of such bottle.

To this end I use in the bottle a rotary agitator, having a shank extending through the cover, and provided with a knob, such agitator being movable lengthwise, besides being capable of being revolved in the cover by the thumb and forefinger of the hand of a person applied to the knob. This agitator has two sets of curved prongs, one of which projects downward toward the bottom of the bottle, and the other upward toward the cover, all being substantially as represented in the drawings, in which—

A denotes the salt holder or bottle, provided with a perforated cap, B, screwed upon its neck a. The agitator G is composed of a cylindrical wire or shank, b, a knob, c, and two series of curved prongs, d e, all arranged in and with the cover, in manner as shown.

By drawing the agitator upward and revolving it, salt that may gather in the cover or stop its holes of discharge may be broken up. So, by depressing the agitator and revolving it within the bottle, salt that may cake in the bottom of such bottle may be broken up. By alternately moving the agitator up and down in the bottle, and at the same time revolving such agitator, the body of the salt may be stirred.

I claim—

The agitator, substantially as described, movable in manner and by means as set forth, in combination and arranged with the bottle and its perforated cap or cover, as specified.

HIRAM J. WHITE.

Witnesses:
R. H. EDDY,
JOHN R. SNOW.

(No Model.)

T. W. BROWN.
OPEN CAP FOR BOTTLES.

No. 244,740.

Patented July 26, 1881.

Fig.1.

Fig.2.

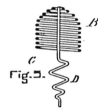

Fig.3.

WITNESSES

INVENTOR

Helen M. Feegan

Thomas W. Brown

Frank L. —

UNITED STATES PATENT OFFICE.

THOMAS W. BROWN, OF BELMONT, MASSACHUSETTS.

OPEN CAP FOR BOTTLES.

SPECIFICATION forming part of Letters Patent No. 244,740, dated July 26, 1881.

Application filed April 8, 1881. (No model.)

To all whom it may concern:

Be it known that I, THOMAS W. BROWN, of Belmont, in the county of Middlesex and State of Massachusetts, have invented a new and useful Improved Open Cap for Bottles, &c., of which the following is a specification.

My invention relates to that class of bottles, &c., which have open caps—that is, such caps as will allow the contents of the bottle or other vessel, when in a granulated or powdered form, to be shaken out, and thus distributed evenly, as may be desired; and it consists in combining with the mouth of a bottle or other containing-vessel a helix spiral wire cap, the wire being so wound that it will allow of the passage of any granulated or powdered substance through the interstices between the several coils of the wire.

In the drawings, Figure 1 is an elevation of my invention, showing the helix spiral cap applied to a bottle. Fig. 2 is a vertical section, showing one method of forming the cap. Fig. 3 is a vertical section of the cap, showing an addition of a central member, which extends downward into the bottle.

This device is intended as a cap or cover for any box, bottle, or other device for holding granulated or powdered material which is to be shaken out for use—as for instance, salt, pepper, mustard, bluing, insect-powder, &c., and is made of different shapes, dimensions, size of wire, width of interstices, &c., to adapt it for the use intended.

The drawings exhibit my invention as applied to a salt or pepper box or bottle, which in this case has a screw-thread formed on its neck.

The cap B is formed of any suitable wire coiled to form a cap-shaped spiral, terminating in a helix, the wire being so loosely wound as to leave interstices between each coil.

In Fig. 3, I have shown a modification of my device, in which I have added to the cap a downwardly-projecting member C, D, which consists in a straight part, C, and the helix D, as shown. This part descends into the bottle and serves to prevent the contents from clogging.

If desirable, that part of the cap that is immediately over the mouth of the bottle may be coned or concaved, so as to form a sinkage at the mouth, instead of a raised surface, as shown in the drawings.

The wire is round, flat, or square in sections, as may be desired.

I claim—

1. The cap B, made of wire coiled to the shape desired, whereby an open cap is formed, substantially as described, and for the purpose set forth.

2. The cap B, made of coiled wire, in combination with the member C D, substantially as described, and for the purpose set forth.

THOMAS W. BROWN.

Witnesses:
  HELEN M. FEEGAN,
  SAMUEL A. OTIS.

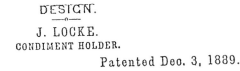

DESIGN.

J. LOCKE.

CONDIMENT HOLDER.

No. 19,460.

Patented Dec. 3, 1889.

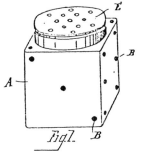

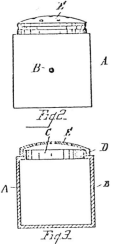

UNITED STATES PATENT OFFICE.

JOSEPH LOCKE, OF TOLEDO, OHIO, ASSIGNOR TO THE W. L. LIBBEY & SON COMPANY, OF SAME PLACE.

DESIGN FOR A CONDIMENT-HOLDER.

SPECIFICATION forming part of Design No. 19,460, dated December 3, 1889.

Application filed October 7, 1889. Serial No. 326,283. Term of patent 3½ years.

To all whom it may concern:

Be it known that I, JOSEPH LOCKE, a citizen of the United States, and a resident of Toledo, in the county of Lucas and State of Ohio, have
5 invented and produced a new and original Design for Condiment and Similar Receptacles; and I do hereby declare that the following is a full, clear, and exact description of the invention, which will enable others skilled in
10 the art to which it appertains to make and use the same, reference being had to the accompanying drawings, and to the letters of reference marked thereon, which form part of this specification.
15 The class to which my design relates is that of condiment and similar receptacles, and the design pertains to the exterior contour and ornamentation thereof.

The drawings represent, in Figure 1, a per-
20 spective view of an article of glassware having an exterior contour and ornamentation in accordance with my design, the article chosen for illustration being a salt or pepper box. Fig. 2 is a side elevation, and Fig. 3 is a lon-
25 gitudinal section.

The leading features of my design are a cubical receptacle having on its faces any desired number of dots or depressions, an annular neck formed on the upper face, and a perforated cover fitted on said neck. 30

In the drawings, A designates the cubical body embellished with dots B in the arrangement of the ordinary dice, so that the dots of the two opposing sides shall aggregate seven. 35

C designates an annular projection formed upon the top side of the cube and provided with a perforated cover E,

The design is very unique and produces a pleasing effect.

What I claim is— 40

The design for condiment or similar receptacles, substantially as shown and described.

In testimony that I claim the foregoing as my own I hereby affix my signature in presence of two witnesses.

JOSEPH LOCKE.

Witnesses:
WILLIAM WEBSTER,
SOLON O. RICHARDSON, Jr.

WITNESSES

Carroll J. Webster

Anna J. Delaney

INVENTOR.

Joseph Locke

By William Webster

Atty

DESIGN.

C. V. HELMSCHMIED.
TABLE VESSEL.

No. 21,878.   Patented Oct. 4, 1892.

Fig.1.

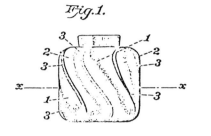

Fig.2.

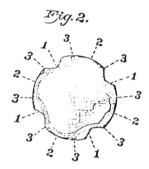

WITNESSES:

INVENTOR
Carl V. Helmschmied,

BY

ATTORNEY

UNITED STATES PATENT OFFICE.

CARL V. HELMSCHMIED, OF MERIDEN, CONNECTICUT, ASSIGNOR TO THE
C. F. MONROE COMPANY, OF SAME PLACE.

DESIGN FOR A TABLE-VESSEL.

SPECIFICATION forming part of Design No. 21,878, dated October 4, 1892.

Application filed August 18, 1892. Serial No. 443,447. Term of patent 3½ years.

To all whom it may concern:

Be it known that I, CARL V. HELMSCHMIED, a citizen of the United States, residing at Meriden, in the county of New Haven and
5 State of Connecticut, have invented and produced a new and original Design for Vessels for Table Use; and I do hereby declare the following to be a full, clear, and exact description of the invention, such as will enable oth-
10 ers skilled in the art to which it appertains to make and use the same.

Referring to the accompanying drawings, Figure 1 is an elevation of a table-salt, showing my design; Fig. 2, a cross-section of the
15 same.

Similar numbers of reference denote like parts in both figures of the drawings.

The leading feature of my design consists in an alternating series of concave and con- 20 vex surfaces spirally disposed in the direction of the height of the vessel, and a spiral rib between such surfaces.

1 denotes the concave, and 2 the convex surfaces.

3 denotes the ribs. 25

I claim—

The design for vessels for table use, substantially as herein shown and described.

In testimony whereof I affix my signature in presence of two witnesses.

CARL V. HELMSCHMIED.

Witnesses:
    WILLIS I. FENN,
    C. F. MONROE.

DESIGN.

A. E. & H. A. SMITH.
SALT HOLDER.

No. 22,342.   Patented Apr. 11, 1893.

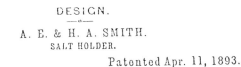

Fig.1.

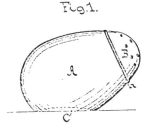

Fig.2.

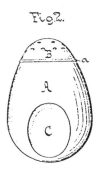

WITNESSES:

INVENTORS
Alfred E. Smith,
Harry A. Smith,
BY
ATTORNEY

UNITED STATES PATENT OFFICE.

ALFRED E. SMITH AND HARRY A. SMITH, OF NEW BEDFORD, MASSACHUSETTS.

DESIGN FOR A SALT-HOLDER.

SPECIFICATION forming part of Design No. 22,342, dated April 11, 1893.

Application filed February 1, 1893. Serial No. 460,615. Term of patent 3¼ years.

To all whom it may concern:

Be it known that we, ALFRED E. SMITH and HARRY A. SMITH, of the city of New Bedford, in the county of Bristol and State of Massa-
5 chusetts, have invented and produced a new and original Design for a Salt-Holder, of which the following is a specification, reference being had to the accompanying drawings, showing the same.

10 Figure 1, is a side view of the salt holder, and Fig. 2, is a bottom or plan view of the same.

The leading feature of our design consists in a receptacle having a segment removed
15 from its outer surface midway the longer and shorter axes of the holder.

In the drawings Fig. 1 shows the new design as it appears from the side when resting in proper position on a table. A is the body which may be of any desired material, the 20 smaller end showing perforations as at B. The field of perforations is terminated by a fancy band *a*.

What we claim is—

The design for a salt holder herein shown 25 and described.

ALFRED E. SMITH.
HARRY A. SMITH.

Witnesses:
EMMA J. SHEEHY,
NATHAN R. GIFFORD.

A. STEFFIN.
SALT BOX OR CONDIMENT HOLDER.

No. 19,120.   Patented May 28, 1889.

Fig.1.

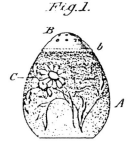

Fig.2.

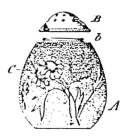

Witnesses: *Inventor.*

UNITED STATES PATENT OFFICE.

ALBERT STEFFIN, OF NEW BEDFORD, MASSACHUSETTS.

DESIGN FOR A SALT-BOX OR CONDIMENT-HOLDER.

SPECIFICATION forming part of Design No. 19,120, dated May 28, 1889.

Application filed November 10, 1887. Serial No. 254,859. Term of patent 7 years.

To all whom it may concern:

Be it known that I, ALBERT STEFFIN, a citizen of the United States, residing at New Bedford, in the county of Bristol and State of
5 Massachusetts, have invented a certain new and useful Design for Salt-Boxes or Condiment Holders and Distributers, of which the following is a specification, reference being had to the accompanying drawings.
10 My invention consists in a new and original design for salt-boxes or condiment holders and distributers, which represents the form of an egg with a flattened base, containing the following features.
15 The accompanying drawings illustrate my design, in which—

Figure 1 shows the box with the cap in place, while Fig. 2 shows the same with the cap raised.

The body A B is oval in form, having a
20 truncated base, a perforated cap or top, B, and the line of demarkation *b*, the body being decorated with artistic decorations C, giving the article a unique and tasteful appearance.

I claim as my invention—
25 A design for salt-boxes or condiment-holders, consisting of a body of oval shape having a truncated base, the perforated top and line of demarkation *b*, and provided with an ornamented surface, as shown.
30 In testimony whereof I affix my signature in presence of two witnesses.

ALBERT STEFFIN.

Witnesses:
  FRED. R. FISH,
  ARTHUR L. BLACKMER.

DESIGN.

A. STEFFIN.
CONDIMENT HOLDER.

No. 22,781.
Patented Sept. 12, 1893.

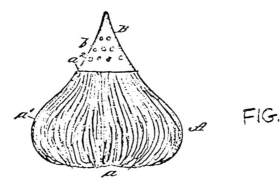

FIG.

UNITED STATES PATENT OFFICE.

ALBERT STEFFIN, OF NEW BEDFORD, MASSACHUSETTS, ASSIGNOR TO THE MOUNT WASHINGTON GLASS COMPANY, OF SAME PLACE.

DESIGN FOR A CONDIMENT-HOLDER.

SPECIFICATION forming part of Design No. 22,781, dated September 12, 1893.

Application filed March 31, 1891. Serial No. 468,617. Term of patent 7 years.

To all whom it may concern:

Be it known that I, ALBERT STEFFIN, a citizen of the United States, residing at New Bedford, in the county of Bristol and State of 5 Massachusetts, have invented and produced a new and original Design for a Condiment or other Holder, of which the following is a specification, reference being had to the accompanying drawing, showing my design.

10 The leading feature of my design is a cone-shaped receptacle having a base of contracted diameter.

A is the receptacle of a general cone-shape, the largest diameter being at a'. From a' 15 upwardly to the apex receptacle A is of constantly decreasing diameter; and from a' to its flattened base, it also constantly decreases in diameter. The apex B is perforated at b and forms the subject-matter of my pending application, Serial No. 468,619, filed March 31, 20 1893, and all rights to the same are expressly reserved. The body of receptacle A is shown as fluted vertically from the base toward apex B, the flutings being somewhat irregular and converging at a^2. 25

What I claim is—

The design for a condiment or other holder herein shown and described.

ALBERT STEFFIN.

Witnesses:
FREDERICK RATCLIFF,
F. K. ALLEN.

Witnesses:
N. E. Renick
H. E. Renick &

Inventor;
Albert Steffin
By his attorney
Edward P. Beach

March 30, 1937. R. I. DORFMAN ET AL Des. 103,910

JAR OR SIMILAR CONTAINER

Filed Jan. 9, 1937

GRECIAN GODDESS

FIG. 1.

FIG. 2.

ROBERT I. DORFMAN AND
EUGENE MUNK, INVENTORS,

BY *Julian J. Wittel,*

their ATTORNEY.

Patented Mar. 30, 1937

Des. 103,910

UNITED STATES PATENT OFFICE

103,910

DESIGN FOR A JAR OR SIMILAR CONTAINER

Robert I. Dorfman and Eugene Munk, New
York, N. Y.

Application January 9, 1937, Serial No. 66,966

Term of patent 14 years

To all whom it may concern:

Be it known that we, Robert I. Dorfman, and Eugene Munk, citizens of the United States and residing at New York, county of Bronx, and State of New York, have invented a new, original, and ornamental Design for a Jar or Similar Container, of which the following is a specification, reference being had to the accompanying drawing, forming a part thereof.

In the drawing:

Fig. 1 is a front view of a jar or similar container embodying our design, and

Fig. 2 is a side view thereof.

We claim:

The ornamental design for a jar or similar container, as shown.

ROBERT I. DORFMAN.
EUGENE MUNK.

J. W. HAINES.
Dredge-Bottle.

No. 204,564.   Patented June 4, 1878.

Fig. 1.

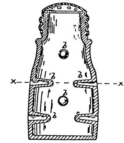

Fig. 2.

Fig. 3.

WITNESSES   INVENTOR

B. W. Williams   *John W. Haines*

John E. Fanning.   By his attys

                        Henry W. Williams atty

UNITED STATES PATENT OFFICE.

JOHN W. HAINES, OF CAMBRIDGE, MASSACHUSETTS.

IMPROVEMENT IN DREDGE-BOTTLES.

Specification forming part of Letters Patent No. **204,564**, dated June 4, 1878; application filed May 6, 1878.

To all whom it may concern:

Be it known that I, JOHN W. HAINES, of Cambridge, in the county of Middlesex and State of Massachusetts, have invented a new and valuable Improvement in Salt-Bottles for Table or Caster Use, of which the following is a specification:

This invention relates to that class of salt-bottles or salt-boxes which are arranged to prevent the salt from forming into lumps, or to break such lumps when formed, and to prevent the clogging of the cap, so that the salt may run easily through the perforations therein.

The devices heretofore used for preventing the lumping of the salt have been of two general kinds. The first kind consisted in attaching metallic stems or projections to the bottom, sides, or cap, against which metallic projections the lumps struck as the bottle was shaken. The second kind consisted of metallic forks or pieces of different shapes placed loosely within the bottle, so that as the bottle is shaken these pieces of metal rattle around therein and break the lumps.

My invention consists in a glass salt bottle or box, blown in a mold of such a shape and construction that the interior of the bottle is furnished with projections or arms extending from the sides or bottom (or both) of the bottle, said arms or projections being integral with the bottle, and of course glass. By this means the necessity of attaching or fastening any arms or stems to the inside of the bottle, or of placing anything therein loosely, is ob-

viated, and all applications of metal pieces of any kind, which are usually unhealthy, and have a tendency to soil and color the salt, are done away with.

In the accompanying drawings, in which similar letters of reference indicate like parts, Figure 1 is an elevation of a salt-bottle embodying my improvement. Fig. 2 is a vertical section of the same. Fig. 3 is a horizontal section upon line *x x*, Fig. 2.

a is an ordinary perforated cap. *b b* are the inwardly-projecting stems or arms, of any proper size and shape, of a piece with the rest of the bottle, the whole being of glass, blown in a mold. These arms *b* may be of any number, and may project either from the sides or bottom, as the mold is constructed.

Of course the bottle described may be used for containing pepper or other articles, if desired.

Having thus fully described my invention, what I claim, and desire to secure by Letters Patent, is—

A glass bottle for table or caster use, for holding salt or other substance, provided with stems or arms *b b*, projecting inwardly from the sides or bottom, or both, said stems or arms being integral with the body of the bottle, substantially as shown, and for the purpose of preventing or destroying lumps therein, as a new article of manufacture.

JOHN W. HAINES.

Witnesses:
HENRY W. WILLIAMS,
B. W. WILLIAMS.

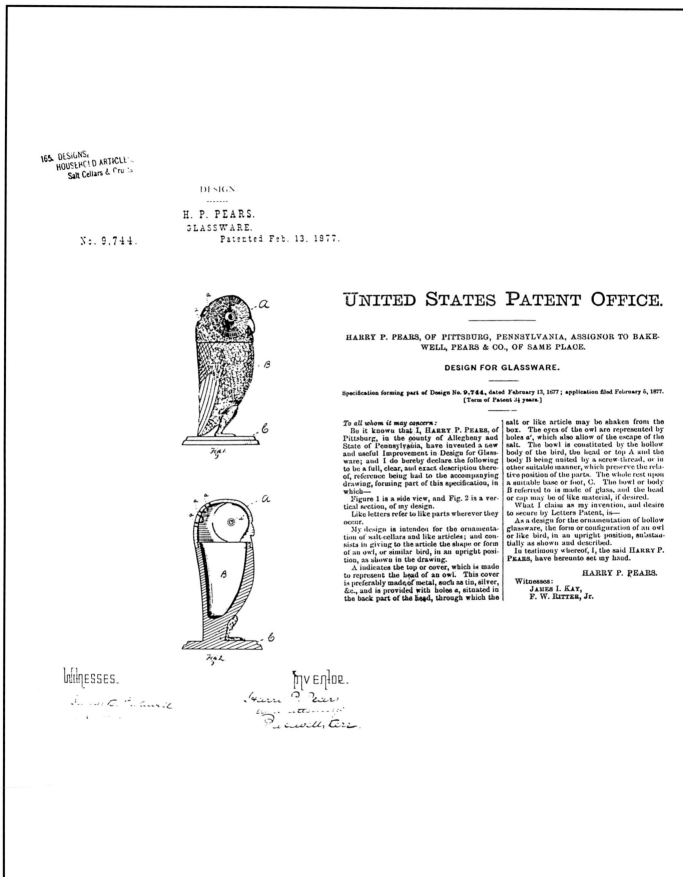

DESIGN

H. P. PEARS.
GLASSWARE.

No. 9,744.   Patented Feb. 13. 1877.

Fig.1

Fig.2

Witnesses.

Inventor.
Harry P. Pears

UNITED STATES PATENT OFFICE.

HARRY P. PEARS, OF PITTSBURG, PENNSYLVANIA, ASSIGNOR TO BAKE-WELL, PEARS & CO., OF SAME PLACE.

DESIGN FOR GLASSWARE.

Specification forming part of Design No. 9,744, dated February 13, 1877; application filed February 5, 1877.
[Term of Patent 3½ years.]

To all whom it may concern:

Be it known that I, HARRY P. PEARS, of Pittsburg, in the county of Allegheny and State of Pennsylvania, have invented a new and useful Improvement in Design for Glassware; and I do hereby declare the following to be a full, clear, and exact description thereof, reference being had to the accompanying drawing, forming part of this specification, in which—

Figure 1 is a side view, and Fig. 2 is a vertical section, of my design.

Like letters refer to like parts wherever they occur.

My design is intended for the ornamentation of salt-cellars and like articles; and consists in giving to the article the shape or form of an owl, or similar bird, in an upright position, as shown in the drawing.

A indicates the top or cover, which is made to represent the head of an owl. This cover is preferably made of metal, such as tin, silver, &c., and is provided with holes a, situated in the back part of the head, through which the salt or like article may be shaken from the box. The eyes of the owl are represented by holes a', which also allow of the escape of the salt. The bowl is constituted by the hollow body of the bird, the head or top A and the body B being united by a screw-thread, or in other suitable manner, which preserve the relative position of the parts. The whole rest upon a suitable base or foot, C. The bowl or body B referred to is made of glass, and the head or cap may be of like material, if desired.

What I claim as my invention, and desire to secure by Letters Patent, is—

As a design for the ornamentation of hollow glassware, the form or configuration of an owl or like bird, in an upright position, substantially as shown and described.

In testimony whereof, I, the said HARRY P. PEARS, have hereunto set my hand.

HARRY P. PEARS.

Witnesses:
JAMES I. KAY,
F. W. RITTER, Jr.

DESIGN.

R. HUNTER.
CONDIMENT HOLDER.

No. 27,132.

Patented June 1, 1897.

Witnesses
Albert B. Blackwood.
B. R. Kelly.

Inventor
Robert Hunter
By Connolly Bro.
Attorneys

THE NORRIS PETERS CO., PHOTO-LITHO., WASHINGTON, D. C.

UNITED STATES PATENT OFFICE.

ROBERT HUNTER, OF ROCHESTER, PENNSYLVANIA, ASSIGNOR TO THE
PHOENIX GLASS COMPANY, OF PITTSBURG, PENNSYLVANIA.

DESIGN FOR A CONDIMENT-HOLDER.

SPECIFICATION forming part of Design No. 27,132, dated June 1, 1897.

Application filed March 13, 1897. Serial No. 627,435. Term of patent 3½ years.

To all whom it may concern:

Be it known that I, ROBERT HUNTER, a citizen of the United States, residing at Rochester, in the county of Beaver and State of Pennsylvania, have invented a Design for a Condiment-Holder or Similar Article; and I do hereby declare the following to be a full, clear, and exact description of the invention, such as will enable others skilled in the art to which it appertains to make and use the same.

This invention has relation to designs for hollow articles, such as condiment-holders; and it consists in the shape and configuration herein shown and described.

In the accompanying drawing the figure is a side view or elevation of an article of tableware embracing my design.

The shape of the article is a conventional representation of the "chrysanthemum" flower, and comprises the bulbous body portion *a* and base *b*, upon which appear in relief and intermingling curves the leaves *d d*. The order and pattern in which the leaves are arranged may be varied without departing from the essential features of the design.

Having described my invention, I claim—

The design for a condiment-holder herein shown and described.

In testimony whereof I affix my signature in presence of two witnesses.

ROBERT HUNTER.

Witnesses:
  H. A. DARROLL,
  CHAS. W. HURST.

D. C. RIPLEY.

Salt and Pepper Dredges.

No. 5,666.   Reissued Nov. 18, 1873.

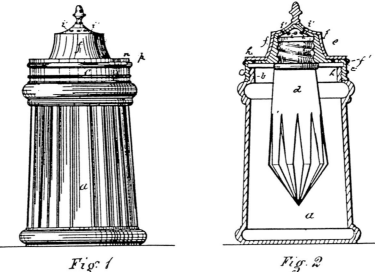

Fig. 1   Fig. 2

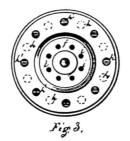

Fig. 3.

Witnesses { James I Kay   Inventor Daniel C. Ripley
           Fred. Standish   by Bakewell Christy & Ken.
                                                his attys

UNITED STATES PATENT OFFICE.

DANIEL C. RIPLEY, OF PITTSBURG, PENNSYLVANIA.

IMPROVEMENT IN SALT AND PEPPER DREDGES.

Specification forming part of Letters Patent No. 142,351, dated September 2, 1873; reissue No. **5,666,** dated November 18, 1873; application filed October 13, 1873.

To all whom it may concern:

Be it known that I, DANIEL C. RIPLEY, of Pittsburg, in the county of Allegheny and State of Pennsylvania, have invented a new and useful Improvement in Salt and Pepper Dredges; and I do hereby declare the following to be a full, clear, and exact description thereof, reference being had to the accompanying drawing forming a part of this specification, in which—

Figure 1 is a side elevation of my improved salt and pepper dredge. Fig. 2 is a vertical section of the same, and Fig. 3 is a plan view of the cap.

Like letters of reference indicate like parts in each.

My invention relates to the construction of an improved dredge for table and culinary uses; and it consists, first, of two distinct and separate chambers or compartments sifting through the same top; and, second, of the combination of the said compartments with a rotating cap, by means of which either compartment may be opened while the other is closed, the perforations in the caps registering with the desired compartment upon the rotation of the cap.

The object of my invention is a dredge which will contain two different condiments.

To enable others skilled in the art to make and use my improvement, I will describe its construction and manner of use.

In the drawing I show a form of my invention which is especially designed for table use.

I make the body or can a of any desired shape or material. I prefer, however, to make it of glass, as it is the cheapest and most suitable. Around its mouth I make a thread, b, upon which I screw a stationary cap, c. The cap c has a threaded socket, e, in its center for the reception of the threaded end of the receptacle d, which extends down into the can a. In the cap c I make two sets of holes or perforations, the first set, h, opening into the can a, and the second set, i, opening into the receptacle d. Upon the face of the cap c I put a turning or rotating cover or cap, f, which is secured by its overlapping lip f', burnished or drawn in around the projecting edge c' of the cap c. The cover f has a slight rotating motion over the face of the cap c, which is limited by a stop, n, extending down into the slot p in the cap c, or by any other equivalent stop device.

The perforations of the two series h and i in the cap c are placed opposite each other. In the cover f I make two similar sets or series of perforations, h' and i', which correspond with the perforations h and i in every respect, except in their relative arrangement, not being placed opposite to, but alternately with each other.

The effect of this arrangement is, that when the two caps are put together, and either two corresponding sets, such as the set i in cap c, and the set i' in the cover f, are brought together, the other two sets, h and h', will be disconnected, as shown in Fig. 3, so as to close the openings from the can a. By turning the cap f the extent of its movement, these perforations will be brought together and the perforations i and i' will be separated, thereby closing the openings from the receptacle d, and opening those from the can a.

The stop device may be omitted, if desired, its object being convenience in registering the perforations in the caps.

The dredge shown is more particularly designed for use with pepper and salt.

It is evident to all that the arrangement of the compartments may be changed, as, for instance, the can a may be divided equally into two compartments by a division-wall extending across it, and the perforations be arranged so that when in use they may be open to the desired compartment and closed to the other.

The utility of my improvement and the advantages arising from its use are evident, and I will not enlarge thereupon.

What I claim as my invention, and desire to secure by Letters Patent, is—

1. A dredge having two compartments with the discharge-openings at one and the same end, as described.

2. The combination, in a dredge, of two

DESIGN.

C. F. MONROE.
SALT CELLAR, &c.

No. 20,788.   Patented June 2, 1891.

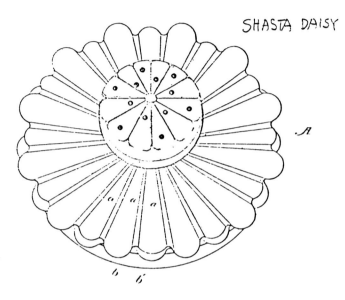

SHASTA DAISY

Witnesses:
A.S. Cushman.

Inventor:
Charles F. Monroe.

By
Arthur M. Harrison

UNITED STATES PATENT OFFICE.

CHARLES F. MONROE, OF MERIDEN, CONNECTICUT.

DESIGN FOR A SALT-CELLAR, &c.

SPECIFICATION forming part of Design No. 20,788, dated June 2, 1891.

Application filed May 5, 1891. Serial No. 391,678. Term of patent 7 years.

To all whom it may concern:

Be it known that I, CHARLES F. MONROE, of Meriden, in the county of New Haven and State of Connecticut, have invented and pro-
5 duced a new and original Design for Salt-Cellars or Pepper-Boxes; and I do hereby declare the following to be a full, clear, and exact description of said invention, reference being had to the accompanying drawing, and to the
10 letters of reference marked thereon, which form a part of this specification.

The said photograph represents one of my salt-cellars as tilted somewhat upon its side to clearly show the leading feature of my de-
15 sign, which consists in the top or upper surface having a scalloped edge with grooves or lines converging toward the center.

A is the upper surface of the salt-cellar, and *a* are lines radiating from the raised center,
20 which supports the perforated sprinkler. The outer edge of the surface is curved between the lines, as at *b* and *b'*, and preferably the said curves are alternately different distances from the center, the whole forming an irregular scalloped edge, and with the lines *a* hav-25 ing the appearance somewhat of a daisy or chrysanthemum, some of the petals of which are shorter than the others.

To enhance the beauty of the design, I may have the portion of the body of the salt-cellar 30 that is just below the outer ends of the shorter petals formed with projecting curves, as at *c*.

This design is for the shape of the upper surface of the body of the salt-cellar and is irrespective of the shape of the lower part 35 and of any painting or other surface ornamentation.

As is obvious, the same design may serve for pepper-boxes.

What I claim is— 40
The design for a salt or pepper box, substantially as shown and described.

In testimony whereof I affix my signature in presence of two subscribing witnesses.

CHARLES F. MONROE.

Witnesses:
HELEN C. BECKWITH,
C. J. HELMSCHMIED.

DESIGN

No. 35,320.

B. CRAWFORD.
CONDIMENT BOX.
(Application filed Oct. 21, 1901.)

Patented Nov. 26, 1901.

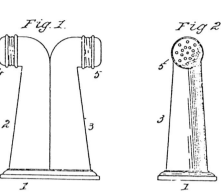

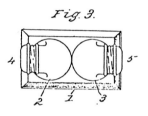

Fig. 1.

Fig 2

Fig. 3.

Witnesses.
Nora Graham
Ira C. Graham

Inventor
Benjamin Crawford
By L. R. Graham
his attorney.

UNITED STATES PATENT OFFICE.

BENJAMIN CRAWFORD, OF CHICAGO, ILLINOIS.

DESIGN FOR A CONDIMENT-BOX.

SPECIFICATION forming part of Design No. 35,320, dated November 26, 1901.

Application filed October 21, 1901. Serial No. 79,491. Term of patent 7 years.

To all whom it may concern:

Be it known that I, BENJAMIN CRAWFORD, of the city of Chicago, county of Cook, and State of Illinois, have invented a new and useful Design for a Condiment-Box, of which the following is a specification.

The box described herein and illustrated in the accompanying drawings is particularly intended to hold salt and pepper for table use; and its essential characteristics reside in a base on which are conjoined two receptacles having their perforated discharge ends presented horizontally in opposite directions.

In the drawings, Figure 1 is a face elevation, Fig. 2 is a side elevation, and Fig. 3 is a plan, of my design.

The base is shown at 1, one receptacle is shown at 2, and the discharge end thereof at 4, while the other receptacle is shown at 3 and the discharge end thereof at 5. The base is oblong, the receptacles are circular and tapering, and the discharge ends are circular in cross-section and perforated, as shown in Fig. 2. The receptacles back one against the other to near their upper ends and then curve outward in opposite directions.

Having described my invention, what I claim as new, and desire to secure by Letters Patent, is—

The design for a condiment-box herein shown and described.

In testimony whereof I sign my name in the presence of two subscribing witnesses.

BENJAMIN CRAWFORD.

Witnesses:
W. B. NICHOLS,
ISHMAEL JONES.

DESIGN.
—o—
N. KOPP.
CLOSED VESSEL WITH PERFORATED COVER.

No. 20,566.   Patented Mar. 10, 1891.

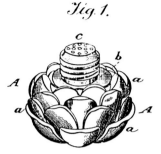

Fig. 1.

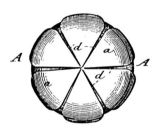

Fig. 2.

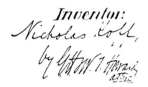

Witnesses:
A. Ruppert.
E. Cruse

Inventor:
Nicholas Kopp,
by Gtt. W. I. Thrain
att'y

UNITED STATES PATENT OFFICE.

NICHOLAS KOPP, OF FOSTORIA, OHIO, ASSIGNOR TO THE FOSTORIA SHADE
AND LAMP COMPANY, OF SAME PLACE.

DESIGN FOR A CLOSED VESSEL WITH PERFORATED COVER.

SPECIFICATION forming part of Design No. 20,566, dated March 10, 1891.

Application filed January 24, 1891. Serial No. 378,979. Term of patent 7 years.

To all whom it may concern:

Be it known that I, NICHOLAS KOPP, a citizen of the United States, residing at Fostoria, in the county of Seneca and State of Ohio, have invented and produced a new and original Design for Closed Vessels with Perforated Covers, of which the following is a specification, reference being had to the accompanying drawings, forming a part thereof.

Figure 1 is a perspective view, and Fig. 2 a view of the under side of my design.

The leading feature of my design consists in the hollow body A, having the outline or shape of a flower of the rosaceous order, of which the rose is a genus, which when viewed in perspective, as in Fig. 1, has its petals *a* standing in the way in which they are ordinarily found in flowers of the order named when in bloom, and from the center of the body rises a neck or tube *b*, surmounted by the perforated cover or cap *c*. On the under side of the design, as seen in Fig. 2, the divisions of the petals are represented by the lines *d*.

This design, which is intended for all classes of closed vessels provided with perforated covers or caps, may be executed in china, glass, or other ware, to which the natural color of the flower may be given, if desired.

What I claim is—

The design for closed vessels with perforated covers herein shown and described, representing a flower of the rosaceous order, of which the rose is a genus, the same comprising the body A, the petals *a*, and the neck or tube *b*, rising centrally from the body and surmounted by a perforated cover, substantially as set forth.

NICHOLAS KOPP.

Witnesses:
J. D. SNYDER,
J. B. GRAHAM.

No. 750,688.

PATENTED JAN. 26, 1904.

L. B. PARKER.
COMPOSITE CONDIMENT HOLDER.
APPLICATION FILED JUNE 13, 1903.

NO MODEL.

Fig. I.

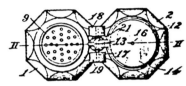

Fig. II.

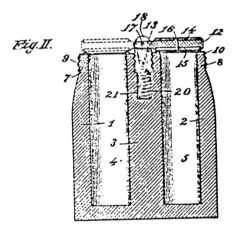

2 Witnesses
H. S. Austin
Frank J. Kent

Inventor:
Lyman B. Parker
By Joseph E. Atkins
Attorney.

UNITED STATES PATENT OFFICE.

LYMAN B. PARKER, OF CHICKASHA, INDIAN TERRITORY.

COMPOSITE CONDIMENT-HOLDER.

SPECIFICATION forming part of Letters Patent No. 750,688, dated January 26, 1904.

Application filed June 13, 1903. Serial No. 161,301. (No model.)

To all whom it may concern:

Be it known that I, LYMAN B. PARKER, of Chickasha, in the Chickasaw Nation, Indian Territory, have invented certain new and use-
5 ful Improvements in Composite Condiment-Holders, of which the following is a complete specification, reference being had to the accompanying drawings.

The object of my invention is to produce
10 improvements in unitary articles for holding a plurality of condiments and for selectively discharging the contents thereof at the will of the manipulator.

In the accompanying drawings, Figure I is
15 a top plan view of a form of embodiment of my invention presented in a two-compartment holder. Fig. II is a section on the line II II of Fig. I, the cap being shown on one side in section and on the other side in dotted lines
20 and the cap-actuating spring being shown in elevation.

Referring to the numerals on the drawings, 1 indicates one compartment, and 2 the other, which are united, as by an integral medial wall
25 or septum 3, into a single article, provided upon opposite sides of the wall 3 with recesses 4 and 5, which constitute the hollow interiors of the compartments 1 and 2, respectively. Each of the compartments is preferably furnished with
30 a cylindrical preferably externally-threaded neck (indicated by the numerals 7 and 8, respectively, and adapted to accommodate one of the usual perforated screw-caps 9 and 10.)

The compartment 2 being provided, for ex-
35 ample, with salt and the compartment 1 with pepper, it is designed that one may help himself at pleasure to either of said condiments in the usual way, but without discharging or depositing any portion of the contents of the
40 other compartment than that which holds the condiment which he selects. Accordingly I provide a cap or disk 12, having a tailpiece 13 and provided upon opposite sides with pads

14 and 15, secured, as by a central pin 16, to
45 the cap or disk 12. To take the place of the pads, the disk may be made of yielding flexible material. The cap or disk 12 is adapted to close either of the recesses 4 and 5 at pleasure, and for that purpose it is preferably piv-
50 oted, as by a pin 17 passing through the tailpiece 13, to lugs 18 and 19, extending upwardly from the compartments 1 and 2 and the septum 3.

Within a recess in the septum and between
55 the lugs 18 and 19 I provide a coiled spring 20, seated at its lower end on the bottom of a spring socket or recess 21 and at the other end secured to the end of the tailpiece 13. The tendency of the spring 20 is to yieldingly
60 urge one or the other padded side of the cap 12 against one or the other of the necks 7 and 8, or, in other words, against one of the screw-caps 9 and 10.

In operation, the recesses 4 and 5 being prop-
65 erly charged, a manipulator turns the cap 12 to one side or the other of the holder and from the open recess thereof causes discharge of its contents, as by shaking in the ordinary way.

What I claim is—

70 In a composite condiment-holder the combination with a plurality of compartments provided with an intermediate spring-socket, of lugs upon opposite sides thereof, a cap provided with a tailpiece pivoted between said
75 lugs, and a trigger-spring seated in the socket and engaging the end of the tailpiece on the other side of the pivot from the cap, to hold said cap firmly over either compartment of the holder.

80 In testimony of all which I have hereunto subscribed my name.

LYMAN B. PARKER.

Witnesses:
M. C. HAECKER,
F. B. HOUSTON.

(No Model.)

L. W. HUSK.
DREDGE BOX.

No. 247,358.   Patented Sept. 20, 1881.

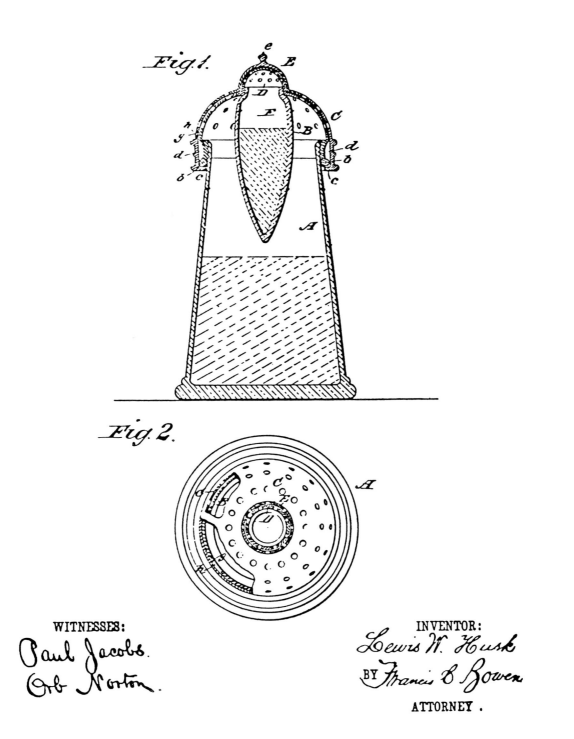

Fig. 1.

Fig. 2.

WITNESSES:
Paul Jacobs.
Orb Norton.

INVENTOR:
Lewis W. Husk
BY Francis C. Bowen
ATTORNEY.

UNITED STATES PATENT OFFICE.

LEWIS W. HUSK, OF ALBANY, NEW YORK.

DREDGE-BOX.

SPECIFICATION forming part of Letters Patent No. 247,358, dated September 20, 1881.

Application filed April 21, 1881. (No model.)

To all whom it may concern:

Be it known that I, LEWIS W. HUSK, of Albany, in the county of Albany and State of New York, have invented certain new and useful Improvements in Dredge-Boxes; and I do hereby declare that the following is a full, clear, and exact description of the invention, that will enable others skilled in the art to which it appertains to make and use the same, reference being had to the accompanying drawings, and to the letters of reference marked thereon, which form a part of this specification.

My invention relates to vessels for holding and distributing separately different kinds of seasonings, such as salt and pepper, and also for powder of various kinds.

The invention consists in a novel construction of a box or vessel containing another box or vessel provided with a foraminous lid and a foraminous cover or cap fitting over and sliding around upon said lid, as hereinafter more particularly described.

In the accompanying drawings, Figure 1 represents a vertical section of a vessel constructed according to my invention; and Fig. 2 is a top view of the same, partly broken away.

A is a vessel or box, constructed of glass, tin, wood, or any other suitable material, made with fluted sides or otherwise, for holding one kind of seasoning, provided with a perforated or foraminous lid, B, thereto attached by means of screw-threads in the usual manner. This lid is provided with a perforated or foraminous dome, D, in its upper part, screw-threaded on part of its inner surface.

F is a vessel or box, screw-threaded at its neck for attaching it to the dome D.

C is a perforated or foraminous cap, having a dome, E, also foraminous, and a knob, c, for revolving it, and fitting closely over and revolving upon the lid B and dome D. It is attached by means of a flange, e, projecting inwardly from its lower part, which is sprung over a bead, b, on the lid B, as shown in the drawings. The perforations or foramina in the dome E and the cap C are arranged in lines radiating from the center thereof; but the radial lines of the foramina in the dome are so directed that they would, if extended, be between the lines of foramina in the other part of the cap, so that when the foramina in the dome of the lid and those in the dome-cap correspond those in the outer and lower parts of the lid and cap do not, thus allowing but one kind of seasoning to be distributed at a time. The cap is prevented from revolving too far by means of a stud, g, and slot h, the stud being either on the lid and working in a slot in the cap, as shown in Fig. 1, or on the cap and working in a slot in the lid, as shown in Fig. 2.

The mode of operation of my invention is as follows: In order to fill the vessel with seasoning the upper parts are unscrewed from the vessel A, which can then be nearly filled, leaving a little space for the material that will be displaced on the replacing of the inner vessel, F. To fill the inner vessel, F, it is unscrewed from the lid B in the ordinary manner.

When it is desired to distribute the seasoning from the inner vessel the cap is turned until the foramina of the domes correspond. To distribute seasoning from the outer vessel the cap is turned in the reverse direction until the foramina of the outer and lower parts of the cap and the lid correspond. The stud g is intended to indicate when the foramina of either part of the cap correspond with the proper parts of the lid by reaching the end of its slot h and preventing further revolution of the cap.

The advantage of my invention over former combined dredge-boxes is that while in my invention one kind of seasoning is perfectly prevented from passing into the vessel containing the other kind, yet it is comparatively simple in construction.

I am aware that combined dredge-boxes have been heretofore made which are much more simple than my invention; but they do not keep the various condiments separate perfectly.

I am also aware that Letters Patent have been heretofore granted for combined dredge-boxes which perfectly prevent the condiments from intermixing with each other; but the inventions so patented have been much more complicated and costly than my invention, and also more delicate and liable to get out of order.

My invention has been particularly described in reference to the construction of a vessel or box containing another vessel, each provided with foraminous tops; but it is equally applicable to the employment of a single vessel provided with tops having perforations in them, as described, so that it can be used for powder and other like substances, if necessary.

Having thus described my invention, what I claim as new, and desire to secure by Letters Patent, is—

The combination of the outer vessel, A, having the lid B, adapted to be screwed thereon, and provided with the bead b, the inner vessel, F, the cap or cover C fitted over B and adapted to be sprung into the bead b, and the stud g and slot h, lid and cover, all arranged and operated herein shown and described.

In testimony that I claim the foregoing I have hereunto set my hand this 21st April, 1881.

LEWIS W. HUSK.

Witnesses:
FRANCIS C. BOWEN,
EDGAR GARRETSON.

(No Model.)

M. THOMSON.
SALT CELLAR.

No. 374,508.　　　　Patented Dec. 6, 1887.

Fig.1.

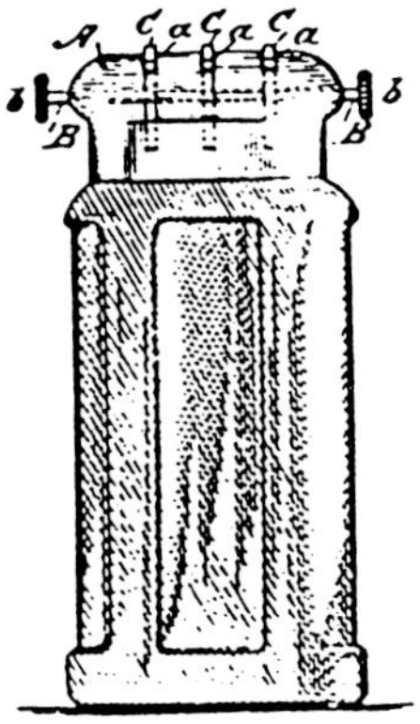

Fig.2.

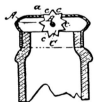

UNITED STATES PATENT OFFICE.

METELLUS THOMSON, OF KENTON, OHIO.

SALT-CELLAR.

SPECIFICATION forming part of Letters Patent No. 374,508, dated December 6, 1887.

Application filed March 25, 1887. Serial No. 232,352. (No model.)

To all whom it may concern:

Be it known that I, METELLUS THOMSON, of Kenton, in the county of Hardin and State of Ohio, have invented a new and useful Improvement in Salt-Cellars, of which the following is a specification.

My invention is an improvement in receptacles especially intended for use as salt-cellars, but which manifestly may be used for pepper and other like articles which it may be desired to distribute in finely-divided portions. Therefore, while the following description and the appended claim may refer to the improvement as pertaining to salt-cellars, it will be understood that I do not desire to be confined to such use.

The invention consists in a salt-cellar top provided with a slot or slots and having a disk or disks operating through said slot, and provided with sockets which receive the salt when within the cellar and discharge the same when the disk is turned to bring the sockets out of the top.

In the drawings, Figure 1 is a side elevation of a salt-cellar provided with my improvements, and Fig. 2 is a partial section thereof drawn through one of the slots of the top.

In the use of the ordinary pepper-box salt-cellars the perforations frequently become clogged up, and by being sometimes clogged and at other times open, at times the salt is discharged quite freely, while at others little or no salt can be obtained. This leads to difficulties in properly seasoning the food at the table, which, while they may appear slight, are, in fact, troublesome and annoying. To avoid this difficulty various devices have been provided for keeping the salt in the cellar finely pulverized, as well as for opening the perforations in the top. By my invention, however, I seek to provide a device which may be easily operated, and the use of which will involve a positive outfeeding of the salt in an even regular quantity, so that the user may employ any quantity of salt desired.

The top A is provided in its upper side with one or more slots, a, usually, and preferably three, as shown. To the top is journaled the shaft B, which extends at right angles to the direction of length of the slots a, and is provided with heads b or similar expedients, by which it may be easily turned. The disk or disks C are secured to this shaft B and turn through the slot or slots a, the number of disks and slots corresponding, as shown. Sockets c are formed in the disks, and such sockets in the turning of the disks are brought into the cellar, where they receive salt when the cellar is inverted, and then out through slots a when they discharge the salt, and by means of this construction the salt may be discharged positively to any desired quantity by the proper turning of the shaft.

The improvement is simple and in practice efficiently serves its end, its operation being easy and its action certain, as will be readily understood from the foregoing description and the accompanying drawings.

Having thus described my invention, what I claim, and desire to secure by Letters Patent, is—

As an improved article of manufacture, the herein-described salt-cellar top provided with a slot, the journaled shaft, and a disk fixed thereto and provided with sockets, the said disk being arranged to operate through the slot of the top, as and for the purposes specified.

METELLUS THOMSON.

Witnesses:
CHARLES SCHRADER,
KARL POERTNER.

WITNESSES:
Fred G. Dieterich
O. B. Turpin.

INVENTOR:
Metellus Thomson

BY Munn & Co
ATTORNEYS.

DESIGN.

J. LOCKE.
CONDIMENT HOLDER.

No. 19,462.

Patented Dec. 3, 1889.

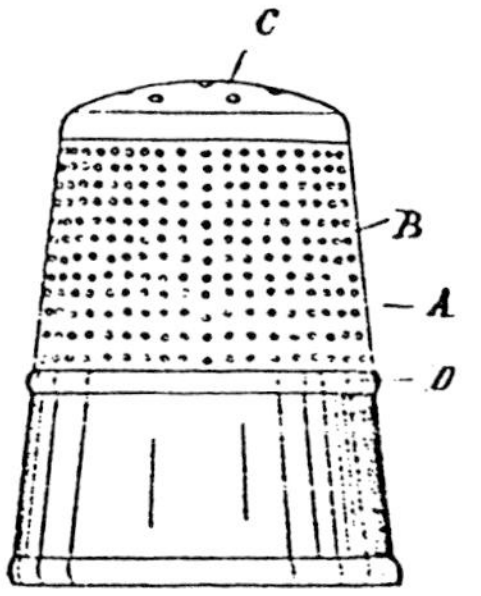

Fig.1.

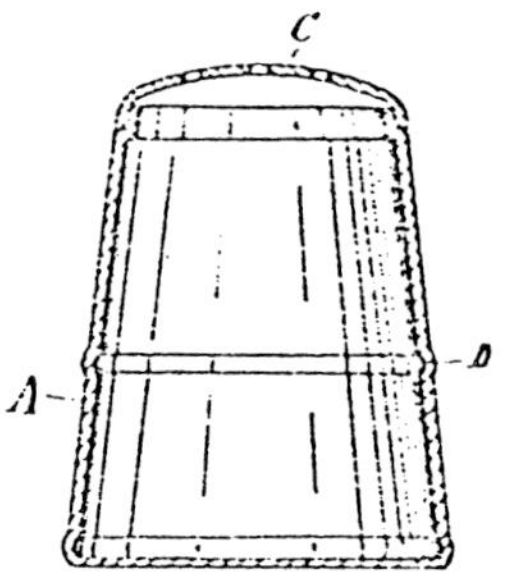

Fig.2.

UNITED STATES PATENT OFFICE.

JOSEPH LOCKE, OF TOLEDO, OHIO, ASSIGNOR TO THE W. L. LIBBEY & SON COMPANY, OF SAME PLACE.

DESIGN FOR A CONDIMENT-HOLDER.

SPECIFICATION forming part of Design No. 19,462, dated December 3, 1889.

Application filed October 7, 1889. Serial No. 326,285. Term of patent 3½ years.

To all whom it may concern:

Be it known that I, JOSEPH LOCKE, a citizen of the United States, and a resident of Toledo, in the county of Lucas and State of 5 Ohio, have invented and produced a new and original Design for Condiment-Receptacles; and I do hereby declare that the following is a full, clear, and exact description of the invention, which will enable others skilled in 10 the art to which it appertains to make and use the same, reference being had to the accompanying drawings, and to the letters of reference marked thereon, which form part of this specification.

15 The class to which my design belongs is that of condiment-receptacles, &c., and has reference to the exterior contour and ornamentation thereof.

The drawing, Figure 1, represents a salt or 20 pepper box embodying my design. Fig. 2 is a longitudinal vertical section thereof.

The leading feature of my design is a receptacle of the character specified in the form of a thimble having a closed bottom and perforated top.

25 A designates the receptacle, in the form of a truncated cone with a portion of the upper part indented, as at B; in representation of the usual indentations of a thimble, and with the upper portion inclosed by a perforated 30 cover C. An annular corrugation D is formed upon the side of the receptacle.

What I claim is—

The design for a condiment-receptacle, substantially as shown and described.

35 In testimony that I claim the foregoing as my own I hereby affix my signature in presence of two witnesses.

JOSEPH LOCKE.

Witnesses:
WILLIAM WEBSTER,
SOLON O. RICHARDSON, Jr.

WITNESSES.

C. and J. Webster.
Anna F. Chaney.

INVENTOR.

Joseph Locke
By William Webster
Atty

DESIGN.
—o—
A. STEFFIN.
SALT CELLAR, &c.

No. 19,539.   Patented Dec. 31, 1889.

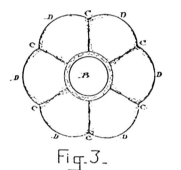

Fig. 3.

TOMATO

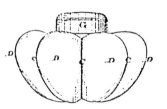

Fig. 1.

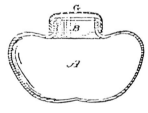

Fig. 2.

UNITED STATES PATENT OFFICE.

ALBERT STEFFIN, OF NEW BEDFORD, MASSACHUSETTS.

DESIGN FOR A SALT-CELLAR, &c.

SPECIFICATION forming part of Design No. 19,539, dated December 31, 1889.

Application filed September 25, 1889. Serial No. 325,106. Term of patent 7 years.

To all whom it may concern:

Be it known that I, ALBERT STEFFIN, designer and decorator, a citizen of the United States, residing at New Bedford, in the county of Bristol and State of Massachusetts, have invented certain new and useful Improvements in Designs for Salt or Sugar Boxes; and I do declare the following to be a, full, clear, and exact description of the invention, such as will enable others skilled in the art to which it appertains to make and use the same, reference being had to the accompanying drawings, and to the letters and figures of reference marked thereon, which form a part of this specification.

My invention relates to designs for salt, pepper, or sugar boxes; and it consists in an article of manufacture made in the form of a tomato and provided with an opening or neck, as will be more fully described hereinafter.

Figure 1 is a side elevation of a box which embodies my invention. Fig. 2 is a vertical section of the same. Fig. 3 is a plan view with the cover removed.

A represents a salt, pepper, or sugar box or receptacle, which is made in the form of a tomato. The opening B into the box is through the neck formed upon its top. This box or receptacle has creases or grooves C in its outer side, and these creases or grooves radiate from a common center, as shown in Fig. 1, forming the rounded portions D in between them. The width of the box or receptacle is greater than its height, and this, in connection with the flattened form and the grooves or creases, gives the box the appearance of a tomato. Over the opening is placed a perforated cover G.

Having thus described my invention, I claim—

The design for a salt, pepper, or sugar box of the form of a tomato and having an opening or neck, substantially as shown and described.

In testimony whereof I affix my signature in presence of two witnesses.

ALBERT STEFFIN.

Witnesses:
G. T. SANFORD,
C. H. BARTLETT.

WITNESSES:

Chas. F. Swift
George H. Swift

INVENTOR:

Albert Steffin
F. W. Lehmann,
Atty.

DESIGN.

S. McKEE.

Pepper-Cruet.

No. 11,744.   Patented April 20, 1880.

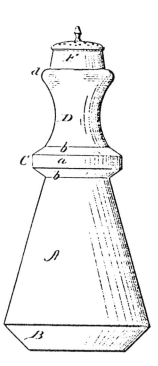

UNITED STATES PATENT OFFICE.

STEWART McKEE, OF PITTSBURG, PENNSYLVANIA.

DESIGN FOR PEPPER-CRUETS.

SPECIFICATION forming part of Design No. 11,744, dated April 20, 1880.

Application filed March 29, 1880. Term of patent 7 years.

To all whom it may concern:

Be it known that I, STEWART McKEE, of Pittsburg, in the county of Allegheny, and in the State of Pennsylvania, have invented certain new and useful Improvements in Designs for Pepper-Cruets; and I do hereby declare that the following is a full, clear, and exact description thereof, reference being had to the accompanying drawing, and to the letters of reference marked thereon, making a part of this specification.

The nature of my design is fully illustrated in the accompanying drawing.

A represents the body of the cruet, made in the form of a truncated cone. The bottom B is tapering in the opposite direction. On top of the cone A is formed a band, C, having a straight surface, a, and upper and lower beveled surfaces, b b. Above this band is the neck D, made concave, and terminating in a circular or convex ridge, d, and a suitable mouth to receive the cap F.

What I claim is—

The design for pepper-cruet, consisting of the conical body A, tapering bottom B, the band C, and neck D, substantially as shown and described.

In testimony that I claim the foregoing I have hereunto set my hand this 16th day of March, 1880.

STEWART McKEE.

Witnesses:
J. J. McCARTHY,
H. AUBREY TOULMIN.

Witnesses:

Inventor:

Notes

The following notes are listed in numerical order alphabetically by glass factory/house. They are normally used as a comment or reference at the bottom of a page, or to add confirmatory evidence to a statement made within a specific section of text. We have deemed it best to consolidate this information within a special section in the interest of brevity and reader convenience.

The Bellaire Goblet Company
[1]See *Findlay Glass* by Measell and Smith, page 65.

Boston & Sandwich Glass Company
[1]*The Glass Industry In Sandwich*, Volumes 2, 3, 4, by Raymond E. Barlow & Joan E. Kaiser.
[2]*The Glass Industry In Sandwich*, Volume 1.
[3]*The Decorating Work of Mary Gregory*, Volume 2, pages 277 through 288.
[4]*The Glass Industry In Sandwich*, Volume 2, page 292.

Cambridge Glass Company
[1]The Kamm pattern name has been endorsed by both Arthur Peterson and A.C. Revi.

Dazell, Gilmore and Leighton Company
[1]See *Findlay Glass* by Measell & Smith, pages 78 & 79.
[2]See *Nineteenth Century Glass* by A.C. Revi, page 208.

The Dithridge Princess Swirl
[1]See Clear Over Cranberry shaker on page 82 in the "Fenton Art Glass Co." section of this book.

George Duncan and Sons
[1]See *American Pressed Glass & Figure Bottles*, by A.C. Revi, pages 142, 143.

Eagle Glass & Manufacturing Company
[1]See *Victorian Colored Pattern Glass*, Book 3, by William Heacock, page 86.

Gillinder and Sons
[1]See *Victorian Colored Pattern Glass*, Book 3 by William Heacock, page 86.

The Helmschmied Manufacturing Company
[1]See *American Art Nouveau Glass* by A.C. Revi, page 288.

The Imperial Glass Company
[1]See *Colored Glassware of the Depression Era 2*, page 160, Hazel Marie Weatherman.

Kokomo Glass Company
[1]See *American Pressed Glass and Figure Bottles*, by A.C. Revi.

Lancaster Glass Works
[1]See *Victorian Colored Pattern Glass*, Book 3, by William Heacock, page 85.

Longwy Faience Company
[1]See *New Dictionary of Marks; Pottery & Porcelain, 1850 to Present*, by Ralph and Terry Kovel.

Model Flint Glass Company
[1]See *Opalescent Glass*, by William Heacock, page 23.

Moser Meierhofen Works
[1]See *Moser Artistry in Glass, 1857-1938* by Gary

Baldwin and Lee Carno. Copyright 1988 by Antique Publications.
[2]See *American Silver Manufacturers: Their Marks, Trademarks and History*, by Dorothy T. Rainwater: Copyright 1966.

Phoenix Glass Company
[1]See *Victorian Colored Pattern Glass*, Book 3 by William Heacock, page 51
[2]See *Collecting Glass*, Volume 3, page 63, by William Heacock.

L.E. Smith Glass Company
[1]See *Depression Glass III* by Sandra Stout, pages 28 and 29.

Steuben Glass Works
[1]See *American Art Nouveau Glass* by A.C. Revi, 1968, Steuben Glass Works chapter.
[2]See *American Art Nouveau Glass* by Revi, pages 134 and 135.

The Thompson Glass Company Limited
[1]See *Victorian Colored Pattern Glass*, Book 7, by William Heacock, page 197.

Tiffany Furnaces
[1]As this book is being written, this shaker along with the Carl Just collection is being prepared for auction in New York City.

The West Virginia Glass Company
[1]See *Old Pattern Glass* according to Heacock, pages 98, 99.

Potpourri
[1]See *Collecting Glass*, Volume II, pages 13–28.
[2]See *Greentown Glass* by J. Measell, picture 205, page 88.
[3]See *The Glass of C.F. Monroe* by Wilfred Cohen, page 152.
[4]See *The Pairpoint Glass Story* by G.C. Avila, page 6.
[5]See *The Glass of C.F. Monroe* by Wilfred Cohen, page 205, illustration 6900.
[6]See Kamm 2, page 26, for pattern details.
[7]See page 133 of *Glass Salt Shakers. 1000 Patterns*, by A.G. Peterson, for more details.
[8]See Heacock 9, page 61.
[9]See Heacock 2, page 70.
[10]See *Glass Salt Shakers: 1000 Patterns* by A.G. Peterson, pages 66 & 143.
[11]See Heacock 6, page 56, Hobbs Brockunier Trade Ad.
[12]See *Collectible Glass* illustration 352 by Theodore & Viola Lagerberg, published by Wallace-Homestead Book Company.
[13]See *Nineteenth Century Glass* by A.C. Revi, pages 268–269.

Bibliography References

Archer, Douglas and Margaret. *Imperial Glass Company*. (catalogue reprint). Collector Books, Paducah, Kentucky.

Barlow, R.E. & J.E. Kaiser. *The Glass Industry In Sandwich, Volumes 1, 2, 3, & 4*. Barlow/Kaiser Publishing Co. Windham, New. Hampshire.

Barnett, Jerry. *Paden City - The Color Co*. Stevens Publishing Co., Astoria, Illinois (Out of Print).

Boyd, Ralph & Louise. *Greentown In Color*. Modlin Printing Co., Marion, Idaho.

Bredehoft, Neila. *Heisey Glass (1925-1938)*. Collector Books, Paducah, Kentucky.

Fauster, Carl U. *Libbey Glass*. Len Beach Press, Toledo, Ohio.

Gardner, Paul V. *The Glass of Frederick Carder*. Crown Publishers, Inc., New York. (1971-2nd edition).

Hartung, Marion. *Northwood Pattern Glass in Color*. Privately Printed by Author (1969). Emporia, Kansas.

Heacock, William. *Encyclopedia of Victorian Colored Pattern Glass*, Vol. 1–7. Antique Publications, Marietta, Ohio.

Heacock, William. *Fenton Books 1, 2, & 3*. Antique Publications, Marietta, Ohio.

Heacock, William. *The Glass Collector*, Vol. 1, 2 and 3. Antique Publications, Marietta, Ohio.

Herrick, Ruth. *Greentown Glass*. 4th Edition (1970). Published privately by the author. Grand Rapids, Michigan (out of print).

Kamm, Minnie W. *Pattern Glass*. (8 books). Antique Publications, Marietta, Ohio.

Lechner, Mildred and Ralph. *The World of Salt Shakers*. Collector Books, Paducah, Kentucky.

McKearin, A.E. *American Glass*. Crown Publishers, New York.

Measell, James & Don E. Smith. *Findlay Glass*. Antique Publications, Marietta, Ohio.

Measell, James. *Greentown Glass*. Grand Rapids, Michigan, Public Museum.

Metz, Alice H. *American Pattern Glass 1 & 2*. Collector Books, Paducah, Kentucky.

Millard, S.T. *Goblets 1 & 2*. Wallace-Homestead Company, Des Moines, Iowa.

Millard, S.T. *Opaque Glass*. (3rd edition, 1953). Central Press, Topeka, Kansas (out of print).

Miller, Everett and Addie. *New Martinsville Glass Story*. Richardson Printing Company. Marietta, Ohio (out of print).

Murray, Dean L. *More Cruets Only*. (1973), Kilgore Graphics Inc., Phoenix, Arizona.

Peterson, A.G. *Glass Patents & Patterns*. (1973), Celery City Printing Company, Sanford, Florida.

Peterson, A.G. *Glass Salt Shakers: 1000 Patterns*. (1970) Wallace-Homestead, Des Moines, Iowa.

Revi, Albert C. *American Art Nouveau Glass*. Crown Publishers, Inc., New York.

Revi, Albert C. *American Pressed Glass and Figure Bottles*. Crown Publishers Inc., New York.

Revi, Albert C. *Nineteenth Century Glass*. Crown Publishers Inc., New York.

Shuman, John A. *American Art Glass*. Collector Books, Paducah, Kentucky.

Stevens, Gerald. *Canadian Glass - 1825-1925*. Ashton-Potter Ltd., Toronto, Canada.

Stevens, Gerald. *Glass In Canada: The First One Hundred Years*. Ashton-Potter, Ltd., Toronto, Canada.

Stout, Sandra. *Complete Book of McKee Glass*. (1972), The Trojan Press, North Kansas City, Missouri.

Stout, Sandra. *Three Books on Depression Glass*. Wallace-Homestead, Des Moines, Iowa.

Pattern Index

Value Guide

The prices listed in this value guide are for shakers pictured in this book. If a pair of shakers is illustrated, then the dollar value given is for that pair. Most of the prices are for single shakers which represent the majority of items depicted. All of the shakers shown are in excellent condition unless otherwise stated in the text.

Page 17
Hexaglory Condiment Set. 500.00-530.00
Page 18
Barrel, Ribbed $900.00-950.00
Pillar, Ribbed ....ea. $975.00-1,025.00
Blue Aurene $1,750.00-1,800.00
Curved Ribbing...............................$2,250.00-2,300.00
Page 19
Findlay Floradine.............................$1,250.00-1,300.00
Rose Findlay Onyx $1,100.00-1,200.00
Holly Amber $510.00-535.00
Tiffany Furnaces $2,100.00
Page 20
Mary Gregory $425.00-450.00
Mary Gregory Type $300.00-325.00
Webb Peachblow ....$1,700.00-$1,750.00
Page 21
Queen Ann $1,550.00-1,600.00
Long Neck Barrel $2,300.00-2,375.00
Page 22
Peachbloom..$480.00-510.00
New England Peachblow Barrel........$2,100.00-2,200.00
Geranium..$490.00-520.00
Stevens & Williams Peachblow..............$525.00-550.00
Page 23
Rose O'Neill Kewpies............................$700.00-750.00
Baseball Player $600.00-650.00
Carnival Corn....................................$975.00-1,050.00
Page 24
Thousand Eye $30.00-37.00
Thumbprint, Ruby..................................$38.00-45.00
Wildflower $34.00-40.00
Cottage...$68.00-75.00
Page 25
Valencia Waffle $24.00-30.00
Hobnail in Square $52.00-60.00
Page 26
Atterbury Twin $90.00-110.00
Rib and Swirl $35.00-50.00
Owl, Big $125.00-138.00
Page 27
Owl, Little ....frosted $125.00-140.00
crystal $95.00-110.00
salt & pepper $250.00-275.00
Page 28
Beatty Honeycomb $60.00-70.00
Beatty Rib $50.00-60.00
Coinspot...$70.00-80.00
Page 29
Flora $72.00-78.00
Flower Mold, Beaumont's $83.00-88.00
Yarn, Bulbous $58.00-65.00
Earlybird...$60.00-65.00
Page 30
Log and Star...$17.00-22.00
Page 31
Christmas Barrel Condiment $450.00-500.00
Christmas Barrel Condiment
Variation $450.00-500.00

Page 32
Panel, Christmas $60.00-125.00
Pearl, Christmas....................................$60.00-80.00
Page 33
Waffle, Octagon $30.00-50.00
Chrysanthemum Base $72.00-80.00
Opal Ribbon, Short................................$70.00-78.00
Page 34
Star of Bethlehem $50.00-60.00
Cambridge #1035...................................$15.00-20.00
Page 35
Coin, Columbian $38.00-45.00
Ribbed Inside $25.00-37.00
Liberty Bell...$85.00-100.00
Page 36
Spirea Band $22.00-30.00
Thumbprint, Swirl-Based $22.00-35.00
Banded Shells $38.00-46.00
Page 37
Beaded Oval Mirror $30.00-40.00
Flower Bouquet $25.00-32.00
Forget-me-not $28.00-35.00
Page 38
Forget-me-not, Tall................................$38.00-50.00
Horseshoe & Aster $75.00-90.00
Marble Glass Box $125.00-140.00
Pleated Skirt...$35.00-42.00
Page 39
Seashell $75.00-87.00
Slag...$70.00-80.00
Slag: Variegated Blue $65.00-80.00
Square S $25.00-35.00
Page 40
Broken Column with Red Dots $80.00-90.00
Radiant $75.00-83.00
Argus Swirl $52.00-65.00
Page 41
Beaded Panel...$28.00-37.00
Beads & Bulges $70.00-85.00
Bulging Leaf ....pr. $60.00-70.00
Bulging Loops $55.00-75.00
Page 42
Bulging Petal...$28.00-42.00
Cone $60.00-70.00
Bulging 3 Petal Condiment Set $375.00-400.00
Page 43
Cord & Tassel, Double............................$48.00-60.00
Cotton Bale $26.00-35.00
Cosmos, Tall $35.00-47.00
Page 44
Criss Cross..$68.00-80.00
Daisy, Long Petal...................................$60.00-74.00
Dahlia, Beaded $60.00-70.00
Page 45
Florette $85.00-100.00
Distended Sides..........................opalware $55.00-65.00
cranberry $60.00-65.00
Fish...$35.00-50.00

Petticoat $45.00-50.00
Seed Pod $35.00-40.00
Winsome $16.00-20.00
Page 180
   X-ray $58.00-65.00
   Fagot $45.00-55.00
   Josephine's Fan $17.00-21.00
   Zanesville $75.00-80.00
Page 181
   Snake Dance $95.00-105.00
   Coil Top (small) $50.00-60.00
Page 182
   Coil Top (large).................clear crystal $40.00-45.00
                        cobalt blue $80.00-85.00
   Blue Aurene ....pr. $1,600.00-1,700.00
Page 183
   Steuben, Crystal..................................$120.00-130.00
   Stevens & Williams Peachblow..............$525.00-550.00
Page 184
   Atlanta, Tarentum's $20.00-25.00
   Beaded Square $25.00-30.00
   Oregon, Tarentum's..............................$33.00-40.00
Page 185
   Georgia Gem $52.00-58.00
   Princeton..$16.00-20.00
   Teardrop, Paneled $98.00-106.00
   Thumbprint, Tarentum's $75.00-80.00
Page 186
   Victoria, Tarentum's..............................$45.00-50.00
   Tile $47.00-55.00
   Summit, The $48.00-57.00
Page 187
   Tiffany...$2,100.00
Page 188
   Acorn, Little $25.00-30.00
   Alabama..$75.00-80.00
Page 189
   Broken Column with Red Dots $80.00-90.00
   California $60.00-65.00
   Colorado...$60.00-70.00
   Carolina $40.00-50.00
Page 190
   Delaware $75.00-85.00
   Diamond & Sunburst Variant $40.00-45.00
   Diamond Mat Band $40.00-50.00
   Florida $45.00-55.00
   Galloway $24.00-30.00
   Heavy Gothic...$47.00-55.00
Page 191
   Hexagon, Block $48.00-55.00
   Hexagon, Six Panel $22.00-28.00
   King's No. 500 ....$30.00-35.00
   Iowa $35.00-40.00
   Maine $33.00-40.00
Page 192
   Lacy Medallion $27.00-34.00
   Mario $78.00-85.00
   Michigan $60.00-70.00
   Millard (Fan and Flute)...........................$40.00-45.00
   Nail $36.00-42.00
Page 193
   Minnesota $32.00-37.00
   Octagon Panel $20.00-25.00

New Jersey $50.00-55.00
Oregon $48.00-55.00
New Hampshire $68.00-76.00
Page 194
   Paneled Palm..$35.00-40.00
   Roman Rosette $70.00-80.00
   Roman Rosette ....set $110.00-120.00
   Pennsylvania $26.00-32.00
   Red Block $55.00-65.00
   Square Block $50.00-60.00
Page 195
   Snail $62.00-70.00
   Swirl, Beaded $30.00-35.00
   Texas $23.00-30.00
   Vermont $70.00-80.00
   Wisconsin..$33.00-40.00
Page 196
   Daisy and Button $6.00-8.00
   English Hobnail, Westmoreland's.............$7.00-11.00
Page 197
   Flute and Crown $33.00-36.00
   Fruit Band $45.00-50.00
   High Hob...$18.00-24.00
   Hundred Eye...$30.00-35.00
Page 198
   Marbleized Caramel...............................$38.00-44.00
   Sterling $23.00-27.00
   Star and Diamond...................................$7.00-9.00
   Optic, West Virginia's.............................$82.00-90.00
Page 199
   Blue Opal $100.00-108.00
   Fandangle $35.00-40.00
   Optic, Nine Rib $30.00-35.00
   IOU $75.00-80.00
Page 200
   Medallion Sprig ....amethyst $115.00-120.00
                 opaque white $25.00-30.00
   Pillar, West Virginia's.............................$30.00-35.00
   Ada $65.00-70.00
Page 201
   Acorn, Footed.......................................$22.00-27.00
   Amberina Sphere..................................$200.00-210.00
   Aztec Carnival $195.00-205.00
   Arched Oval $32.00-38.00
   Banded Sphere $15.00-20.00
   Baby Thumbprint, Bulging $155.00-160.00
Page 202
   Barrel Custard $125.00-130.00
   Barrel, Dual Molded $90.00-100.00
   Barrel English $230.00-250.00
   Barrel, Flat Top $95.00-108.00
   Barrel, IVT $85.00-95.00
Page 203
   Barrel, Little $62.00-75.00
   Barrel, Ringed $19.00-25.00
   Barrel, Opalescent................................$70.00-80.00
   Baseball Player.....................................$600.00-650.00
   Barrel, Narrow.....................................$130.00-145.00
Page 204
   Bead Band $18.00-25.00
   Barrel, Souvenir $27.00-30.00
   Beaded Diamond and Scroll $30.00-35.00
   Beaded Panel, Concave..........................$32.00-38.00

Books on Antiques and Collectibles

Most of the following books are available from your local book seller or antique dealer, or on loan from your public library. If you are unable to locate certain titles in your area you may order by mail from COLLECTOR BOOKS, P.O. Box 3009, Paducah, KY 42002-3009. Add $2.00 for postage for the first book ordered and $.30 for each additional book. Include item number, title and price when ordering. Allow 14 to 21 days for delivery. All books are well illustrated and contain current values.

Books on Glass and Pottery

1810	American Art Glass, Shuman	$29.95
2016	Bedroom & Bathroom Glassware of the Depression Years	$19.95
1312	Blue & White Stoneware, McNerney	$9.95
1959	Blue Willow, 2nd Ed., Gaston	$14.95
1627	Children's Glass Dishes, China & Furniture II, Lechler	$19.95
1892	Collecting Royal Haeger, Garmon	$19.95
1373	Collector's Ency of American Dinnerware, Cunningham	$24.95
2133	Collector's Ency. of Cookie Jars, Roerig	$24.95
2017	Collector's Ency. of Depression Glass, 9th Ed., Florence	$19.95
2209	Collector's Ency. of Fiesta, 7th Ed., Huxford	$19.95
1439	Collector's Ency. of Flow Blue China, Gaston	$19.95
1961	Collector's Ency. of Fry Glass, Fry Glass Society	$24.95
2086	Collector's Ency. of Gaudy Dutch & Welsh, Schuman	$14.95
1813	Collector's Ency. of Geisha Girl Porcelain, Litts	$19.95
1915	Collector's Ency. of Hall China, 2nd Ed., Whitmyer	$19.95
1358	Collector's Ency. of McCoy Pottery, Huxford	$19.95
1039	Collector's Ency. of Nippon Porcelain I, Van Patten	$19.95
2089	Collector's Ency. of Nippon Porcelain II, Van Patten	$24.95
1665	Collector's Ency. of Nippon Porcelain III, Van Patten	$24.95
1447	Collector's Ency. of Noritake, Van Patten	$19.95
1037	Collector's Ency. of Occupied Japan I, Florence	$14.95
1038	Collector's Ency. of Occupied Japan II, Florence	$14.95
1719	Collector's Ency. of Occupied Japan III, Florence	$14.95
2019	Collector's Ency. of Occupied Japan IV, Florence	$14.95
1715	Collector's Ency. of R.S. Prussia II, Gaston	$24.95
1034	Collector's Ency. of Roseville Pottery, Huxford	$19.95
1035	Collector's Ency. of Roseville Pottery, 2nd Ed., Huxford	$19.95
1623	Coll. Guide to Country Stoneware & Pottery, Raycraft	$9.95
2077	Coll. Guide Country Stone. & Pottery, 2nd Ed., Raycraft	$14.95
1523	Colors in Cambridge, National Cambridge Society	$19.95
1425	Cookie Jars, Westfall	$9.95
1843	Covered Animal Dishes, Grist	$14.95
1844	Elegant Glassware of the Depression Era, 4th Ed., Florence	$19.95
1845	Ency. of U.S. Marks on Pottery, Porcelain & Clay, Lehner	$19.95
2024	Kitchen Glassware of the Depression Years, 4th Ed., Florence	$19.95
1465	Haviland Collectibles & Art Objects, Gaston	$19.95
1917	Head Vases Id & Value Guide, Cole	$14.95
1392	Majolica Pottery, Katz-Marks	$9.95
1669	Majolica Pottery, 2nd Series, Katz-Marks	$9.95
1919	Pocket Guide to Depression Glass, 7th Ed., Florence	$9.95
1438	Oil Lamps II, Thuro	$19.95
1670	Red Wing Collectibles, DePasquale	$9.95
1440	Red Wing Stoneware, DePasquale	$9.95
1958	So. Potteries Blue Ridge Dinnerware, 3rd Ed., Newbound	$14.95
2221	Standard Carnival Glass, 3rd Ed., Edwards	$24.95
2222	Standard Carnival Glass Price Guide, 1991, 8th Ed., Edwards	$7.95
1814	Wave Crest, Glass of C.F. Monroe, Cohen	$29.95
1848	Very Rare Glassware of the Depression Years, Florence	$24.95
2140	Very Rare Glassware of the Depression Years, Second Series	$24.95

Books on Dolls & Toys

1887	American Rag Dolls, Patino	$14.95
2079	Barbie Fashion, Vol. 1, 1959-1967, Eames	$24.95
1514	Character Toys & Collectibles 1st Series, Longest	$19.95
1750	Character Toys & Collectibles, 2nd Series, Longest	$19.95
2021	Collectible Male Action Figures, Manos	$14.95
1529	Collector's Ency. of Barbie Dolls, DeWein	$19.95
1066	Collector's Ency. of Half Dolls, Marion	$29.95
2151	Collector's Guide to Tootsietoys, Richter	$14.95
2082	Collector's Guide to Magazine Paper Dolls, Young	$14.95
1891	French Dolls in Color, 3rd Series, Smith	$14.95
1631	German Dolls, Smith	$9.95
1635	Horsman Dolls, Gibbs	$19.95
1067	Madame Alexander Collector's Dolls, Smith	$19.95
2025	Madame Alexander Price Guide #16, Smith	$7.95
2185	Modern Collector's Dolls, Vol. I, Smith, 1991 Values	$17.95
2186	Modern Collector's Dolls, Vol. II, Smith, 1991 Values	$17.95
2187	Modern Collector's Dolls, Vol. III, Smith, 1991 Values	$17.95
2188	Modern Collector's Dolls, Vol. IV, Smith, 1991 Values	$17.95
2189	Modern Collector's Dolls Vol. V, Smith, 1991 Values	$17.95

1540	Modern Toys, 1930-1980, Baker	$19.95
2218	Patricia Smith Doll Values, Antique to Modern, 7th Ed.	$12.95
1886	Stern's Guide to Disney	$14.95
2139	Stern's Guide to Disney, 2nd Series	$14.95
1513	Teddy Bears & Steiff Animals, Mandel	$9.95
1817	Teddy Bears & Steiff Animals, 2nd, Mandel	$19.95
2084	Teddy Bears, Annalees & Steiff Animals, 3rd, Mandel	$19.95
2028	Toys, Antique & Collectible, Longest	$14.95
1648	World of Alexander-Kins, Smith	$19.95
1808	Wonder of Barbie, Manos	$9.95
1430	World of Barbie Dolls, Manos	$9.95

Other Collectibles

1457	American Oak Furniture, McNerney	$9.95
1846	Antique & Collectible Marbles, Grist, 2nd Ed.	$9.95
1712	Antique & Collectible Thimbles, Mathis	$19.95
1880	Antique Iron, McNerney	$9.95
1748	Antique Purses, Holiner	$19.95
1868	Antique Tools, Our American Heritage, McNerney	$9.95
2015	Archaic Indian Points & Knives, Edler	$14.95
1426	Arrowheads & Projectile Points, Hothem	$7.95
1278	Art Nouveau & Art Deco Jewelry, Baker	$9.95
1714	Black Collectibles, Gibbs	$19.95
1666	Book of Country, Raycraft	$19.95
1960	Book of Country Vol II, Raycraft	$19.95
1811	Book of Moxie, Potter	$29.95
1128	Bottle Pricing Guide, 3rd Ed., Cleveland	$7.95
1751	Christmas Collectibles, Whitmyer	$19.95
1752	Christmas Ornaments, Johnston	$19.95
1713	Collecting Barber Bottles, Holiner	$24.95
2132	Collector's Ency. of American Furniture, Vol. I, Swedberg	$24.95
2018	Collector's Ency. of Graniteware, Greguire	$24.95
2083	Collector's Ency. of Russel Wright Designs, Kerr	$19.95
1634	Coll. Ency. of Salt & Pepper Shakers, Davern	$19.95
2020	Collector's Ency. of Salt & Pepper Shakers II, Davern	$19.95
2134	Collector's Guide to Antique Radios, Bunis	$16.95
1916	Collector's Guide to Art Deco, Gaston	$14.95
1537	Collector's Guide to Country Baskets, Raycraft	$9.95
1437	Collector's Guide to Country Furniture, Raycraft	$9.95
1842	Collector's Guide to Country Furniture II, Raycraft	$14.95
1962	Collector's Guide to Decoys, Huxford	$14.95
1441	Collector's Guide to Post Cards, Wood	$9.95
1629	Doorstops, Id & Values, Betoria	$9.95
1716	Fifty Years of Fashion Jewelry, Baker	$19.95
2213	Flea Market Trader, 7th Ed., Huxford	$9.95
1668	Flint Blades & Proj. Points of the No. Am. Indian, Tully	$24.95
1755	Furniture of the Depression Era, Swedberg	$19.95
2081	Guide to Collecting Cookbooks, Allen	$14.95
1424	Hatpins & Hatpin Holders, Baker	$9.95
1964	Indian Axes & Related Stone Artifacts, Hothem	$14.95
2023	Keen Kutter Collectibles, 2nd Ed., Heuring	$14.95
2216	Kitchen Antiques - 1750–1940, McNerney	$14.95
1181	100 Years of Collectible Jewelry, Baker	$9.95
2137	Modern Guns, Identification & Value Guide, Quertermous	$12.95
1965	Pine Furniture, Our Am. Heritage, McNerney	$14.95
2080	Price Guide to Cookbooks & Recipe Leaflets, Dickinson	$9.95
2164	Primitives, Our American Heritage, McNerney	$9.95
1759	Primitives, Our American Heritage, 2nd Series, McNerney	$14.95
2026	Railroad Collectibles, 4th Ed., Baker	$14.95
1632	Salt & Pepper Shakers, Guarnaccia	$9.95
1888	Salt & Pepper Shakers II, Guarnaccia	$14.95
2220	Salt & Pepper Shakers III, Guarnaccia	$14.95
2141	Schroeder's Antiques Price Guide, 10th Ed.	$12.95
2096	Silverplated Flatware, 4th Ed., Hagan	$14.95
2027	Standard Baseball Card Pr. Gd., Florence	$9.95
1922	Standard Bottle Pr. Gd., Sellari	$14.95
1966	Standard Fine Art Value Guide, Huxford	$29.95
2085	Standard Fine Art Value Guide Vol. 2, Huxford	$29.95
2078	The Old Book Value Guide, 2nd Ed	$19.95
1923	Wanted to Buy	$9.95
1885	Victorian Furniture, McNerney	$9.95

Schroeder's Antiques Price Guide

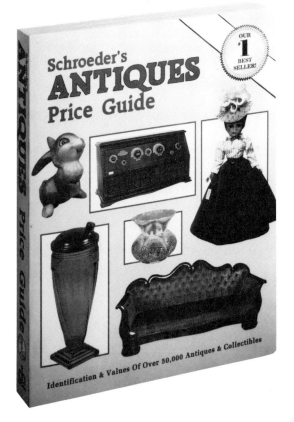

Schroeder's Antiques Price Guide has become THE household name in the antiques & collectibles field. Our team of editors work year-round with more than 200 contributors to bring you our #1 best-selling book on antiques & collectibles.

With more than 50,000 items identified & priced, *Schroeder's* is a must for the collector & dealer alike. If it merits the interest of today's collector, you'll find it in *Schroeder's*. Each subject is represented with histories and background information. In addition, hundreds of sharp original photos are used each year to illustrate not only the rare and unusual, but the everyday "fun-type" collectibles as well -- not postage stamp pictures, but large close-up shots that show important details clearly.

Our editors compile a new book each year. Never do we merely change prices. Accuracy is our primary aim. Prices are gathered over the entire year previous to publication, from ads and personal contacts. Then each category is thoroughly checked to spot inconsistencies, listings that may not be entirely reflective of actual market dealings, and lines too vague to be of merit. Only the best of the lot remains for publication. You'll find *Schroeder's Antiques Price Guide* the one to buy for factual information and quality.

No dealer, collector or investor can afford not to own this book. It is available from your favorite bookseller or antiques dealer at the low price of $12.95. If you are unable to find this price guide in your area, it's available from Collector Books, P.O. Box 3009, Paducah, KY 42002-3009 at $12.95 plus $2.00 for postage and handling.

8½ x 11", 608 Pages   **$12.95**

COLLECTOR BOOKS
A Division of Schroeder Publishing Co., Inc.